# Developing Java Beans

# THE JAVA SERIES™

Exploring Java

Java Threads

Java Network Programming

Java Virtual Machine

Java AWT Reference

Java Language Reference

Java Fundamental Classes Reference

Developing Java Beans

Database Programming with JDBC and Java

*Also from O'Reilly*

Java in a Nutshell, Second Edition

# Developing Java Beans

Robert Englander

O'REILLY®

*Beijing · Cambridge · Farnham · Köln · Paris · Sebastopol · Taipei · Tokyo*

*Developing Java Beans*
by Robert Englander

Copyright © 1997 O'Reilly & Associates, Inc. All rights reserved.
Printed in the United States of America.

Published by O'Reilly & Associates, Inc., 101 Morris Street, Sebastopol, CA 95472.

**Editor:** Mike Loukides

**Production Editor:** David Futato

**Printing History:**

        June 1997:        First Edition

ISBN: 1-56592-289-1

[M]

*For my daughter Jessica*

# Table of Contents

# *Preface*

JavaBeans is one of the most important developments in Java™ since its inception. It is Java's component architecture, which allows components built with Java to be used in graphical programming environments. Graphical development environments let you configure components by specifying aspects of their visual appearance (like the color or label of a button) in addition to the interactions between components (what happens when you click on a button or select a menu item). This means that someone can use a graphical tool to connect some Beans together and make an application without actually writing any Java code—in fact, without doing any programming at all. Developing an application isn't necessarily a matter of producing thousands of lines of code that can only be read by computer professionals. It's more like working with Lego blocks: you can build large structures using snap-together pieces. The result is that applications can be created by people who are good at designing user interfaces and aspects of the interaction between the user and the computer. The guts of an application can be written by software developers, who are great at coding, but not necessarily good at understanding users. This is how it should be, and in fact how it is in many other industries. The engineer who designed the engine of your car is certainly not the same person who designed the interior. JavaBeans allows us to make the same kind of distinction in the software business.

As Beans become widely available, we will see more developers using them to build applications. But before these applications can be built, someone has to build the components. That's what this book is all about.

You won't find any hype in this book, and you won't find vague descriptions of technology that may or may not appear in the future. JavaBeans is here now, and programmers must have the information at hand to begin creating components.

So if you're ready to get right into the techniques and concepts used by the Java-Beans architecture, and if you want to understand the underpinnings of the technology that makes it work, this book is for you.

## Intended Audience

This book is for everyone who wants to know how to build reusable components using the JavaBeans architecture and Java class libraries. It is designed to be used by programmers, students, and professionals that are already familiar with Java, so it doesn't concentrate on any of the basic concepts or syntax of the language. However, if you are experienced with other object-oriented languages such as C++ or Smalltalk, you should be able to follow along. If you aren't familiar with Java, you may want to keep a book on the Java language close by, like the *Java Language Reference* (O'Reilly). In any case, the material should prove useful to both novice and experienced programmers.

One chapter discusses the interaction between JavaBeans and ActiveX components, and has some examples using Visual Basic. I assume that readers interested in this topic are already familiar with VB and the ActiveX component architecture, and don't attempt to explain them. Many good books on Visual Basic are available if you need an introduction.

## A Moment in Time

The JavaBeans architecture continues to evolve. This book describes the technology in its first release, coinciding with version 1.1 of the Java Development Kit. The concepts and techniques that I cover will continue to be relevant in future Java releases, and new things will no doubt be added along the way. With the rapid rate of change that Java is currently undergoing, the best that any book can do is capture a moment in time.

## How the Book Is Organized

The chapters in this book are organized so that each one builds upon the information presented in previous chapters, so it's best if you read the chapters in order.

*Chapter 1, Introduction*

> This chapter provides a general description of the component model, followed by an overview of the JavaBeans architecture.

*Chapter 2, Events*

> This chapter describes the event model introduced in Java 1.1. It covers event listener interfaces, event objects, and event sources, and covers the semantics

of event delivery. Topics also include design patterns, event listener registration, and multicast and unicast events.

*Chapter 3, Event Adapters*

This chapter describes how to use event adapters to simplify an event listener, and how to adapt an object to an event listener interface. Topics include demultiplexing, using low-level reflection to create generic adapters, event filtering, and event queuing.

*Chapter 4, Properties*

This chapter describes properties, the named attributes that define the state and behavior of a component. Properties represent some part of the Bean that is likely to be manipulated by nontraditional programming techniques such as visual editors. Topics include design patterns, accessor methods, indexed properties, bound and constrained properties, and property-related events.

*Chapter 5, Persistence*

This chapter describes the use of object serialization provided by Java 1.1 for saving and restoring the state of a Bean. It discusses what can and can't be stored and how storage and retrieval is accomplished. Topics include automatic and class-specific serialization, serializing an object's class hierarchy, class versioning and compatibility, and serialized versions of Beans.

*Chapter 6, JAR Files*

This chapter describes the Java Archive (JAR) file, used to package one or more Beans, classes, or associated resource files. The *jar* utility provided with the JDK is discussed, along with manifest entries, and how to use them to identify a component as a Bean.

*Chapter 7, The BeanBox Tool*

This chapter introduces the BeanBox program, a visual Bean-testing tool provided with the Beans Development Kit (BDK). It describes how to include your Beans for testing in the BeanBox, how to wire Beans together based on their events and properties, and how to save and restore a collection of inter-operating Beans.

*Chapter 8, Putting It All Together*

This chapter takes all of the concepts and techniques described in the previous chapters and uses them to develop a fully functioning example. This example includes some Beans, as well as supporting classes, that all work together to create a temperature simulator. The Beans that are developed are wired together using traditional programming, as well as the BeanBox testing tool.

*Chapter 9, Introspection*

This chapter introduces the introspection mechanism used to expose the events, methods, and properties of a Bean. It describes how to create special Java classes that explicitly provide this information for your Beans.

*Chapter 10, Property Editors and Customizers*

This chapter describes property editors, the Java classes that are used by programming tools to provide visual editors for changing a Bean's property values. It shows you how to use the standard property editors, and how to create your own custom property editors. Customizers are interfaces to customize the behavior and/or appearance of an entire Bean. This chapter shows you how to create your own customizer, as well as how to use a property editor as part of your customizer.

*Chapter 11, ActiveX*

This chapter describes the JavaBeans ActiveX Bridge, a tool that allows you to package your Beans as ActiveX components. The mapping between the two technologies is discussed, as well as those parts of JavaBeans that don't map well to ActiveX. You will also see how Beans can be used in an ActiveX container.

*Appendix A, Design Patterns*

All of the design patterns that are introduced throughout the book are put here for easy reference.

*Appendix B, The java.beans Package*

This is a basic class reference for all of the classes and interfaces in the `java.beans` package. Each class and interface has a brief description, along with a class definition that shows its methods.

# *Conventions Used in This Book*

`Constant Width` is used for:

- Anything that might appear in a Java program, including keywords, operators, data types, constants, method names, variable names, class names, and interface names, and also for Java packages.

- Command lines and options that should be typed verbatim on the screen.

*Italic* is used for:

- Pathnames, filenames, and Internet addresses, such as domain names and URLs. Italic is also used for Bean properties and executable files.

# Acknowledgments

I was first introduced to Java by my friend Rinaldo DiGiorgio. He tried to convince me that Java was going to be big, and that I should get involved. Eventually, I broke down and followed his advice. More recently, he had to twist my arm to take a hard look at JavaBeans, and subsequently to write this book. I am grateful to Rinaldo for pointing me in the right direction.

My sincere thanks go to Mitch Duitz, Hugh Lynch, and John Zukowski for their detailed technical reviews of the book, and for providing valuable feedback. They managed to find errors, point out omissions, and offer advice that makes this a better book than it would have been without their help. Thanks to Max Spivak and Jonathan Knudsen for reading the draft and offering their comments and suggestions. My appreciation also goes to Mike Loukides, the book's editor, for believing this was an important book to write and for helping me to do so.

A thank you is due to the O'Reilly design and production crew: David Futato, the production editor and copyeditor for the book; Nancy Kotary for proofreading and quality control; Seth Maislin, who produced the index; Edie Freedman, who designed the cover; Nancy Priest, for internal design; Chris Reilley and Rob Romano, who were responsible for the figures; and Sheryl Avruch, the production manager.

I also have to thank my friends and family for putting up with me while I was writing. Everyone's encouragement helped me to finish this project.

# How to Contact Us

We have tested and verified the information in this book to the best of our ability, but you may find that features have changed (or even that we have made mistakes!). Please let us know about any errors you find, as well as your suggestions for future editions, by writing to:

> O'Reilly & Associates, Inc.
> 101 Morris Street
> Sebastopol, CA 95472
> 1-800-998-9938 (in the U.S. or Canada)
> 1-707-829-0515 (international/local)
> 1-707-829-0104 (FAX)

You can also send us messages electronically. To be put on the mailing list or request a catalog, send email to:

> *info@oreilly.com*

To ask technical questions or comment on the book, send email to:

> *bookquestions@oreilly.com*

We have a web site for the book, where we'll list examples, errata, and any plans for future editions. You can access this page at:

> *http://www.oreilly.com/catalog/javabeans/*

For more information about this book and others, see the O'Reilly web site:

> *http://www.oreilly.com*

## Providing Feedback to the Author

I've tried to be accurate and complete in my description of JavaBeans, but it's inevitable that there will be errors and omissions. If you find any mistakes, if you think I've left something out, or if you have any suggestions for a future edition of this book, please let me know. In addition to contacting O'Reilly, you may contact me directly at *rob@mindstrm.com*. The JavaBeans architecture will continue to change over time, and this book will certainly attempt to keep up with those changes.

## Retrieving Examples Online

Much of the code in this book is available for download. On the World Wide Web, go to *http://www.oreilly.com/catalog/javabeans/*. You can also retrieve the files via FTP (either with your web browser or another FTP client) at *ftp://ftp.oreilly.com/published/oreilly/java/javabeans/*.

1

# *Introduction*

As software developers, we are constantly being asked to build applications in less time and with less money. And, of course, these applications are expected to be better and faster than ever before. Object-oriented techniques and component software environments are in wide use now, in the hope that they can help us build applications more quickly. Development tools like Microsoft's Visual Basic have made it easier to build applications faster by taking a building-block approach to software development. Such tools provide a visual programming model that allows you to include software components rapidly in your applications.

The JavaBeans architecture brings the component development model to Java, and that's the subject of this book. But before we get started, I want to spend a little time describing the component model, and follow that with a general overview of JavaBeans. If you already have an understanding of these subjects, or you just want to get right into it, you can go directly to Chapter 2, *Events*. Otherwise, you'll probably find that the information in this chapter sets the stage for the rest of the book.

## *The Component Model*

Components are self-contained elements of software that can be controlled dynamically and assembled to form applications. But that's not the end of it. These components must also interoperate according to a set of rules and guidelines. They must behave in ways that are expected. It's like a society of software citizens. The citizens (components) bring functionality, while the society (environment) brings structure and order.

1

JavaBeans is Java's component model. It allows users to construct applications by piecing components together either programmatically or visually (or both). Support of visual programming is paramount to the component model; it's what makes component-based software development truly powerful.

The model is made up of an architecture and an API (Application Programming Interface). Together, these elements provide a structure whereby components can be combined to create an application. This environment provides services and rules, the framework that allows components to participate properly. This means that components are provided with the tools necessary to work in the environment, and they exhibit certain behaviors that identify them as such. One very important aspect of this structure is containment. A container provides a context in which components can interact. A common example would be a panel that provides layout management or mediation of interactions for visual components. Of course, containers themselves can be components.

As mentioned previously, components are expected to exhibit certain behaviors and characteristics in order to participate in the component structure and to interact with the environment, as well as with other components. In other words, there are a number of elements that, when combined, define the component model. These are described in more detail in the following sections.

## Discovery and Registration

Class and interface discovery is the mechanism used to locate a component at run-time and to determine its supported interfaces so that these interfaces can be used by others. The component model must also provide a registration process for a component to make itself and its interfaces known. The component, along with its supported interfaces, can then be discovered at run-time. Dynamic (or late) binding allows components and applications to be developed independently. The dependency is limited to the "contract" between each component and the applications that use it; this contract is defined by interfaces that the component supports. An application does not have to include a component during the development process in order to use it at run-time; it only needs to know what the component is capable of doing. Dynamic discovery also allows developers to update components without having to rebuild the applications that use them.

This discovery process can also be used in a design-time environment. In this case, a development tool may be able to locate a component and make it available for use by the designer. This is important for visual programming environments, which are discussed later.

## Raising and Handling of Events

An event is something of importance that happens at a specific point in time. An event can take place due to a user action such as a mouse click—when the user clicks a mouse button, an event takes place. Events can also be initiated by other means. Imagine the heating system in your house. It contains a thermostat that sets the desired comfort temperature, keeps track of the current ambient temperature, and notifies the boiler when its services are required. If the thermostat is set to keep the room at 70 degrees Fahrenheit, it will notify the boiler to start producing heat if the temperature dips below that threshold. Components will send notifications to other objects when an event takes place in which those objects have expressed an interest.

## Persistence

Generally, all components have state. The thermostat component has state that represents the comfort temperature. If the thermostat were a software component of a computer-based heating control system, we would want the value of the comfort temperature to be stored on a non-volatile storage medium (such as the hard disk). This way if we shut down the application and brought it back up again, the thermostat control would still be set to 70 degrees. The visual representation and position of the thermostat relative to other components in the application would be restored as well.

Components must be able to participate in their container's persistence mechanism so that all components in the application can provide application-wide persistence in a uniform way. If every component were to implement its own method of persistence, it would be impossible for an application container to use components in a general way. This wouldn't be an issue if reuse weren't the goal. If we were building a monolithic temperature control system we might create an application-specific mechanism for storing state. But we want to build the thermostat component so that it can be used again in another application, so we have to use a standard mechanism for persistence.

## Visual Presentation

The component environment allows the individual components to control most of the aspects of their visual presentation. For example, imagine that our thermostat component includes a display of the current ambient temperature. We might want to display the temperature in different fonts or colors depending on whether we are above, below, or at the comfort temperature. The component is free to choose the characteristics of its own visual presentation. Many of these characteristics will be properties of the component (a topic that will be discussed later). Some of these visual properties will be persistent, meaning that they represent some state of the control that will be saved to, and restored from, persistent storage.

Layout is another important aspect of visual presentation. This concerns the way in which components are arranged on the screen, how they relate to one another, and the behavior they exhibit when the user interacts with them. The container object that holds an assembly of components usually provides some set of services related to the layout of the component. Let's consider the thermostat and heating control application again. This time, the user decides to change the size of the application window. The container will interact with the components in response to this action, possibly changing the size of some of the components. In turn, changing the size of the thermostat component may cause it to alter its font size.

As you can see, the container and the component work together to provide a single application that presents itself in a uniform fashion. The application appears to be working as one unit, even though with the component development model, the container and the components probably have been created separately by different developers.

## Support of Visual Programming

Visual programming is a key part of the component model. Components are represented in toolboxes or palettes. The user can select a component from the toolbox and place it into a container, choosing its size and position. The properties of the component can then be edited in order to create the desired behavior. Our thermostat control might present some type of user interface to the application developer to set the initial comfort temperature. Likewise, the choice of font and color will be selectable in a similar way. None of these manipulations require a single line of code to be written by the application developer. In fact, the application development tool is probably writing the code for you. This is accomplished through a set of standard interfaces provided by the component environment that allow the components to publish, or expose, their properties. The development tool can also provide a means for the developer to manipulate the size and position of components in relation to each other. The container itself may be a component and allow its properties to be edited in order to alter its behavior.

# The JavaBeans Architecture

JavaBeans is an architecture for both using and building components in Java. This architecture supports the features of software reuse, component models, and object orientation. One of the most important features of JavaBeans is that it does not alter the existing Java language. If you know how to write software in Java, you know how to use and create Beans. The strengths of Java are built upon and extended to create the JavaBeans component architecture.

Although Beans are intended to work in a visual application development tool, they don't necessarily have a visual representation at run-time (although many will). What this does mean is that Beans must allow their property values to be changed through some type of visual interface, and their methods and events should be exposed so that the development tool can write code capable of manipulating the component when the application is executed.

Creating a Bean doesn't require any advanced concepts. So before I go any further, here is some code that implements a simple Bean:

```
public class MyBean implements java.io.Serializable
{
    protected  int theValue;

    public MyBean()
    {
    }

    public void setMyValue(int newValue)
    {
        theValue = newValue;
    }

    public int getMyValue()
    {
        return theValue;
    }
}
```

This is a real Bean named *MyBean* that has state (the variable theValue) that will automatically be saved and restored by the JavaBeans persistence mechanism, and it has a property named *MyValue* that is usable by a visual programming environment. This Bean doesn't have any visual representation, but that isn't a requirement for a JavaBean component.

JavaSoft is using the slogan "Write once, use everywhere." Of course "everywhere" means everywhere the Java run-time environment is available. But this is very important. What it means is that the entire run-time environment required by JavaBeans is part of the Java platform. No special libraries or classes have to be distributed with your components. The JavaBeans class libraries provide a rich set of default behaviors for simple components (such as the one shown earlier). This means that you don't have to spend your time building a lot of support for the Beans environment into your code.

The design goals of JavaBeans are discussed in Sun's white paper, "Java Beans: A Component Architecture for Java." This paper can be found on the JavaSoft web site at *http://splash.javasoft.com/beans/WhitePaper.html*. It might be interesting to review these goals before we move on to the technology itself, to provide a little insight into why certain aspects of JavaBeans are the way they are.

## Compact and Easy

JavaBeans components are simple to create and easy to use. This is an important goal of the JavaBeans architecture. It doesn't take very much to write a simple Bean, and such a Bean is lightweight—it doesn't have to carry around a lot of inherited baggage just to support the Beans environment. If a Bean does not require the advanced features of the architecture, it doesn't get them, nor does it get the code that goes with them. This is an important concept. The JavaBeans architecture scales upward in complexity, not downward like other component models. This means it really is easy to create a simple Bean. (The previous example shows just how simple a Bean can be.)

## Portable

Since JavaBeans components are built purely in Java, they are fully portable to any platform that supports the Java run-time environment. All platform specifics, as well as support for JavaBeans, are implemented by the Java virtual machine. You can be sure that when you develop a component using JavaBeans it will be usable on all of the platforms that support Java (version 1.1 and beyond). These range from workstation applications and web browsers to servers, and even to devices such as PDAs and set-top boxes.

## Leverages the Strengths of the Java Platform

JavaBeans uses the existing Java class discovery mechanism. This means that there isn't some new complicated mechanism for registering components with the run-time system.

As shown in the earlier code example, Beans are lightweight components that are easy to understand. Building a Bean doesn't require the use of complex extensions to the environment. Many of the Java supporting classes are Beans, such as the windowing components found in `java.awt`.

The Java class libraries provide a rich set of default behaviors for components. Use of Java Object Serialization is one example—a component can support the persistence model by implementing the `java.io.Serializable` interface. By conforming to a simple set of design patterns (discussed later in this chapter), you can expose properties without doing anything more than coding them in a particular style.

## Flexible Build-Time Component Editors

Developers are free to create their own custom property sheets and editors for use with their components if the defaults aren't appropriate for a particular component. It's possible to create elaborate property editors for changing the value of specific properties, as well as create sophisticated property sheets to house those editors.

Imagine that you have created a Sound class that is capable of playing various sound format files. You could create a custom property editor for this class that listed all of the known system sounds in a list. If you have created a specialized color type called PrimaryColor, you could create a color picker class to be used as the property editor for PrimaryColor that presented only primary colors as choices.

The JavaBeans architecture also allows you to associate a custom editor with your component. If the task of setting the property values and behaviors of your component is complicated, it may be useful to create a component wizard that guides the user through the steps. The size and complexity of your component editor is entirely up to you.

# JavaBeans Overview

The JavaBeans white paper defines a Bean as follows:

> A Java Bean is a reusable software component that can be manipulated visually in
> a builder tool.

Well, if you have to sum it up in one sentence, this is as good as any. But it's pretty difficult to sum up an entire component architecture in one sentence. Beans will range greatly in their features and capabilities. Some will be very simple and others complex; some will have a visual aspect and others won't. Therefore, it isn't easy to put all Beans into a single category. Let's take a look at some of the most important features and issues surrounding Beans. This should set the stage for the rest of the book, where we will examine the JavaBeans technology in depth.

## Properties, Methods, and Events

Properties are attributes of a Bean that are referenced by name. These properties are usually read and written by calling methods on the Bean specifically created for that purpose. A property of the thermostat component mentioned earlier in the chapter could be the comfort temperature. A programmer would set or get the value of this property through method calls, while an application developer using a visual development tool would manipulate the value of this property using a visual property editor.

The methods of a Bean are just the Java methods exposed by the class that implements the Bean. These methods represent the interface used to access and manipulate the component. Usually, the set of public methods defined by the class will map directly to the supported methods for the Bean, although the Bean developer can choose to expose only a subset of the public methods.

Events are the mechanism used by one component to send notifications to another. One component can register its interest in the events generated by another. Whenever the event occurs, the interested component will be notified by having one of its methods invoked. The process of registering interest in an event is carried out simply by calling the appropriate method on the component that is the source of the event. In turn, when an event occurs a method will be invoked on the component that registered its interest. In most cases, more than one component can register for event notifications from a single source. The component that is interested in event notifications is said to be *listening* for the event.

## Introspection

Introspection is the process of exposing the properties, methods, and events that a JavaBean component supports. This process is used at run-time, as well as by a visual development tool at design-time. The default behavior of this process allows for the automatic introspection of any Bean. A low-level reflection mechanism is used to analyze the Bean's class to determine its methods. Next it applies some simple design patterns to determine the properties and events that are supported. To take advantage of reflection, you only need to follow a coding style that matches the design pattern. This is an important feature of JavaBeans. It means that you don't have to do anything more than code your methods using a simple convention. If you do, your Beans will automatically support introspection without you having to write any extra code. Design patterns are explained in more detail later in the chapter.

This technique may not be sufficient or suitable for every Bean. Instead, you can choose to implement a BeanInfo class which provides descriptive information about its associated Bean explicitly. This is obviously more work than using the default behavior, but it might be necessary to describe a complex Bean properly. It is important to note that the BeanInfo class is separate from the Bean that it is describing. This is done so that it is not necessary to carry the baggage of the Bean-Info within the Bean itself.

If you're writing a development tool, an `Introspector` class is provided as part of the Beans class library. You don't have to write the code to accomplish the analysis, and every tool vendor uses the same technique to analyze a Bean. This is important to us as programmers because we want to be able to choose our development tools and know that the properties, methods, and events that are exposed for a given component will always be the same.

## Customization

When you are using a visual development tool to assemble components into applications, you will be presented with some sort of user interface for customizing Bean attributes. These attributes may affect the way the Bean operates or the way it looks on the screen. The application tool you use will be able to determine the properties that a Bean supports and build a property sheet dynamically. This property sheet will contain editors for each of the properties supported by the Bean, which you can use to customize the Bean to your liking. The Beans class library comes with a number of property editors for common types such as `float`, `boolean`, and `String`. If you are using custom classes for properties, you will have to create custom property editors to associate with them.

In some cases the default property sheet that is created by the development tool will not be good enough. You may be working with a Bean that is just too complex to customize easily using the default sheet. Beans developers have the option of creating a customizer that can help the user to customize an instance of their Bean. You can even create smart wizards that guide the user through the customization process.

Customizers are also kept separate from the Bean class so that it is not a burden to the Bean when it is not being customized. This idea of separation is a common theme in the JavaBeans architecture. A Bean class only has to implement the functionality it was designed for; all other supporting features are implemented separately.

## Persistence

It is necessary that Beans support a large variety of storage mechanisms. This way, Beans can participate in the largest number of applications. The simplest way to support persistence is to take advantage of Java Object Serialization. This is an automatic mechanism for saving and restoring the state of an object. Java Object Serialization is the best way to make sure that your Beans are fully portable, because you take advantage of a standard feature supported by the core Java platform. This, however, is not always desirable. There may be cases where you want your Bean to use other file formats or mechanisms to save and restore state. In the future, JavaBeans will support an alternative externalization mechanism that will allow the Bean to have complete control of its persistence mechanism.

## Design-Time vs. Run-Time

JavaBeans components must be able to operate properly in a running application as well as inside an application development environment. At design-time the component must provide the design information necessary to edit its properties and customize its behavior. It also has to expose its methods and events so that the design tool can write code that interacts with the Bean at run-time. And, of course, the Bean must support the run-time environment.

## Visibility

There is no requirement that a Bean be visible at run-time. It is perfectly reasonable for a Bean to perform some function that does not require it to present an interface to the user; the Bean may be controlling access to a specific device or data feed. However, it is still necessary for this type of component to support the visual application builder. The component can have properties, methods, and events, have persistent state, and interact with other Beans in a larger application. An "invisible" run-time Bean may be shown visually in the application development tool, and may provide custom property editors and customizers.

## Multithreading

The issue of multithreading is no different in JavaBeans than it is in conventional Java programming. The JavaBeans architecture doesn't introduce any new language constructs or classes to deal with threading. You have to assume that your code will be used in a multithreaded application. It is your responsibility to make sure your Beans are thread-safe. Java makes this easier than in most languages, but it still requires some careful planning to get it right. Remember, thread-safe means that your Bean has anticipated its use by more than one thread at a time and has handled the situation properly.

## Security

Beans are subjected to the same security model as standard Java programs. You should assume that your Bean is running in an untrusted applet. You shouldn't make any design decisions that require your Bean to be run in a trusted environment. Your Bean may be downloaded from the World Wide Web into your browser as part of someone else's applet. All of the security restrictions apply to Beans, such as denying access to the local file system, and limiting socket connections to the host system from which the applet was downloaded.

If your Bean is intended to run only in a Java application on a single computer, the Java security constraints do not apply. In this case you might allow your Bean to behave differently. Be careful, because the assumptions you make about security could render your Bean useless in a networked environment.

## Using Design Patterns

The JavaBeans architecture makes use of patterns that represent standard conventions for names, and type signatures for collections of methods and interfaces. Using coding standards is always a good idea because it makes your code easier to understand, and therefore easier to maintain. It also makes it easier for another programmer to understand the purpose of the methods and interfaces used by your component. In the JavaBeans architecture, these patterns have even more significance. A set of simple patterns are used by the default introspection mechanism to analyze your Bean and determine the properties, methods, and events that are supported. These patterns allow the visual development tools to analyze your Bean and use it in the application being created. The following code fragment shows one such pattern:

```
public void setTemperatureColor(Color newColor)
{
    . . .
}

public Color getTemperatureColor()
{
    . . .
}
```

These two methods together use a pattern that signifies that the Bean contains a property named *TemperatureColor* of type Color. No extra development is required to expose the property. The various patterns that apply to Beans development will be pointed out and discussed throughout this book. I'll identify each pattern where the associated topic is being discussed.

---

*NOTE*        The use of the term "design pattern" here may be confusing to some readers. This term is commonly used to describe the practice of documenting a reusable design in object-oriented software. This is not entirely different than the application of patterns here. In this case, the design of the component adheres to a particular convention, and this convention is reused to solve a particular problem.

---

As mentioned earlier, this convention is not a requirement. You can implement a specific BeanInfo class that fully describes the properties, methods, and events supported by your Bean. In this case, you can name your methods anything you please.

# JavaBeans vs. ActiveX

JavaBeans is certainly not the first component architecture to come along. Microsoft's ActiveX technology is based upon COM, their component object model. ActiveX offers an alternative component architecture for software targeted at the various Windows platforms. So how do you choose one of these technologies over the other? Organizational, cultural, and technical issues all come into play when making this decision. ActiveX and JavaBeans are not mutually exclusive of each other—Microsoft has embraced Java technology with products like Internet Explorer and Visual J++, and Sun seems to have recognized that the desktop is dominated by Windows and has targeted Win32 as a strategic platform for Java. It is not in anyone's best interest to choose one technology to the exclusion of another. Both are powerful component technologies. I think we should choose a technology because it supports the work we are doing, and does so in a way that meets the needs of the customer.

The most important question is how Beans will be used by containers that are designed specifically to contain ActiveX controls. Certainly, all Beans will not also be ActiveX controls by default. To address the need to integrate Beans into the world of ActiveX, an ActiveX Bridge is available that maps the properties, methods, and events exposed by the Bean into the corresponding mechanisms in COM. This topic is covered in detail in Chapter 11, *ActiveX*.

# Getting Started

If you plan to play along, you should make sure that you have installed the latest versions of the Java Development Kit (JDK) and the Beans Development Kit (BDK). Both of these can be downloaded from the JavaSoft web site at *http://java.sun.com/*.*

Remember that if you don't have a browser that supports JDK1.1, you will have to run your applets in the *appletviewer* program that is provided in the JDK. At the time of this writing, the only browser that supports JDK1.1 is HotJava.

The chapters in this book are arranged so that they build on concepts presented in preceding chapters. I suggest that you try to follow along in order. Of course, this is entirely up to you. If you are comfortable with the technology, you may find that you can jump around a bit.

---

* Beans development requires JDK1.1; however, JDK1.1.1 is now available.

In this chapter:
• *The Java Event Model*
• *Events in the AWT Package*

2

# Events

Events are messages sent from one object to another, notifying the recipient that something interesting has happened. The component sending the event is said to *fire* the event; the recipient is called a *listener*, and is said to *handle* the event. Many objects can listen for a particular event; thus, components must be able to fire an event to an arbitrary number of objects. (Java allows you to define events that can have at most one listener, but outside of this special case, you must assume that there can be many listeners.) Likewise, an object is free to listen for as many different events as it desires.

The process of firing and handling events is a common feature of windowing systems. Many programmers learned how to write software using this mechanism when they began writing code for Microsoft Windows or the X Windows system. Now the techniques of object-oriented programming are showing us that the event model can be used for applications other than windowing. Firing and handling events is one of two ways that objects communicate with each other. The other is by invoking methods on each other. We will see shortly that these two mechanisms can be one and the same.

## The Java Event Model

The JavaBeans architecture takes advantage of the event model that was introduced in version 1.1 of the Java language. Beans are treated the same as every other object within the event model. In fact, there is nothing at all about the event model that is specific to Beans. This is a common theme in JavaBeans. The Beans component model is designed to take advantage of features that are already available in Java. This is not to say that some of those features were not designed with Beans in mind, because apparently they were. But in many cases the features that are needed by Beans are generic enough to be provided by a core Java class library, making them available to any Java class whether or not it happens to be a Bean.

An event source object sends a notification that an event occurred by invoking a method on the target, or "listening," object. The notification mechanism uses standard Java methods. There is no new language construct or programming syntax required to create such a method. Every event has a specific notification method associated with it. When the event occurs, the associated method is invoked on every object that is listening for it. The method itself describes to the caller which event has taken place. When this method is called, an object is passed as an argument that contains specific information about that particular instance of the event. This object always contains a reference to the object that was the source of the event: it allows the object receiving the event to identify the sender, and is particularly important if an object listens for the same event from several sources. Without this reference, we would have no way of determining which object sent the event. The combination of the method called and the data sent completely defines the event.

The Java event model is comprised of *event objects*, *event listeners*, and *event sources*. These objects interoperate in a standard way, using method invocation to facilitate firing and handling events. Figure 2-1 is a simple diagram of this interaction. The event listener registers itself with the event source to receive event notifications. At some point the event source fires an event with the event object as a parameter, and the event listener handles the event.

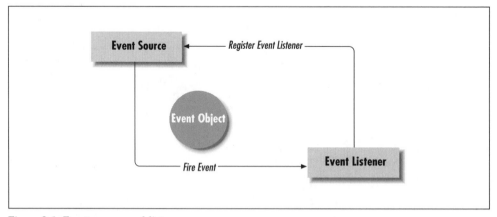

*Figure 2-1. Event sources and listeners*

The Java package `java.util` provides basic support for the event model. It provides a base class for event objects, as well as a base interface for event listeners. All of the classes and interfaces in the Java class libraries that use the event model make use of these classes. When you are developing Beans, or any other Java class that leverages the event model, you will be working directly with these classes and interfaces or their subclasses.

## Event Objects

An event object encapsulates the information that is specific to an instance of an event. For example, an event that represents a mouse click might contain the position of the mouse pointer, and possibly a way of indicating which mouse button was used. This object is passed as the parameter to an event notification method.

The class `java.util.EventObject` is used as the base class for all event objects. It contains a reference to the object that generated the event, along with a method for retrieving that object. It can also render itself as a human-readable string. Like many Java classes, it does this by overriding the `toString()` method. Table 2-1 shows the public methods provided by the `java.util.EventObject` class.

*Table 2-1. Public Methods of EventObject*

| Method | Description |
|---|---|
| `public EventObject(Object source)` | The constructor for the event. It takes the event source object as a parameter. |
| `public Object getSource()` | Returns the object that generated the event. |
| `public String toString()` | Renders the event object in human-readable form. |

Whenever you define an event object for passing information related to a particular event, you should create a subclass of `java.util.EventObject`. By convention, these classes should end in the word *Event*. This helps to quickly identify their purpose to programmers. All of the event subclasses provided by the core Java class libraries follow this convention. Later in this chapter we'll look at some of the classes and interfaces used by the `java.awt.event` package for dealing with events. There you'll notice that this convention is followed, as well as with others that I'll be mentioning.

You are free to pass instances of `java.util.EventObject` when notifying listener objects of events, but you'll probably want to create event-specific subclasses for this purpose. Subclassing allows you to evolve the object over time without redefining any method signatures that take the base class as an argument; it's also useful to ensure that only the desired event type is passed as a parameter during event firing. Equally important is that the event object is part of what defines the event. If you were to use `java.util.EventObject` without subclassing, you would be allowing any (in fact, every) event type to be passed to the event's recipients. This means we could pass a mouse event object when a keyboard event occurs. This is most definitely not a good design practice. You should always subclass

java.util.EventObject even if you don't need to provide any additional information in the event object. If you want to create a new event type without
providing any additional information, your code might look something like this:

```
public class SimpleEvent extends java.util.EventObject
{
    // construct the simple event type
    SimpleEvent(Object source)
    {
        super(source);
    }
}
```

In most cases you will need to extend the basic java.util.EventObject class in
order to fully describe the event. As we'll see later, the event notification method
has no way of distinguishing between event instances. It's up to the event object to
provide the information that uniquely describes a specific instance of an event.
The subclass encapsulates the information related to the event and provides any
methods required to access and manipulate that data.

Before creating a realistic event class, a word about the examples in this book. I
use a set of classes and interfaces to illustrate the concepts throughout each
chapter. As new topics are introduced we'll build on our work. We'll be developing a package for a temperature control simulator. The package is named
BeansBook.Simulator, and it will include classes for things like thermostats,
boilers, and air conditioners. Any useful examples that are not specific to the simulator will be put into another package called BeansBook.util. Although many of
the examples are contrived, they make use of all of the features of Beans development. So by the time we're done, you will have seen all of the concepts applied in
working code.

The simulator is driven by changes in temperature. As the ambient temperature
in our simulated system changes, various objects are going to react. Immediately
we see a need for an event that signals a change in temperature. For our simulator
we will store all temperatures in Celsius. Let's start with the code for a simple
temperature change event object:

```
package BeansBook.Simulator;

public class TempChangedEvent extends java.util.EventObject
{
    // the new temperature value in Celsius
    protected double theTemperature;

    // constructor
    public TempChangedEvent(Object source, double temperature)
    {
```

```
        // pass the source object to the superclass
        super(source);

        // save the new temperature
        theTemperature = temperature;
    }

    // get the temperature value
    public double getTemperature()
    {
        return theTemperature;
    }
}
```

The constructor for the TempChangedEvent class takes the source object and new temperature value as parameters. The source object is passed on to the superclass and the new temperature is stored. The method getTemperature() is provided to allow the new temperature value to be retrieved from the object. We'll see in a later chapter that the getTemperature() method actually conforms to the design pattern for read-only properties.

## Event Listeners

An event listener is an object that needs to be notified when certain events occur. Event notifications are made through method invocations on the listening object, with the event object passed as a parameter. But in order to fire an event, the event source must know what listener method to call. This information is contained in an event-listener interface that defines the methods called to fire an event notification. Any class that wants to receive notifications of the event would implement that interface.

All event-listener interfaces inherit from the base interface java.util.Event-Listener. This interface doesn't actually define any methods. It is used to tag an interface as one that is used for providing event notifications.

By convention, all event-listener interfaces have names ending in the word *Listener*. Just like the convention for event objects described previously, this helps to identify the purpose of the interface. All of the event-listener interfaces provided by the core Java class libraries follow this convention.

An event-listener interface can contain any number of methods, each one corresponding to a different event. These methods are combined in order to collect a set of closely related event notifications into a single interface. If an object wants to listen for the events provided by a source object, it has to implement the associated interface.

Let's create an interface for handling event notifications whenever the ambient temperature in our simulator changes. Later we'll define some kind of object that keeps track of the ambient temperature in the system and generates events when that temperature changes, but for now let's just concentrate on the event listener, which looks as follows:

```
package BeansBook.Simulator;

public interface TempChangeListener extends java.util.EventListener
{
    // this method is called whenever the ambient temperature changes
    void tempChanged(TempChangedEvent evt);
}
```

The methods that are defined in the event-listener interfaces should conform to the standard design pattern for event notification methods. This allows the programmer to quickly understand the purpose of the methods without having to dig through piles of documentation. The method signature for an event-listener method is as follows:

```
void <eventOccurenceMethodName>(<EventObjectType> evt);
```

The event occurrence method name should describe the event. In this example, the method name clearly describes the event that is being fired, tempChanged. The event object type is passed when the event is fired. As described earlier, this object must be derived from the class java.util.EventObject. You can also include a *throws* clause that lists any checked exceptions that might be thrown when this method is invoked.

In some cases it may be beneficial to create a hierarchy of event-listener interfaces. This would allow you to combine the most common event notification methods in a single interface, and to use that interface as the superclass of another interface that adds another set of methods. This can be useful if there are a number of events that most objects listen for, while there are others that only a few objects would be interested in. It would be a nuisance to the programmer to have to implement every event notification method when many of them are of no interest. For example, our simulator system may contain an object that sends basic temperature change events, as well as events sent when the freezing and boiling points for water are crossed. These events may only be interesting to a small subset of potential listeners, and it may be common for these objects to also deal with standard temperature change events. We could derive another listener interface from the TempChangeListener that includes these less frequently used methods. This interface might look like the following:

```
package BeansBook.Simulator;
```

```
public interface AdvancedTempChangeListener
        extends TempChangeListener
{
    // this method is called if the temperature drops below the freezing
    // point of water
    void tempBelowFreezing(TempChangedEvent evt);

    // this method is called if the temperature rises above the boiling
    // point of water
    void tempAboveBoiling(TempChangedEvent evt);
}
```

By creating this hierarchy of event-listener interfaces we are making it easier for client objects, because only one of the interfaces has to be implemented. This also makes it easier for the client object to be upgraded to the advanced interface at a later time without having to change its implementation of the original event methods.

## Event Sources

Event sources are objects that fire events. These objects implement methods which allow the listener to register, and subsequently unregister, its interest in the events it generates. The developer of an object that is interested in the events associated with a source object must implement the appropriate event-listener interface and register its interest in those events. Event-listener registration methods are used for this purpose. The client object invokes a method to add itself as a listener for a specific set of events defined by the associated event-listener interface. The client object can subsequently unregister its interest in those events if it no longer wants to receive them.

The methods used for registration should conform to the standard design pattern for event-listener registration. The method signatures are as follows:

```
public void add<ListenerType>(<ListenerType> listener);
public void remove<ListenerType>(<ListenerType> listener);
```

This pattern identifies the object that implements these methods as an event source for the event-listener interface of type <ListenerType>. The client object invokes the add<ListenerType> method to register an interest in the events supported by the associated interface. When the client object is no longer interested in receiving these event notifications it invokes the corresponding remove<ListenerType> method.

Multiple listeners can be registered with a source for a given set of events. When an event occurs it will be fired to all of the event-listener objects. This is called *multicast event delivery*. It is important to note that the JavaBeans specification does not dictate the event firing order for multicast event sources. This means that it is up to the implementer of the source object to decide the order in which event listeners will be notified for a given event. It would be a good idea to document this information for your users. This might require nothing more than a statement that the firing order is undefined, or you may want to specify a firing order based on the order of registration or some other criterion that is appropriate for your component. Either way, it is a good idea to document it. The same holds true if an event listener is registered more than once, or if a nonexistent event listener is unregistered—what happens is also implementation-dependent, and should be documented. For instance, it might be perfectly legitimate to register an event listener twice. Maybe you would just ignore a registration request for an event listener that is already registered, or maybe you would throw an exception.

Now that we have discussed what is required of an event source, let's continue with our temperature simulator. Let's start to build an object that simulates ambient air temperature, and call this a `Temperature` object. By default it will start with a temperature of 22.2 degrees Celsius (my idea of a comfortable temperature), but this can be overridden by using the constructor that takes a starting temperature as a parameter. This object supports the generation of basic temperature change events, but not the advanced temperature change events we discussed earlier. For now, the code is shown here:

```java
import java.util.Vector;

public class Temperature
{
    // the current temperature in Celsius
    protected double currentTemp = 22.2;

    // the collection of objects listening for temperature changes
    private Vector tempChangeListeners = new Vector();

    // the constructors
    public Temperature(double startingTemp)
    {
        currentTemp = startingTemp;
    }

    public Temperature()
    {
    }

    // add a temperature change listener
    public synchronized void
    addTempChangeListener(TempChangeListener l)
    {
        // add a listener if it is not already registered
        if (!tempChangeListeners.contains(l))
```

```
    {
        tempChangeListeners.addElement(l);
    }
}

// remove a temperature change listener
public synchronized void
removeTempChangeListener(TempChangeListener l)
{
    // remove it if it is registered
    if (tempChangeListeners.contains(l))
    {
        tempChangeListeners.removeElement(l);
    }
}

// notify listening objects of temperature changes
protected void notifyTemperatureChange()
{
    // create the event object
    TempChangedEvent evt = new TempChangedEvent(this, currentTemp);

    // make a copy of the listener object vector so that it cannot
    // be changed while we are firing events
    Vector v;
    synchronized(this)
    {
        v = (Vector) tempChangeListeners.clone();
    }

    // fire the event to all listeners
    int cnt = v.size();
    for (int i = 0; i < cnt; i++)
    {
        TempChangeListener client =
            (TempChangeListener)v.elementAt(i);
        client.tempChanged(evt);
    }
}
}
```

The Temperature class uses a Vector to manage its listeners. When it needs to fire an event, it loops through all the elements in the Vector, calling tempChanged() for each one. While this is the simplest way to manage event listeners, you should be aware that it isn't the only way. Management strategies differ primarily in the data structure used to hold the listeners. A linked list is an obvious choice; AWT uses a curious object called an AWTEventMulticaster, which maintains a binary tree of listeners. If you're brave, you can try subclassing the multicaster in your own code.

So far we haven't talked about how the Temperature object changes its temperature, or even how its current temperature can be accessed. That stuff will be handled when we talk about properties. For now we're just dealing with the events. Let's create a listener object that registers an interest in temperature change events. Maybe a Thermometer class would be useful. This object implements the TempChangeListener so that it can keep track of the current ambient temperature. We start out with the following code for the Thermometer class:

```
package BeansBook.Simulator;

public class Thermometer implements TempChangeListener
{
    // a reference to the temperature object that we are monitoring
    protected Temperature theTemperature;

    Thermometer(Temperature temperature)
    {
        theTemperature = temperature;

        // register for temperature change events
        theTemperature.addTempChangeListener(this);
    }

    // handle the temperature change events
    public void tempChanged(TempChangedEvent evt)
    {
        // do something with the temperature that we can retrieve
        // by calling evt.getTemperature()
    }
}
```

## Event-Listener Methods with Multiple Parameters

I've already mentioned that event notification methods should pass a single argument which is a subclass of java.util.EventObject. But there may be times when it doesn't make sense to limit yourself to this pattern. You may find yourself writing code that interfaces with environments that require that more information is passed when an event is fired, or you just might feel that passing one argument is too confining.

Although it is not recommended, you can define event notification method signatures that contain any number of parameters. The design pattern for the signature is as follows:

```
void <eventOccurenceMethodName>(<parameter list>);
```

The parameters of this method do not have to be instances of EventObject. They can be any valid class or Java primitive.

It is important to stop and think about why you are creating such a method. Is it necessary because you are interfacing to native code? Does it truly provide a degree of flexibility that could not be provided by subclassing an existing event object and encapsulating the extra data? Is there some other way that the desired behavior could be implemented? Maybe you could take advantage of event adapters, a topic that we will study in detail in the next chapter. These are important questions, and you should ask them if you find yourself writing components that fire events using this style of method signature. But if ultimately you find that this is the best way to implement a particular event method, fear not! Visual application development environments are not supposed to discriminate between event notification methods that follow either of the described design patterns. Programming to this type of method by hand doesn't present any real problems, except that it might be a little confusing to someone that expects the method signature to take a single parameter.

## Unicast Event Propagation

So far we have assumed that event delivery is always multicast, supporting any number of event listeners for a single event-listener interface. But some event source objects may not want to support multiple listeners. There can be various reasons for this: for instance, the performance of a particular system or the design itself may dictate that an object support only one event listener. This is known as a unicast event source.

The design pattern for registering interest in a unicast event is almost identical to that of a multicast event, and it looks like the following:

```
public void add<ListenerType>(<ListenerType> listener)
        throws java.util.TooManyListenersException;
public void remove<ListenerType>(<ListenerType> listener);
```

The only difference between the unicast pattern and the multicast pattern is the throws clause with the exception java.util.TooManyListenersException. This pattern indicates that the source object supports only one listener for the listener type specified. Invoking the add<ListenerType> method on a unicast source registers the specified listener only if no other listener is currently registered; otherwise, the java.util.TooManyListenersException is thrown. The nice thing about this arrangement is that source objects can migrate to a multicast event model without breaking any client code.

The name TooManyListenersException may not be the best one. It does not indicate that the source object supports only one listener, only that it has an upper limit. Imagine that you wanted to create an event source that takes up to three listeners, but not more. It seems that you would use the same pattern to model this. The pattern itself can't actually enforce a unicast event model. Maybe that is the kind of flexible interpretation that the JavaBeans designers were aiming for, although I doubt it. This pattern really looks like a way of defining that there are a limited number of listeners that can be supported by the event source, but the spec says that this pattern reflects a unicast event source, so if you see this pattern, you should assume only one listener.

## Exceptions

One concern is that an exception might be thrown while an event is being fired. Event-listener methods are allowed to throw checked exceptions that must be handled by the caller. It is up to the implementer of the event source object to decide what to do when an exception is thrown. In the case of a multicast event source, the implementer may decide not to continue with delivery of event notifications to the remaining listeners. Notice that I said that event listeners are allowed to throw checked exceptions. In actuality, it is entirely possible that an unchecked exception could be thrown. You could wash your hands of this because an unchecked exception is probably due to a bug in the listener object. But since it is likely that your components will be used by a wide variety of bug-ridden applications, it's probably best to let those applications crash somewhere other than in your code. Whatever behavior you choose to implement, the most important thing to do is document it.

## Synchronous Event Delivery

Events are delivered by a source object to a listener in a synchronous manner, using a method invocation. This method call takes place on the caller's thread, which may not be the same one that the listener normally runs on. In many cases this may not present a problem, but for some applications it could be unacceptable to tie up the event source while a listening object processes an event notification. Imagine what would happen if you were writing a controller class for the antilock braking system in an automobile. The object might be designed to send an event to another object that controls the pressure response in the brake pedal. If the pressure control is slow to process the event it might stop the brake controller from maintaining the correct braking pressure. The results could be disastrous! In Chapter 3, *Event Adapters*, we'll look at a few techniques for dealing with this type of problem.

## Multiple Threads

There are a number of issues regarding threads that must be considered when you are designing event sources and event listeners. You simply can't assume that the event notification is being delivered on the same thread that created your listening object. In fact, you should assume that this is not the case. Under these conditions, it is necessary for you to protect your code from multithreaded access by using the synchronization constructs available to you in Java.

You have to be very careful when deciding what methods or blocks of code are going to be synchronized. With events, you have to remember that while your code is calling into the methods of some other object, it is possible that the same object may be making calls back to you from another thread. This can lead to deadlock.

Here are some guidelines that might help you to avoid the common pitfalls of synchronization as they relate to the event model. Event source objects should not hold onto their own internal locks when they are invoking event-listener methods on other objects. This means you should be careful not to call listener methods from within a synchronized block of code or from within a synchronized method. This is particularly important when an event source object is looping through its collection of event listeners in order to fire a multicast event. On the other hand, it is perfectly reasonable for an object to implement its event-listening methods as synchronized methods. This is the best way to protect your event-handling methods from being called from multiple threads at the same time.

A listener can unregister itself while the event is being delivered to another object. This means that the collection object you are using to keep track of event listeners could have been modified in the process. A subsequent access of the listener collection could result in a run-time exception. Therefore, make a copy of the collection of event listeners before any notifications take place, and perform the copy within a synchronized block of code. You might have noticed that I used this technique in the earlier example code for the notifyTemperatureChange() method of the Temperature class. Here it is again:

```
protected void notifyTemperatureChange()
    {
    // create the event object
    TempChangedEvent evt = new TempChangedEvent(this, currentTemp);

    // make a copy of the listener object vector so that it cannot
    // be changed while we are firing events
    Vector v;
    synchronized(this)
        {
```

```
            v = (Vector) tempChangeListeners.clone();
        }

        // fire the event to all listeners
        int cnt = v.size();
        for (int i = 0; i < cnt; i++)
        {
            TempChangeListener client = (TempChangeListener)v.elementAt(i);
            client.tempChanged(evt);
        }
    }
```

The method itself is not synchronized. The Vector that contains the listening objects is cloned within a synchronized block of code. Be sure not to simply assign the Vector to a temporary variable, as this does nothing more than create another reference to it. The clone() method actually creates a new object with an exact copy of the contents of the original. Notice that I end the block of synchronized code before I start firing the event. This is really important. Whenever you fire an event to a listener, there is the chance that the listener will call back to you on another thread. If you fire the event from within a synchronized block, there is a chance that the call made by the other thread will result in deadlock. Again, the basic rule of thumb is to avoid firing events from within synchronized blocks.

This solves the problem for the event source, but what about the event listener? With this scheme it is entirely possible that an event listener could receive an event after it has successfully unregistered itself from the event source. Although a different implementation might avoid this problem, your listening object can't count on it. So when you design your event-listener objects, you'll have to consider the possibility that your object can receive an event notification even after it has unregistered its interest in the event, and your design should deal with this possibility gracefully.

## *Events in the AWT Package*

The components in the java.awt package use the same event model that I've just described. Many of the components in the package send event notifications for things such as mouse clicks, button presses, and window resizings. There are a number of standard classes and interfaces available in java.awt.event for dealing with such events and event notifications. It's interesting to take a look at some of these more closely to see how they are used and how they behave. This will give you some more insight into how the event model works, and how it is employed by one of the core Java packages.

java.awt.Component is the base class for many components in the AWT package. It provides a great deal of functionality that is shared by all components. As such, there are also a number of events that are fired by all components. These events are grouped into a number of event-listener interfaces, which provide methods that are invoked when their associated events occur. Each of these interfaces extends `java.util.EventListener`. For each of these event-listener interfaces, there is also an event object class used to encapsulate any specific information related to an instance of the event. These event classes all extend the class `java.awt.AWTEvent`, which is a subclass of `java.util.EventObject`.

Let's take a look at one of the event interfaces supported by the `java.awt.Compo-`nent class. This interface, `java.awt.event.MouseListener`, is used to provide notifications of events that are generated due to the pointer moving into or out of the frame of a component, or a mouse button press. The interface definition for `java.awt.event.MouseListener` looks like the following:

```
public interface MouseListener extends EventListener
{
    // generated whenever a mouse button is clicked while the mouse
    // pointer is over the component
    public abstract void mouseClicked(MouseEvent e);

    // generated when the mouse pointer crosses into the boundary
    // of the component
    public abstract void mouseEntered(MouseEvent e);

    // generated when the mouse pointer crosses outside of the boundary
    // of the component
    public abstract void mouseExited(MouseEvent e);

    // generated when a mouse button is pressed while the mouse pointer
    // is over the component
    public abstract void mousePressed(MouseEvent e);

    // generated when a mouse button is released while the mouse pointer
    // is over the component
    public abstract void mouseReleased(MouseEvent e);
}
```

All of the methods in the `MouseListener` interface take a single parameter. This parameter is of type `java.awt.event.MouseEvent`, and is used to encapsulate the information that is related to a specific instance of the event. This class inherits from a rather lengthy class hierarchy, so I won't bother going into the features provided by each of its superclasses. Table 2-2 shows some of the methods that are provided by the `MouseEvent` class. It is not a complete listing, but it's enough to give you a feel for the class.

*Table 2-2. Methods for Working with MouseEvents*

| Method | Description |
|---|---|
| `public int getX()` | Returns the *x* position of the event relative to the source component. |
| `public int getY()` | Returns the *y* position of the event relative to the source component. |
| `public synchronized Point getPoint()` | Returns the *x, y* position of the event relative to the source component. |
| `public synchronized void`<br>`    translatePoint(int x, int y)` | Translates the coordinate position of the event by *x, y*. |
| `public int getClickCount()` | Return the number of mouse clicks associated with this event. |

Notice that the `getX()` and `getY()` methods are not synchronized, but the `getPoint()` method is. There is no reason to synchronize the `getX()` and `getY()` methods because the values they return do not depend on each other. But when you call `getPoint()`, you are asking for both the *x* and *y* coordinate values at one time. In this case these values are expected to be consistent in relation to each other. If the method wasn't synchronized, there's a chance that one of the values might be changed before the method returns.

Next we will examine the class `java.awt.Button`. This class implements the standard pushbutton object. Obviously this class adds functionality to the base `java.awt.Component` class to provide button behavior. This includes the way the component is drawn, the ability to associate a textual label with the object, and an event (`ActionEvent`) that notifies a listener that the button has been pushed. But an interface is not defined just to handle the event generated by pushing the button. There are quite a few components in the AWT package that have similar action-style events. For example, every item in a menu is a subclass of `Component`. When a menu item is selected, an action event is generated. Instead of defining a new type of event for each component, a generic action event exists that is used by all components that fit the action event model. The interface associated with the action event is named `java.awt.event.ActionListener`, the interface definition of which looks like the following:

```
public interface ActionListener extends java.util.EventListener
{
    // generated when an action is performed on a component
    void actionPerformed(ActionEvent e);
}
```

The `actionPerformed()` method takes an `ActionEvent` object as its sole parameter. Just like the `MouseEvent` object, this object is used to provide information specific to an action event.

Getting back to the `java.awt.Button` class, it should be clear that it is a source of the events handled by both `MouseListener` and `ActionListener`, as well as others that I have not covered here. So if an object wanted to receive notifications of mouse events, it would call the following method on the button (which is actually provided by the base `Component` class):

```
public void addMouseListener(MouseListener listener);
```

Likewise, if an object wanted to receive action event notifications from the button, it would register itself by calling the following method provided by the `Button` class:

```
public void addActionListener(ActionListener listener);
```

Now we can talk about how to go about listening for events generated by the button. The following code implements a simple applet that contains a push-button. When the button is pressed the phrase *Button Pressed* is printed to the console. This means that the applet must implement the `ActionListener` interface in order to receive the action event notification. The applet also keeps track of when the mouse pointer enters and exits the button, and it prints to the console the phrases *Mouse Entered* and *Mouse Exited,* respectively. Therefore, it also implements the `MouseListener` interface. Here's the code for this applet:

```
import java.applet.*;
import java.awt.*;
import java.awt.event.*;

// the applet class definition
public class ExampleApplet1 extends Applet
        implements ActionListener, // to receive action events
                   MouseListener   // to receive mouse events
{
    // the button
    protected Button theButton;

    // the applet initialization
    public void init()
    {
        // add the button to the applet
        theButton = new Button("Press Me");
        add(theButton);

        // make this applet an action listener
        theButton.addActionListener(this);

        // make this applet a mouse listener
        theButton.addMouseListener(this);
    }
```

```
    // this gets called when the button is pressed
    public void actionPerformed(ActionEvent e)
    {
        System.out.println("Button Pressed");
    }


    // this gets called when the mouse pointer enters the button
    public void mouseEntered(MouseEvent e)
    {
        System.out.println("Mouse Entered");
    }


    // this gets called when the mouse pointer exits the button
    public void mouseExited(MouseEvent e)
    {
        System.out.println("Mouse Exited");
    }


    // this gets called on a mouse click over the button.
    // this is NOT the same as a button press, which results in
    // an action event being generated
    public void mouseClicked(MouseEvent e)
    {
    }


    // this gets called when a mouse button is pressed over the button
    public void mousePressed(MouseEvent e)
    {
    }


    // this gets called when a mouse button is released over the button
    public void mouseReleased(MouseEvent e)
    {
    }
}
```

One question that comes to mind at this point is how the event model works with inheritance. In other words, what happens if I want to extend an existing java.awt component to perform some function when an event takes place? For instance, let's say I was creating a button that automatically updated its label to reflect the number of times it had been pressed. One way to accomplish this would be to make the new button an ActionListener on itself. This way it would be informed of the event just like any other listener. The code would look like this:

```
import java.awt.*;
import java.awt.event.*;

class UpdatingButton extends Button
    implements ActionListener
```

```
{
    // number of times pressed
    protected int count = 0;

    // constructors
    UpdatingButton()
    {
        this("");
    }

    UpdatingButton(String str)
    {
        super(str);

        // register as an action listener on myself
        addActionListener(this);
    }

    // called when the button is pressed
    public void actionPerformed(ActionEvent e)
    {
        // bump the count and update the label
        count++;
        setLabel(String.valueOf(count));
    }
}
```

This approach is perfectly legitimate, and in fact works just fine in this example. But we know one of the strengths of the JavaBeans model is that it supports inheritance. So there must be another way to accomplish this. The java.awt.Button class, as an action event source, implements a protected interface with the following signature:

```
protected void processActionEvent(ActionEvent e);
```

This method is called whenever an action event notification is going to be fired. By overriding this method, a subclass of java.awt.Button can intercept action event notifications before they are fired. This allows you to perform any function you want either before or after the notifications take place.

Normally, events will not be generated unless there are corresponding event listeners registered. To force the processActionEvent() method to be called even if no listeners are registered, you'll have to make a call to enableEvents() with the appropriate event masks for the events you are interested in. The code for the self-updating button now looks like this:

```
import java.awt.*;
import java.awt.event.*;
```

```java
class UpdatingButton extends Button
{
    // number of times pressed
    protected int count = 0;

    // constructors
    UpdatingButton()
    {
        this("");
    }

    UpdatingButton(String str)
    {
        super(str);

        // enable action events
        enableEvents(AWTEvent.ACTION_EVENT_MASK);
    }

    protected void processActionEvent(ActionEvent e)
    {
        // make sure listeners are notified
        super.processActionEvent(e);

        // bump the count and update the label
        count++;
        setLabel(new Integer(count).toString());
    }
}
```

# 3

# Event Adapters

It may have already occurred to you that the event model could get unmanageable rather quickly. For instance, if a given object wanted to listen for events from a large number of event source objects, it would have to implement the interfaces for every one. This may not be the best approach if only a few of the events that are supported by the event listener interfaces are of interest. Another problem occurs when an object is listening for events from two or more objects that are sources of the same event types. Since an object can only implement an event listener interface once, it would have to figure out for itself which object was the source of the event.

Neither of these problems is insurmountable, but each can (and often will) lead to code that is hard to read and even harder to maintain. One way of dealing with this is to introduce another object—an *event adapter*—between the event source and the event target. The purpose of this object is to adapt the source to the specific needs of the target: thus the name. Figure 3-1 shows a diagram of the object interaction using an adapter.

## Demultiplexing

Because a listener object can receive event notifications from multiple sources, it is said to be a multiplexing event receiver. For example, let's say that our Thermometer object was designed to track temperatures from two locations at the same time. This means that it is going to receive temperature change events from two Temperature objects. These notifications will both take place by invoking the one and only tempChanged() method that is implemented by the Thermometer. We might find it more appropriate to have different methods in our Thermometer

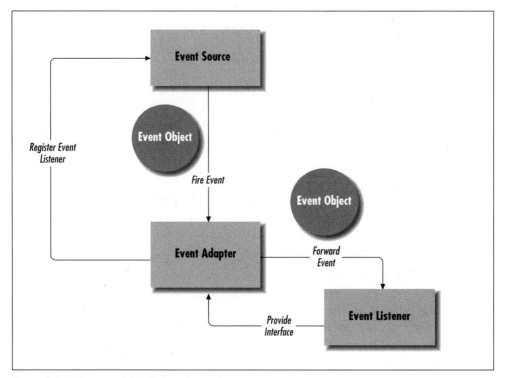

*Figure 3-1. Using an adapter to handle events*

class to deal with events from our two `Temperature` objects. Let's say we have the following two methods for dealing with temperature changes:

```
// handle changes to Temperature object 1
protected void temperature1Changed(double newTemp)
{
}

// handle changes to Temperature object 2
protected void temperature2Changed(double newTemp)
{
}
```

Until now, the implementation of the `tempChanged()` method would have to figure out for itself which `Temperature` object generated the event, and then invoke the appropriate handler method. The code for routing events would look something like this:

```
public void tempChanged(TempChangeEvent evt)
{
    if (temperature1 == evt.getSource())
    {
```

```
        temperature1Changed(evt.getTemperature());
    }
    else if (temperature2 == evt.getSource())
    {
        temperature2Changed(evt.getTemperature());
    }
}
```

This code doesn't look so bad. But imagine what it would look like if there were ten Temperature objects firing events on a single Thermometer object. Now take it a step further. What if our event source were capable of firing five different event types? The amount of code we would need just to route events to the appropriate method could grow very large.

## Adapter Classes

Instead of this approach, we could insert adapters between the Thermometer object and each of its Temperature objects. These adapters would receive the temperature change events from their associated Temperature object. Each adapter would in turn invoke the appropriate method on the Thermometer. These adapters have the affect of demultiplexing the events. The diagram in Figure 3-2 shows how adapters can be used.

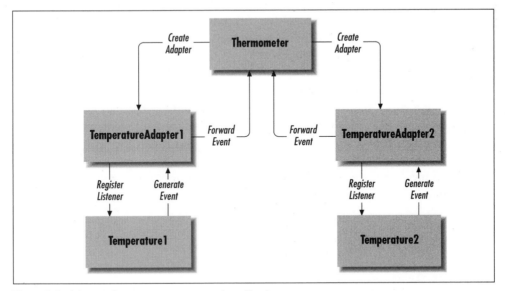

*Figure 3-2. Adapters in a temperature control application*

Each adapter receives a temperature change event from a single Temperature source. So there is a one-to-one relationship between an event source and an event adapter, and a one-to-many relationship between an event target and an adapter. We start by creating a base adapter class that implements a single event listener interface. This class will do nothing with the received events. This base adapter is designed to be subclassed to serve a specific target object. Let's take a look at the code for the base TemperatureAdapter class:

```
package BeansBook.Simulator;

public class TemperatureAdapter implements TempChangeListener
{
    // the constructor
    public TemperatureAdapter(Temperature t)
    {
        // register for events
        t.addTempChangeListener(this);
    }

    // handle the event
    public void tempChanged(TempChangedEvent evt)
    {
        // forward the event
    }
}
```

The constructor takes a Temperature object as a parameter, and registers itself as an event listener for this object. There is an empty implementation of the tempChanged() method for receiving temperature change events. If we were adapting an interface that had several methods, we would provide a default empty implementation for each one. This is done so that a subclass can choose to handle only those events that it is interested in by overriding the associated methods. The rest of the events will be handled by the default methods, which simply do nothing. We subclass this adapter to create an adapter that can be used by the Thermometer object. This new adapter takes a Thermometer object as a parameter in its constructor, and it saves this parameter so that it can forward events to the Thermometer object when they are received. The tempChanged() method is overridden to invoke the appropriate method on the target Thermometer. We'll create a different adapter for each Temperature source:

```
public class TemperatureAdapter1 extends TemperatureAdapter
{
    protected Thermometer target;

    // the constructor
    TemperatureAdapter1(Thermometer targ, Temperature t)
    {
        // pass this to the superclass
        super(t);
```

```
        target = targ;
    }

    public void tempChanged(TempChangedEvent evt)
    {
        target.temperature1Changed(evt.getTemperature());
    }
}

public class TemperatureAdapter2 extends TemperatureAdapter
{
    protected Thermometer target;

    // the constructor
    TemperatureAdapter2(Thermometer targ, Temperature t)
    {
        // pass this to the superclass
        super(t);

        target = targ;
    }

    public void tempChanged(TempChangedEvent evt)
    {
        target.temperature2Changed(evt.getTemperature());
    }
}
```

## Using Inner Classes

There are a couple of problems with this approach. The subclassed adapters and the Thermometer have a circular dependency. Each of these classes depends upon each other. This creates a problem when you are compiling your code. The Thermometer class expects the adapter class to be compiled previously, since it needs to reference it, and the adapter expects the same thing about the Thermometer. So which one do we compile first? This circular dependency is a sign that we need to provide a closer physical relationship between the Thermometer and adapter classes. Since the adapters are specific to the Thermometer class, they don't have to be public, so we can move the code for the adapters into the same file as the Thermometer class. Now that we have a coupled relationship, we might as well make things a little simpler by using Java inner classes to implement the adapters. An inner class is one that is encapsulated within the scope of another class. Since the inner class shares the scope of the encapsulating class, it has access to its data and member functions. The following code shows the Thermometer class with the two adapters implemented as inner classes:

```
package BeansBook.Simulator;
```

```java
public class Thermometer
{
    // references to the two temperature objects that we are monitoring
    protected Temperature theTemperature1;
    protected Temperature theTemperature2;

    // the temperature change adapters
    protected TemperatureAdapter1 tempAdapter1;
    protected TemperatureAdapter2 tempAdapter2;

    // the first adapter class
    class TemperatureAdapter1 extends TemperatureAdapter
    {
        TemperatureAdapter1(Temperature t)
        {
            super(t);
        }

        public void tempChanged(TempChangedEvent evt)
        {
            temperature1Changed(evt.getTemperature());
        }
    }

    // the second adapter class
    class TemperatureAdapter2 extends TemperatureAdapter
    {
        TemperatureAdapter2(Temperature t)
        {
            super(t);
        }

        public void tempChanged(TempChangedEvent evt)
        {
            temperature2Changed(evt.getTemperature());
        }
    }

    // constructor
    Thermometer(Temperature temperature1, Temperature temperature2)
    {
        // save references to the temperature objects
        theTemperature1 = temperature1;
        theTemperature2 = temperature2;

        // create the adapters
        tempAdapter1 = new TemperatureAdapter1();
        tempAdapter2 = new TemperatureAdapter2();
    }
```

```
    // handle changes to Temperature object 1
    protected void temperature1Changed(double newTemp)
    {
    }

    // handle changes to Temperature object 2
    protected void temperature2Changed(double newTemp)
    {
    }
}
```

Notice that this Thermometer class doesn't implement the TempChangeListener interface anymore. This is because the adapters are handling the temperature change events on its behalf. When the adapters receive an event notification, they forward the message on to the associated Thermometer method. The adapters each extend the base TemperatureAdapter class. The adapter constructors pass the corresponding Temperature object to the base class, and they forward the new temperature to the corresponding method of the Thermometer class. Before forwarding the event, the adapter extracts the new temperature from the TempChangedEvent object that was sent by the Temperature object.

Adapters are a good technique for decoupling an event listener from an event source. It also works well when you have more than one source firing the same type of event on a listener. But so far we've done nothing to reduce the overall complexity of the code. We need an adapter object for each event source, and we have to create a new adapter for each target object that it forwards events to. So we're going to end up with a large number of new adapter classes that cannot be reused by others. What we really want is a generic adapter: an adapter that is specific to an event source, but not specific to an event target. Such an adapter would eliminate any dependency between the adapter and the object to which it forwards its events.

## Generic Adapters

How can we create a TemperatureAdapter class that is not coupled to a specific target class? We need some way of telling the adapter how to forward an event to the target. In the earlier examples, the TemperatureAdapter class had knowledge about the methods available in the Thermometer class. But this is no good, because we want to decouple the adapter from the target. Normally we would define an interface for the target object to implement, but if we did, we would have the same problem we had before the adapter was introduced. The proposed interface can be implemented only once, so again we would have no way of knowing which adapter was forwarding the event to us.

Let's take a closer look at what we're trying to do here. We're actually trying to create a mapping from the event forwarded by an instance of a given adapter to a method on the listening object, without forcing the listener to declare that it implements any particular Java interface. We want multiple instances of a specific adapter to forward their events to different methods on the same target, as shown in Figure 3-3.

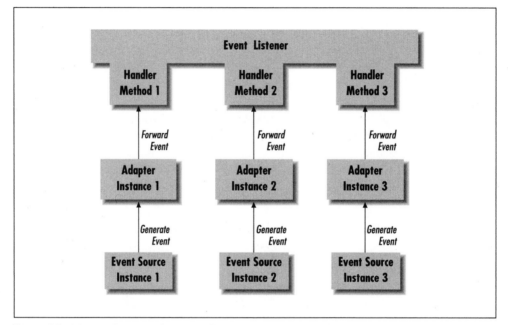

*Figure 3-3. Adapters for events from several sources*

In order to do this in a generic way, we need a mechanism for telling the adapter at run-time which method to invoke when it forwards an event. If we were programming in C++, we could use function pointers to accomplish this. The adapter would be handed a pointer to a function that conforms to a specific signature, and this method would be called by the adapter to forward the event. But in Java we don't have that option. We have only objects and interfaces at our disposal. Or do we?

## *Using Java Reflection*

The Java reflection API is designed for analyzing Java objects and classes at run-time. Amongst other things, the reflection mechanism allows you to discover methods at run-time. The methods are represented by an instance of the class `java.lang.reflect.Method`. We'll be able to associate an instance of this class to an instance of an adapter. The methods that will be invoked by the adapter must conform to a specific signature, and you'll see shortly how we ensure that they do.

### Finding the class

The `java.lang.Class` class contains a static method called `forName()`. This method takes a string parameter containing the fully qualified class name and returns an instance of `java.lang.Class`. If the class does not exist, the exception `java.lang.ClassNotFoundException` will be thrown. The following example shows how to get the `Class` object for the `java.awt.Button` class:

```
try
{
    Class theClass = Class.forName("java.awt.Button");
}
catch (java.lang.ClassNotFoundException e)
{
}
```

You can also obtain the `Class` object associated with any Java object that is already instantiated. The `Object` class provides a method called `getClass()`, which returns the associated instance of `java.lang.Class`. Using `getClass()` allows for the possibility that the class wasn't loaded by the default class loader. If we already had an instance of `java.awt.Button`, we could get its `Class` object as follows:

```
java.awt.Button theButton = new java.awt.Button("Sample");
try
{
    Class theClass = theButton.getClass();
}
catch (java.lang.ClassNotFoundException e)
{
}
```

Probably the easiest technique for getting a `Class` object is to assign it the static definition of the class you are looking for. You can specify the static class definition by appending *.class* to the class name. Here's an example:

```
Class theClass = java.awt.Button.class;
```

### Finding the method

Once we have determined the `Class` object, we can get an instance of `java.lang.reflect.Method` for any of the methods implemented by the object. The `java.lang.Class` class contains a method named `getMethod()`, which takes the name of the method as a `String` as one parameter, and an array of `Class` objects as the other parameter. This array contains the instances of `java.lang.Class` for each parameter in the method signature. If there are no parameters in the method you are reflecting, you can pass null in place of the array. Finally, the java.lang.reflect.Method class has a method named invoke(), which is used to invoke the method. It takes the target Object as the first parameter, and an Object array as the second parameter. This array is used to pass the parameters to the method being invoked. But not all parameters will be a subclass of Object. What if you have parameters that are one of the primitive Java types, such as int or float? In those cases you'll have to use the static object representation of that type. As you know, each primitive data type has a corresponding object type; for instance the type float has a corresponding class called Float. Each of the object versions of the primitives contain a static field named TYPE that is used to represent its primitive counterpart as an object. For example, the object representation of float would be java.lang.Float.TYPE. The following code shows how we could find the setLabel() method of the java.awt.Button class, and then invoke it.

```
try
{
    // get the button class
    java.awt.Button theButton = new java.awt.Button("Sample");
    Class theClass = theButton.getClass();

    // get the string parameter class
    java.lang.Class paramClasses[] = { java.lang.String.class };

    // find the method
    java.lang.reflect.Method mthd = theClass.getMethod("setLabel"
                                                        paramClasses);

    // now invoke it, changing the label to "Did It"
    Object param[] = { new String("Did It") };
    mthd.invoke(theButton, param);
}
catch (java.lang.IllegalAccessException e)
{
}
catch (java.lang.ClassNotFoundException e)
{
}
catch (java.lang.NoSuchMethodException e)
{
}
catch (java.lang.InvocationTargetException e)
{
}
```

## Single Instance Adapters

This technique allows us to create an adapter that uses reflection to find the method that handles events. But we will still need an instance of this adapter for every event source. It would be nice to build the generic adapter so that we only need one instance of it to handle events from multiple event sources, and forward those events to different methods on a single target. Figure 3-4 shows this.

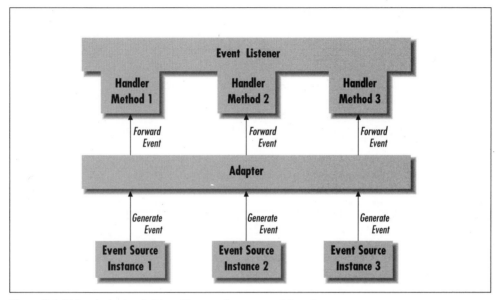

*Figure 3-4. Using a single adapter with several sources and targets*

Let's create a generic adapter object that adapts the `TempChangedListener` interface to any arbitrary target object, and that can handle multiple `Temperature` objects as event sources. The only requirement for the target object is that the signature of the methods that the adapter will forward events to looks as follows:

```
public void <methodName>(BeansBook.Simulator.TempChangeEvent evt);
```

The only new method needed for the `GenericTemperatureAdapter` class is `registerEventHandler()`; it takes a `Temperature` object and a method name as parameters. This method is used to associate the event-handling method on the target object with a specific `Temperature` event source. When the adapter receives a `tempChanged` event, it will forward it to the method on the target with the name passed into this parameter. The adapter uses a hash table to store these mappings. When the event is received, the source object is retrieved from the `TempChanged-Event`. This object is then used to look up the associated event-handling method object in the hash table. The code for this adapter is shown here.

```java
package BeansBook.Simulator;

import java.lang.reflect.*;
import java.util.*;

public class GenericTemperatureAdapter
        implements TempChangeListener // the adapter receives the events
{
    // the target object
    protected Object theTarget;

    // the class of the target object
    protected Class theTargetClass;

    // the class array for the parameters used for
    // the target method
    protected final static Class paramClasses[] =
                { BeansBook.Simulator.TempChangedEvent.class };

    // the mapping of source objects to callback methods
    protected Hashtable mappingTable = new Hashtable();

    // constructor
    public GenericTemperatureAdapter(Object target)
    {
        theTarget = target;
        theTargetClass = target.getClass();
    }

    // add an event source, along with the name of the method to call
    // on the target when the event is received
    public void registerEventHandler(Temperature tmp, String methodName)
                throws NoSuchMethodException
    {
        Method mthd = theTargetClass.getMethod(methodName, paramClasses);
        tmp.addTempChangeListener(this);
        mappingTable.put(tmp, mthd);
    }

    // implement the listener method
    public void tempChanged(TempChangedEvent evt)
    {
        try
        {
            // invoke the registered method on the target
            Method mthd = (Method)mappingTable.get(evt.getSource());
            Object params[] = { evt };
            mthd.invoke(theTarget, params);
        }
```

```
        catch (IllegalAccessException e)
        {
            System.out.println(e);
        }
        catch (InvocationTargetException e)
        {
            System.out.println(e);
        }
    }
```

Now that we've got an adapter, let's rewrite the Thermometer class to use it. This is pretty straightforward stuff. We can get rid of the inner class adapters, and use one instance of GenericTemperatureAdapter instead. In the earlier example, the methods temperature1Changed() and temperature2Changed() took an instance of double as the parameter. This was because the inner class adapters pulled the new temperature from the event object before the methods were called. The new adapter, GenericTemperatureAdapter, just passes the event object to the target method, so we need to change the parameter type for these methods from double to TempChangedEvent.

```
package BeansBook.Simulator;

public class Thermometer
{
    // references to the two temperature objects that we are monitoring
    protected Temperature theTemperature1;
    protected Temperature theTemperature2;

    // the temperature change adapter
    protected GenericTemperatureAdapter tempAdapter;

    // constructor
    Thermometer(Temperature temperature1, Temperature temperature2)
    {
        // save references to the temperature objects
        theTemperature1 = temperature1;
        theTemperature2 = temperature2;

        // create the adapter
        tempAdapter = new GenericTemperatureAdapter(this);

        // register the handler methods
        try
        {
            tempAdapter.registerEventHandler(theTemperature1,
                                "temperature1Changed");
            tempAdapter.registerEventHandler(theTemperature2,
                                "temperature2Changed");
        }
```

```
        catch (NoSuchMethodException e)
        {
            System.out.println(e);
        }
    // handle changes to Temperature object 1
    public void temperature1Changed(TempChangedEvent evt)
    {
    }

    // handle changes to Temperature object 2
    public void temperature2Changed(TempChangedEvent evt);
    {
    }
}
```

# Event Adapters in the AWT Package

The java.awt.event package provides adapters for various event-listener types. These adapters are nothing more than empty shells that implement the methods in the various listener interfaces. These adapters don't provide much added value, but you can subclass them to build basic demultiplexing adapters. They relieve you from having to implement every interface method yourself, although the burden is quite small.

Let's look at an example. The following chunk of code is the listing for the java.awt.event.FocusAdapter class:

```
    public class FocusAdapter implements FocusListener
    {
        public FocusAdapter()
        {
        }

        public void focusGained(FocusEvent e)
        {
        }

        public void focusLost(FocusEvent e)
        {
        }
    }
```

So, as you can see, these adapters aren't all that helpful. You'll find an adapter class in java.awt.event for every event-listener interface that has more than one method in it. I think the fact that these adapters are provided at all is an indication that the technique is expected to be widely used. But I expect that more complex adapters will find more use than these.

## A Generic Button Adapter

It's common for a dialog box or other window to contain multiple Button objects—a perfect place to make use of an intelligent adapter. The Generic-TemperatureAdapter class shown earlier can be easily modified for this purpose. Let's create an adapter that will handle the ActionListener interface for multiple buttons, and will forward the ActionEvent to a method on the target object. Here's the code for the GenericButtonAdapter class:

```java
package BeansBook.util;

import java.awt.*;
import java.awt.event.*;
import java.lang.reflect.*;
import java.util.*;

public class GenericButtonAdapter
        implements ActionListener // the adapter receives the events
{
    // the target object
    protected Object theTarget;

    // the class of the target object
    protected Class theTargetClass;

    // the class array for the parameters used for
    // the target method
    protected final static Class paramClasses[] =
                        { java.awt.event.ActionEvent.class };

    // the mapping of source objects to callback methods
    protected Hashtable mappingTable = new Hashtable();

    // constructor
    public GenericButtonAdapter(Object target)
        throws ClassNotFoundException
    {
        theTarget = target;
        theTargetClass = target.getClass();
    }

    // add an action object to listen for, along with the
    // method to call on the target when the action event
    // is received
    public void registerActionEventHandler(Button btn,
                                            String methodName)
                throws NoSuchMethodException
    {
        Method mthd = theTargetClass.getMethod(methodName, paramClasses);
        btn.addActionListener(this);
```

```
        mappingTable.put(btn, mthd);
    }

    // implement the listener method
    public void actionPerformed(ActionEvent evt)
    {
        try
        {
            // invoke the registered method on the target
            Method mthd = (Method)mappingTable.get(evt.getSource());

            Object params[] = { evt };
            mthd.invoke(theTarget, params);
        }
        catch (IllegalAccessException e)
        {
            System.out.println(e);
        }
        catch (InvocationTargetException e)
        {
            System.out.println(e);
        }
    }
}
```

Now let's create a simple applet that makes use of the adapter. The applet contains three buttons, labeled *Button 1* through *Button 3*. The applet also has three handler methods that, when invoked, print a message to the console that contains the name of the message handler and the label of the button that was pressed. The applet is trivial, but it illustrates how the adapter is used. The code for the applet is shown below:

```
import java.applet.*;
import java.awt.*;
import java.awt.event.*;
import java.util.*;
import BeansBook.util.*;

public class ExampleApplet2 extends Applet
{
    // the buttons
    protected Button b1 = new Button("Button 1");
    protected Button b2 = new Button("Button 2");
    protected Button b3 = new Button("Button 3");

    // the adapter
    protected GenericButtonAdapter adapter;

    // the applet initialization
    public void init()
```

```
    {
        // add the buttons to the applet
        add(b1);
        add(b2);
        add(b3);

        try
        {
            adapter = new GenericButtonAdapter(this);
            adapter.registerActionEventHandler(b1, "handleB1");
            adapter.registerActionEventHandler(b2, "handleB2");
            adapter.registerActionEventHandler(b3, "handleB3");
        }
        catch (ClassNotFoundException e)
        {
            System.out.println(e);
        }
        catch (NoSuchMethodException e)
        {
            System.out.println(e);
        }
    }

    public void handleB1(ActionEvent e)
    {
        Button b = (Button)e.getSource();
        System.out.println("handleB1 called for button " + b.getLabel());
    }

    public void handleB2(ActionEvent e)
    {
        Button b = (Button)e.getSource();
        System.out.println("handleB2 called for button " + b.getLabel());
    }

    public void handleB#(ActionEvent e)
    {
        Button b = (Button)e.getSource();
        System.out.println("handleB3 called for button " + b.getLabel());
    }
}
```

When you run this applet, it appears as shown in Figure 3-5.

If you were to press the buttons on the applet consecutively, the following output would be printed to your console window:

```
handleB1 called for button Button 1
handleB2 called for button Button 2
handleB3 called for button Button 3
```

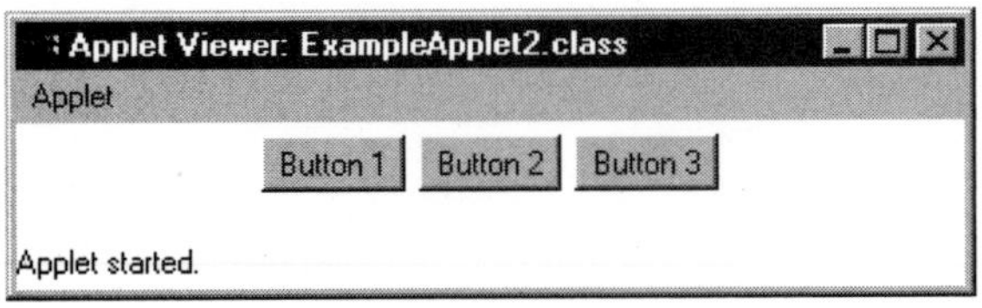

*Figure 3-5. An applet using a generic adapter*

# Event Filtering

Adapters can be used for filtering out events that don't meet certain criteria. The adapter would analyze the information contained in the event and decide whether to forward it to the target object. This could be useful when the event source generates many events and only a small number of them are interesting to the listener.

For example, let's say that we were going to monitor the temperature in our simulator with a special listener that is interested only in temperature changes above or below certain values. We could create an adapter that filters out all temperature change events where the new temperature is between a low and a high threshold value. The GenericTemperatureAdapter can be easily modified to perform this task. The new adapter might be called a GenericTemperature-ThresholdAdapter. We add data members to store the threshold temperatures and assign them default values as follows:

```
protected double lowThreshold = 0.0;
protected double highThreshold = 100.0;
```

Now we need a way to assign the threshold values. For our example, we create methods for getting and setting these values. You'll see in Chapter 4, *Properties*, that these values represent properties of the adapter. The new methods of the GenericTemperatureThresholdAdapter look like this:

```
public void setLowThreshold (double low)
{
    lowThreshold = low;
}

public double getLowThreshold()
{
    return lowThreshold;
}

public void setHighThreshold(double high)
{
    highThreshold = high;
}
```

```
public double getHighThreshold()
{
    return highThreshold;
}
```

Now we need to modify the code that does event notifications to perform the filtering. Before we even look up the method that is associated with the source of the event, we compare the new temperature to our threshold values. We only forward the event if the new temperature falls below the low or above the high threshold. The modified code for the tempChanged() method is shown below:

```
// implement the listener method
public void tempChanged(TempChangedEvent evt)
{
    // compare the new temperature against the threshold
    if (evt.getTemperature() < lowThreshold ||
        evt.getTemperature() > highThreshold)
    {
        try
        {
            // invoke the registered method on the target
            Method mthd = (Method)mappingTable.get(evt.getSource());
            Object params[] = { evt };
            mthd.invoke(theTarget, params);
        }
        catch (IllegalAccessException e)
        {
            System.out.println(e);
        }
        catch (InvocationTargetException e)
        {
            System.out.println(e);
        }
    }
}
```

## Event Queuing

So far, everything we've done assumes that events are being generated synchronously. We've also assumed that this wouldn't create a problem for the object that generates the events. Remember that events are fired on the caller's thread. In some cases, this thread may have other work to do. If we write event-handler methods that do a great deal of work before returning to the caller, we may hold up the caller's thread longer than is safe. Holding up the caller's thread could also be a problem if it is important that all event listeners be notified quickly. Since the delivery order of events is generally undefined, it would be unfair (or worse) to hold up the delivery of an event to one listener because another is slow to respond.

We could assume that if an event generator didn't want to be interrupted for long periods of time, it would be implemented to protect itself from this possibility. But another approach is to use an event adapter that queues events and forwards them to the target object on another thread. This type of asynchronous delivery allows the thread that originally fired the event to continue doing whatever it wants, because the method call it made when firing the event returns almost immediately.

Let's create an example to illustrate how to build this type of adapter. We have a worker object that runs a thread every 200 milliseconds in order to update a counter. This object will be called a `Poller`. On every third update it generates a `PollEvent` to a listening object that implements the `PollerListener` interface, and it also prints the string "Value: $x$," where $x$ represents the value of the counter. Here's the code.

```java
import java.util.*;

class PollEvent extends EventObject
{
    // the event value
    protected int value;

    // constructor takes source and value
    PollEvent(Object source, int value)
    {
        // pass the source to the superclass
        super(source);

        // save the value
        this.value = value;
    }

    // return the event value
    public int getValue()
    {
        return value;
    }
}

interface PollerListener
{
    public abstract void pollSent(PollEvent e);
}
```

```
class Poller extends Thread
{
   // a counter
   protected int cnt = 0;

   // the listener
   protected PollerListener listener = null;

   // the constructor
   public Poller()
   {
      // start my thread
      start();
   }

   // add the listener
   public void addPollerListener(PollerListener l)
                  throws TooManyListenersException
   {
      if (listener != null)
      {
         throw new TooManyListenersException();
      }

      listener = l;
   }

   // remove the listener
   public void removePollerListener(PollerListener l)
   {
      if (listener == l)
      {
         listener = null;
      }
   }

   // the run loop for this thread
   public synchronized void run()
   {
      // loop forever
      for (;;)
      {
         try
         {
            // we sleep for 200 milliseconds at a time
            this.sleep(200);

            // bump the counter
            cnt++;
```

```
                    // every 3rd time, fire the event
                    if ((cnt % 3) == 0)
                    {
                        // print out which event we're firing
                        System.out.println("Value: " + cnt);

                        // fire the event
                        if (listener != null)
                        {
                            listener.pollSent(new PollEvent(this, cnt));
                        }
                    }
                }
                catch (InterruptedException e)
                {
                }
            }
        }
    }
```

With no listener object, the `Poller` loops unimpeded. It bumps its counter every 200 milliseconds, and with every third update it prints its message. Now let's introduce an object called a `Watcher` that implements the `PollerListener` interface. Whenever the event is fired on the `Watcher`, it prints out the value of the event it received and sleeps for 2 full seconds. This will interfere with the `Poller` run loop, because the synchronous delivery of events results in the `Poller` thread being held up by the event handling method of the `Watcher` object. The code for the `Watcher`, as well as the application code to get the whole thing started, is given below:

```
class Watcher implements PollerListener
{
    // the poller object
    protected Poller poller = new Poller();

    // the constructor
    public Watcher()
    {
        // register as the event listener
        try
        {
            poller.addPollerListener(this);
        }
        catch (TooManyListenersException e)
        {
        }
    }
```

```
        // the event handler simulates work by sleeping for
        // 2 seconds before returning
        public void pollSent(PollEvent evt)
        {
            try
            {
                System.out.println("Received Event Number: " +
                                    evt.getValue());
                Thread.sleep(2000);
            }
            catch (InterruptedException e)
            {
            }
        }
    }


    public class Example3
    {
        // the application entry point
        public static void main(String[] args)
        {
            // create the watcher object
            Watcher h = new Watcher();
        }
    }
```

Since Example3 is an application, not an applet, you can run it by issuing the following on the command line:

```
java Example3
```

When you do so, the following will be printed to your console window:

```
Value: 3
Received Event Number: 3
Value: 6
Received Event Number: 6
Value: 9
Received Event Number: 9
Value: 12
Received Event Number: 12
Value: 15
Received Event Number: 15
Value: 18
Received Event Number: 18
Value: 21
Received Event Number: 21
```

You can see from this output that the Poller thread is being held up by the Watcher object. The Poller thread is supposed to be looping every 200 milliseconds to update the counter, printing its message every third update. So we would expect to see a few "Value: $x$" messages for each "Received Event: $x$" message. This is clearly not happening. We can correct this by introducing an asynchronous queuing adapter between the Poller and Watcher objects. This adapter queues the events received from the Poller, and it fires the events to the Watcher from its own notification thread, allowing the Poller to continue its work. The code for the PollerAdapter class is shown below:

```java
class PollerAdapter extends Thread implements PollerListener
{
    // the event queue
    protected Vector queue = new Vector();

    // the real listener
    protected PollerListener listener;

    public PollerAdapter(PollerListener l, Poller p)
    {
        // save a reference to the target listener
        listener = l;

        // register myself as the event listener
        try
        {
            p.addPollerListener(this);
        }
        catch (TooManyListenersException e)
        {
        }

        // start my thread
        start();
    }

    // receive events
    public synchronized void pollSent(PollEvent e)
    {
        // add an element to the queue
        synchronized (queue)
        {
            queue.addElement(e);
        }

        this.notify();
    }

    // the run loop of the thread
    public void run()
    {
        // loop forever
```

```
        for (;;)
        {
           // suspend until there is work to do
           try
        {
           this.wait();
        }
        catch (Exception e)
        {
        }

           // clone the queue so we don't tie up anyone else
           Vector tempQueue;
           synchronized (queue)
           {
               tempQueue = (Vector)queue.clone();

               // delete the ones we have from the real queue
               queue.removeAllElements();
           }

           // empty the queue in FIFO order and notify listener
           while (!tempQueue.isEmpty())
           {
               PollEvent evt = (PollEvent)tempQueue.elementAt(0);
               tempQueue.removeElementAt(0);
               listener.pollSent(evt);
           }
        }
    }
}
```

We have to make some changes to the Watcher class as well. We need an instance of the PollerAdapter class, and the Watcher constructor will be modified to use the adapter instead of being the PollerListener itself. Notice that the Watcher still implements the PollerListener interface because that is the way the adapter forwards the events to it. The code for the Watcher now looks like this:

```
class Watcher implements PollerListener
{
    // the poller object
    protected Poller poller = new Poller();

    // the adapter
    protected PollerAdapter adapter;

    // the constructor
    public Watcher()
    {
```

```java
      // create the adapter
      adapter = new PollerAdapter(this, poller);
   }

   // the event handler simulates work by sleeping for
   // 2 seconds before returning
   public void pollSent(PollEvent evt)
   {
      try
      {
         System.out.println("Received Event Number: " +
                            evt.getValue());
         Thread.sleep(2000);
      }
      catch (InterruptedException e)
      {
      }
   }
}
```

Now let's run Example3 again. This time the events are being queued by the
PollerAdapter, so the Poller thread can continue running without interference.
The following output is generated when the program runs:

```
Value: 3
Received Event Number: 3
Value: 6
Value: 9
Value: 12
Value: 15
Received Event Number: 6
Value: 18
Value: 21
Value: 24
Received Event Number: 9
Value: 27
Value: 30
Value: 33
Received Event Number: 12
Value: 36
Value: 39
Value: 42
Received Event Number: 15
Value: 45
```

# 4

# *Properties*

Properties are named attributes or characteristics. They define the behavior and state of an object. For instance, the current temperature value of the `Temperature` object is a property, as are the high and low temperature thresholds of the `GenericTemperatureThresholdAdapter` from the previous chapter. Properties are referenced by their name and can have any type, including primitives such as `int`, and class and interface types such as `java.awt.Color`. The name of the low threshold property is *LowThreshold*, and its type is `double`. Properties are usually part of the persistent state of an object. This will be dealt with later in Chapter 5, *Persistence.*

Properties are exposed to visual programming tools and scripting environments, as well as to traditional Java programming. They are manipulated in a visual programming tool through some kind of property-editing interface. In a scripting environment, properties are exposed through a field-style syntax such as *Object.Property* =*value,* and *value* = *Object.Property.* These are syntactical conveniences provided by the scripting environment. As a Beans developer, you'll expose your properties as described in the rest of this chapter.

## *Accessing Properties*

An object's properties are accessed by calling methods that are defined for setting and getting the property value. Any property that can be read will have an associated method for getting its value. Likewise, any property that can be written will have an associated method for setting its value. We'll see shortly that objects don't always provide both access mechanisms for every property. Properties can be read/write, read-only, or write-only.

The methods used for getting and setting property values should conform to the standard design pattern for properties. These methods are allowed (but not required) to throw checked exceptions. The method signatures are as follows:

```
public void set<PropertyName>(<PropertyType> value);
public <PropertyType> get<PropertyName>();
```

The existence of a matching pair of methods that conform to this pattern represents a read/write property with the name <PropertyName> of the type <PropertyType>. If only the get() method exists, the property is considered to be read-only; if only the set() method exists, the property is considered to be write-only.

If the <PropertyType> is boolean, the get() method can be replaced or augmented with a method that uses the following signature:

```
public boolean is<PropertyName>();
```

Let's look back at the Temperature class. The current temperature is stored within an object of type Temperature, but up until now we have not provided a way to access that value. So now we can add a read-only property called *CurrentTemperature*. The code for the Temperature class will now include the following:

```
package BeansBook.Simulator;

import java.util.Vector;

public class Temperature
{
    // the current temperature in Celsius
    protected double currentTemp = 22.2;

    [The rest of the existing code goes here]

    // the get method for property CurrentTemperature
    public double getCurrentTemperature()
    {
        return currentTemp;
    }

}
```

It is important to recognize that properties are not defined by data members of the object's class. One reason for this is that it would break encapsulation. More importantly, properties can be computed when they are needed without having to be stored explicitly. In an earlier example we described a Thermometer class that tracked temperatures from two locations. We could define a property called *NumberOfLocations*. This is a read-only property that describes how many locations are being tracked by the thermometer. In this case we don't need to explicitly store a data member for this property, we just know that the value is always 2. We could add a property get method to access this value, as follows:

```
public int getNumberOfLocations()
{
    return 2:
}
```

Although our thermometer isn't a visual component yet, imagine that at some point it will be capable of displaying the temperature from one of its source thermometers. Let's design the Thermometer so that it is capable of displaying temperatures in either Celsius or Fahrenheit. We call this property *DisplayingCelsius*, and we expose it using a boolean data type. Remember that this doesn't refer to the way that the property is stored internally, only the way that the property is exposed externally. If Celsius is not used, then Fahrenheit is being used, and vice versa. We'll put off implementing the property until later. So the code for the Thermometer class now looks like this:

```
package BeansBook.Simulator;

public class Thermometer implements TempChangeListener
{
    // a reference to the temperature object that we are monitoring
    protected Temperature theTemperature;

    Thermometer(Temperature temperature)
    {
        theTemperature = temperature;

        // register for temperature change events
        theTemperature.addTempChangeListener(this);
    }

    // handle the temperature change events
    public void tempChanged(TempChangedEvent evt)
    {
        // do something with the temperature that we can retrieve
        // by calling evt.getTemperature()
    }

    // the get method for the DisplayingCelsius property
    public boolean isDisplayingCelsius()
    {
        ...
    }
```

```
// an alternate get method for the DisplayingCelsius property
public boolean getDisplayingCelsius()
{
    return isDisplayingCelsius();
}

// the set method for the DisplayingCelsius property
public void setDisplayingCelsius(boolean value)
{
    ...
}
}
```

In this example I've provided both forms of the get method for the `boolean` property *DisplayingCelsius*. You'll notice that the only method that has an implementation so far is `getDisplayingCelsius()`, which does nothing but call the `isDisplayingCelsius()` method. We'll fill in the code later.

---

*TIP*            Whenever two methods are provided that perform the same func-
                 tion, it is a good idea to implement one in terms of the other. There
                 is no requirement to do this, but it is a good programming practice.
                 Following this guideline will eliminate the need to repeat code, and
                 to modify multiple areas of code when the implementation changes.

---

Normally when a property value is changed, the object will react in some way. Later, when our `Thermometer` object is capable of displaying a temperature value, we will have to implement code that reacts to a change to the *DisplayingCelsius* property by redisplaying the temperature according to the temperature units being used (Celsius or Fahrenheit).

## Indexed Properties

So far we have been talking about properties that have only one value. For each named property, we have a single associated value. But this is not always the best way to represent properties; sometimes a property is better modeled as having multiple values. You can create properties that are actually an ordered collection of values associated with a single name. The individual values are accessed using an integer index, much the same way you would with an array.

There is an additional design pattern for indexed properties. The <Property-Type> in the standard property method design pattern may be an array, as follows:

```
public <PropertyType>[] get<PropertyName>();
public void set<PropertyName>(<PropertyType>[] value);
```

These methods are used to access the entire array of property values at one time. An additional method can be used to provide access to individual values in the property array. The method signatures for this pattern are:

```
public <PropertyType> get<PropertyName>(int index);
public void set<PropertyName>(int index, <PropertyType> value);
```

As with the single value pattern, these methods are allowed to include a *throws* clause for throwing checked exceptions. Specifically, the indexed methods may throw a `java.lang.ArrayIndexOutOfBoundsException` if an index is used that is outside the bounds of the property array. Although this is an important aspect of indexed properties, it isn't required for the indexed properties pattern. Since the indexed properties are considered ordered collections, I think the indexed `get()` and `set()` methods should always declare the `ArrayIndexOutOfBoundsException`. It might have been better to make it a requirement for this pattern.

Imagine that we are building a system that tracks stock prices in real time. First, let's think about building a watch list object that keeps track of prices for a set of stocks. We'll call this class a `WatchList`. We then define a property of the `WatchList` called *Stocks* which contains a list of stocks for which prices are being tracked. The type of the *Stocks* property is a `String` array, and each individual stock is represented by a `String`. We also implement a read-only property called *StockCount* that returns the number of stocks in the `WatchList`. The code looks like this:

```
import java.util.*;

public class WatchList
{
    // a vector that contains the actual stock names
    protected Vector stocks = new Vector();

    // constructor
    public WatchList()
    {
    }

    // the get method for the StockCount property
    public synchronized int getStockCount()
    {
        // the StockCount property is derived from the size of the
        // stocks Vector
        return stocks.size();
    }

    // get method for Stocks property array
    public synchronized String[] getStocks()
    {
```

```
        // we don't currently deal with the case where the watch list
        // is empty

        // allocate an array of strings for the stock names
        String[] s = new String[getStockCount()];

        // copy the elements of the stocks Vector into the string array,
        // and then return the array
        stocks.copyInto(s);
        return s;
    }

    // set method for Stocks property array
    public synchronized void setStocks(String[] s)
    {
        // the existing list of stocks is removed in favor of the
        // new set of stocks

        // set the size of the stocks vector to match the length
        // of the new array
        stocks.setSize(s.length);

        // copy the values into the stocks vector
        for (int i = 0; i < s.length; i++)
        {
            // use the single stock set method
            try
            {
                setStocks(i, s[i]);
            }
            catch (ArrayIndexOutOfBoundsException e)
            {
            }
        }
    }

    // get method for single element of Stocks property
    public synchronized String getStocks(int index)
                throws ArrayIndexOutOfBoundsException
    {
        // make sure the index is in bounds
        if (index < 0 || index >= getStockCount())
        {
            throw new ArrayIndexOutOfBoundsException();
        }

        // get the stock and return it
        String s = (String)stocks.elementAt(index);
        return s;
    }
```

```
        // set an individual element of the Stocks property array
        public synchronized void setStocks(int index, String stock)
                    throws ArrayIndexOutOfBoundsException
    {
        // make sure the index is in bounds
        if (index < 0 || index >= getStockCount())
        {
            throw new ArrayIndexOutOfBoundsException();
        }

        // change the stock at the specified index
        stocks.setElementAt(stock, index);
    }
}
```

# Bound Properties

In the previous example, property changes can take place when one of the
setStocks() methods are invoked. This results in the state of the WatchList
being changed. What would happen if two objects were using the WatchList and
one of them changed the *Stocks* property? It's possible that users of the WatchList
will want to know if its properties are changed.

A Bean component can provide change notifications for its properties. These notifications take the form of events, and they conform to the event model described
in the earlier chapters. Properties that support change notifications are known as
*bound* properties, because other objects can bind themselves to changes in their
value.

## Non-Specific Property Binding

An object can bind itself to non-specific property changes. In this case the source
object sends notifications to the bound object whenever the value of one of its
bound properties has changed. The notification takes the form of a
java.beans.PropertyChangeEvent. The public methods for this class are shown
below, without their implementations:

```
    public class java.beans.PropertyChangeEvent
        extends java.util.EventObject
    {
        // contructor
        PropertyChangeEvent(Object source,          // the source of the event
                        String propertyName,     // the property name
                        Object oldValue,         // the old value
                        Object newValue);        // the new value
```

```
    // get the new value of the property
    public Object getNewValue();

    // get the old value of the property
    public Object getOldValue();

    // get the event propagation id
    public Object getPropagationId();

    // get the name of the property that changed
    public String getPropertyName();

    // set the event propagation id
    public void setPropagationId();
}
```

The java.beans.PropertyChangeEvent class treats old and new values as instances of class Object. If the property that changed uses one of the primitive data types like int or float, you'll have to use the object version of the type here, such as java.lang.Integer or java.lang.Float. It is possible that when the event is fired the old or new values are not known, or that multiple values have changed. In this case null can be returned from the getOldValue() or getNewValue() method. This is also true of the property name. If multiple properties have changed, the getPropertyName() method may return null. The PropertyChangeEvent also contains something called a *propagation ID*. This is reserved for future use. If you receive a PropertyChangeEvent and then in turn generate and fire another PropertyChangeEvent, you must propagate the propagation ID as well.

A PropertyChangeEvent for a bound property should only be fired after its internal state has been updated. This means that the event signifies a change that has already taken place. If an object supports bound properties, it will provide the following methods for registering and unregistering the associated event listeners:

```
    public void addPropertyChangeListener(PropertyChangeListener p);
    public void removePropertyChangeListener(PropertyChangelistener p);
```

The java.beans.PropertyChangeListener interface extends the base Java class java.util.EventListener. This interface supports a single method called propertyChange(), which takes only one parameter as an argument, of type java.beans.PropertyChangeEvent. If an object wants to receive notifications of bound property changes, it would implement the java.beans.PropertyChange-Listener interface and register itself with the source object by calling its addPropertyChangeListener() method. A diagram of this interaction is shown in Figure 4-1.

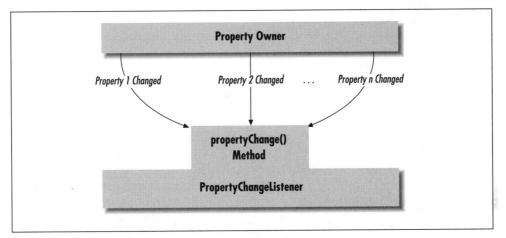

*Figure 4-1. Notifying a listener that a property has changed*

Let's go back to our Temperature class. Earlier we added a read-only property to this class named *CurrentTemperature*. If we wanted to implement this as a bound property, we would implement the addPropertyChangeListener() and remove-PropertyChangeListener() methods. Then whenever *CurrentTemperature* changed, we would fire a PropertyChangeEvent to all listeners. Originally we designed the Temperature class to fire a TempChangedEvent to listeners that implement the TempChangeListener interface. For now we'll remove the code related to the firing of TempChangeEvent events. Now that we understand properties, let's modify the Temperature class to fire the PropertyChangeEvent instead. Because the object does not keep track of the previous temperature, the oldValue parameter of the PropertyChangeEvent constructor is set to null. The code would now look like this:

```java
package BeansBook.Simulator;

import java.beans.*;
import java.util.Vector;

public class Temperature
{
    // the current temperature in Celsius
    protected double currentTemp = 22.2;

    // the collection of objects listening for property changes
    protected Vector propChangeListeners = new Vector();

    // the constructors
    public Temperature(double startingTemp)
    {
```

```java
        this();
        currentTemp = startingTemp;
    }

    public Temperature()
    {
    }

    // the get method for property CurrentTemperature
    public double getCurrentTemperature()
    {
        return currentTemp;
    }

    // add a property change listener
    public synchronized void
    addPropertyChangeListener(PropertyChangeListener l)
    {
        // add a listener if it is not already registered
        if (!propChangeListeners.contains(l))
        {
            propChangeListeners.addElement(l);
        }
    }

    // remove a property change listener
    public synchronized void
    removePropertyChangeListener(PropertyChangeListener l)
    {
        // remove it if it is registered
        if (propChangeListeners.contains(l))
        {
            propChangeListeners.removeElement(l);
        }
    }

    // notify listening objects of CurrentTemperature property changes
    protected void notifyTemperatureChange()
    {
        // create the event object
        PropertyChangeEvent evt =
            new PropertyChangeEvent(this, "CurrentTemperature",
                                    null, new Double(currentTemp));

        // make a copy of the listener object vector so that it cannot
        // be changed while we are firing events
        Vector v;
        synchronized(this)
        {
```

```
            v = (Vector) propChangeListeners.clone();
        }

        // fire the event to all listeners
        int cnt = v.size();
        for (int i = 0; i < cnt; i++)
        {
            PropertyChangeListener client =
                        (PropertyChangeListener)v.elementAt(i);
            client.propertyChange(evt);
        }
    }
}
```

With this change in place, we have to change the implementation of the Thermom-eter class as well. Instead of implementing the TempChangeListener interface it will implement the PropertyChangeListener interface. We remove the tempChanged() method and replace it with a propertyChange() method. For the sake of simplicity, let's revert to the case where the Thermometer works with a single Temperature object named theTemperature instead of the two that we worked with previously. The code for the changed constructor and property-Change() method is shown below:

```
// constructor
Thermometer(Temperature temperature)
{
    theTemperature = temperature;

    // register for property change events
    theTemperature.addPropertyChangeListener(this);
}

// handle the property change events
public void propertyChange(PropertyChangeEvent evt)
{
    // determine if the CurrentTemperature property of the temperature
    // object is the one that changed
    if (evt.getSource() == theTemperature &&
        evt.getPropertyName() == "CurrentTemperature")
    {
        Temperature t = (Temperature)evt.getSource();

        // get the new value object
        Object o = evt.getNewValue();

        double newTemperature;

        if (o == null)
        {
```

```
        // go back to the object to get the temperature
        newTemperature = t.getCurrentTemperature();
    }
    else
    {
        // get the new temperature value
        newTemperature = ((Double)o).doubleValue();
    }
  }
}
```

The propertyChange() method first determines if the source of the event was its
instance of the Temperature class, and if the property that changed is called
*CurrentTemperature*. If these two things are true, the source is cast to type Temperature and the new value object is retrieved from the event object. Since the new
value object can be null, there is a check for that condition. If it is null, it goes
back to the source to get the value of the *CurrentTemperature* property. If it isn't
null, the value is retrieved directly from the new value object.

A support class called java.beans.PropertyChangeSupport can be used to fire
property change events to the registered listeners. You can either inherit from this
class, or directly use an instance of it. PropertyChangeSupport implements the
java.io.Serializable interface, which we discuss in Chapter 5. The method
signatures of this class are as follows:

```
public class java.beans.PropertyChangeSupport
    implements java.io.Serializable
{
    // construct the object
    public PropertyChangeSupport(Object source);

    // add a property change listener
    public synchronized void
    addPropertyChangeListener(PropertyChangeListener l);

    // fire a property change event to any listeners
    public void firePropertyChange(String propertyName, Object oldValue,
                                   Object newValue);

    // remove a property change listener
    public synchronized void
    removePropertyChangeListener(PropertyChangeListener l);
}
```

We could reimplement the Temperature class by inheriting from the Property-
ChangeSupport class. This would eliminate the code that deals with the property
change events. Note that the version of the constructor that takes no parameters
calls the superclass constructor to make itself the event source. Although we

aren't going to keep the Temperature class like this, here's what the code would look like if we did:

```
package BeansBook.Simulator;

import java.beans.*;
import java.util.Vector;

public class Temperature extends PropertyChangeSupport
{
    // the current temperature in Celsius
    protected double currentTemp = 22.2;

    // the constructors
    public Temperature(double startingTemp)
    {
        this();
        currentTemp = startingTemp;
    }

    public Temperature()
    {
        super(this);
    }

    // the get method for property CurrentTemperature
    public double getCurrentTemperature()
    {
        return currentTemp;
    }

    // notify listening objects of CurrentTemperature property changes
    protected void notifyTemperatureChange()
    {
        // fire the event
        firePropertyChange("CurrentTemperature",
                        null, new Double(currentTemp));
    }
}
```

# Constrained Properties

To this point we've assumed that all the property changes that take place are acceptable. Often this will not be the case; it's possible that an attempt to set a property to a given value will be unacceptable and therefore rejected. The simple case is when the object that owns the property wants to reject the change, but there may be times when another object wants a chance to voice its disapproval. Properties that go through this approval process are known as *constrained properties*.

The design pattern for setting and getting constrained properties is similar to the design pattern for properties that are not constrained. The difference is that the set method declares that it throws the exception java.beans.PropertyVetoException. The method signatures look as follows:

```
public <PropertyType> get<PropertyName>();
public void set<PropertyName>(<PropertyType> value)
           throws java.beans.PropertyVetoException;
```

## Binding to Non-Specific Constrained Properties

Those objects that want to participate in the approval process for a change to a constrained property must implement the java.beans.VetoableChangeListener interface. This interface contains a method called vetoableChange() that takes a single parameter of type PropertyChangeEvent. This method may throw the java.beans.PropertyVetoException if it wants to reject the change. Objects that support constrained properties must provide methods for registering and unregistering VetoableChangeListener objects. The methods should look like the following:

```
public void addVetoableChangeListener(VetoableChangeListener p);
public void removeVetoableChangeListener(VetoableChangelistener p);
```

It's possible for the object that owns the property to reject a change itself. So if a set<PropertyName>() method is called with an unacceptable property value, the java.beans.PropertyVetoException can be thrown. If the owning object does not reject the change, it must send notifications to all registered VetoableChangeListener objects. This interaction is shown in Figure 4-2.

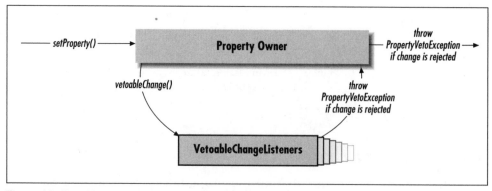

*Figure 4-2. Vetoable property changes*

A VetoableChangeEvent for a constrained property should be fired before the actual value of the property has changed. This gives any VetoableChangeListener a chance to reject the change when its vetoableChange() method is called. The event source must catch the `java.beans.PropertyVetoException`. If a listener throws the exception, the source object must fire a new `Vetoable-ChangeEvent` to all the registered `VetoableChangeListener` objects, using the current value for the property. This is necessary because if there were multiple listeners, some of them may already have been notified of the change that was subsequently rejected. So the second round of events gives those listeners the opportunity to revert to the old value. In this case, any `PropertyVetoException` that is thrown can be caught and ignored. The convention that the second round of `PropertyVetoExceptions` can be ignored prevents infinite loops in which no satisfactory value can be found.

When a listener is informed of a change to a constrained property, it should not assume that the change has already taken place, because some other object may veto the change. If this happens, the listener will be notified again with the property reverted to its old value. Unfortunately, there is no way for the listener to know if the change will be universally accepted at the time of the first notification. So what should the listening object do? For example, let's say that we have a dialog box that includes a component that allows the user to enter the font size to use for all of the controls on the dialog. This font sizer may have a constrained property named *FontSize*. All of the controls on the dialog are registered listeners implementing the `java.beans.VetoableChangeListener` interface, and each control has its own notion of the maximum font size. When each is notified of a request to change the value of the *FontSize* property, each compares the proposed value to its own maximum and throws the `java.beans.PropertyVetoException` if the value is too high. The control that rejects the change may do so after other controls have already been notified, in which case the previously notified controls may already have repainted themselves with the new font size. Now that another control has subsequently rejected the change, all of the controls will be notified again with the old font size value. The result is that the controls have to repaint themselves again. This is certainly not visually appealing, and is potentially time-consuming as well.

The JavaBeans architecture addresses this issue by stating that properties can be both bound and constrained at the same time. In this case the property owner should fire a `VetoableChangeEvent` before the property value is actually changed. If no `VetoableChangeListener` rejects the change, the property value should be changed and then the `PropertyChangeEvent` should be fired. The dialog controls I just discussed could be registered with the font sizer as both a `PropertyChange-Listener` and a `VetoableChangeListener` at the same time. This would allow one of the controls to reject the change when the `vetoableChange()` method is called, but defer reacting to it until the `propertyChange()` method gets called.

Another way to deal with this kind of problem is to have each control inform the font sizer of its maximum font size at initialization time. This way the font sizer itself will have the opportunity to reject an unacceptable change to the *FontSize* property before any of the listening objects are ever notified.

The class java.beans.VetoableChangeSupport is provided to make managing constrained properties easier. You can either inherit from this class or use an instance of it. The public methods of VetoableChangeSupport are shown here:

```
public class java.beans.VetoableChangeSupport
        implements java.io.Serializable
{
    // construct the object
    public VetoableChangeSupport(Object source);

    // add a vetoable change listener
    public synchronized void
            addVetoableChangeListener(VetoableChangeListener l);

    // fire a vetoable change event to any listeners
    public void fireVetoableChange(String propertyName, Object oldValue,
                                    Object newValue)
            throws java.beans.PropertyVetoException;

    // remove a vetoable change listener
    public synchronized void
            removeVetoableChangeListener(VetoableChangeListener l);
}
```

The fireVetoableChange() method performs a valuable service. It fires the VetoableChangeEvent to all registered listeners, and if any of them veto the change it refires the event to all listeners to revert them to the old property value and then rethrows the java.beans.PropertyVetoException. This can be a real convenience, as we will see in the next example.

Let's look again at our Thermometer class. If an instance of this class is used to control a heating device, we might have a property of the Thermometer named *MinimumTemperature*. This is a read/write property that is used to set the temperature threshold that will trigger the turning on and off of the connected heating device. When the temperature drops 1 degree below this threshold, the heater will be turned on. The heater will be shut off when the temperature reaches the *MinimumTemperature* value. Let's constrain the *MinimumTemperature* value to be no less than 10 degrees Celsius (50 degrees Fahrenheit), the minimum value that the Thermometer class itself will allow. The relevant additions to the Thermometer class are shown next.

```
package BeansBook.Simulator;

import java.beans.*;

public class Thermometer implements PropertyChangeListener
{
    // the minimum temperature threshold value defaults to
    // 15 degrees Celsius
    protected double minTemperature = 15.0;

    // the support object for constrained properties
    protected VetoableChangeSupport constrainedHandler;

    // constructor
    Thermometer(Temperature temperature)
    {
        theTemperature = temperature;

        // register for property change events
        theTemperature.addPropertyChangeListener(this);

        // construct the constrained property support object
        constrainedHandler = new VetoableChangeSupport(this);
    }

    [The existing code goes here]

    // add a VetoableChangeListener
    public void addVetoableChangeListener(VetoableChangeListener l)
    {
        // defer to the support handler
        constrainedHandler.addVetoableChangeListener(l);
    }

    // remove a VetoableChangeListener
    public void removeVetoableChangeListener(VetoableChangeListener l)
    {
        // defer to the support handler
        constrainedHandler.removeVetoableChangeListener(l);
    }

    // get the MinimumTemperature property value
    public double getMinimumTemperature()
    {
        return minTemperature;
    }

    // set the MinimumTemperature property value
    public void setMinimumTemperature(double newVal)
        throws PropertyVetoException
```

```
    {
        // let's check against our own criterion first
        if (newVal < 10.0)
        {
            PropertyChangeEvent e = new PropertyChangeEvent(this,
    "MinimumTemperature", null, new Double(newVal));
            throw new PropertyVetoException("Bad MinimumTemperature", e);
        }

        // defer to the support handler
        constrainedHandler.fireVetoableChange("MinimumTemperature",
                new Double(minTemperature), new Double(newVal));

        // if the previous call did not throw an exception, then we are
        // free to make the change
        minTemperature = newVal;
    }
}
```

The setMinimumTemperature() method first checks to see that the new value is not less than the absolute minimum value of 10 degrees Celsius. If it's not, the fireVetoableChange() method is called on the support object. This method handles all of the details of notifying the registered VetoableChangeListener objects and reverting them to the old value if any of them reject the change. If the change is rejected, the PropertyVetoException will be thrown. If not, the last line saves the new value of the property.

## *Handling Events for Specific Properties*

If a Bean component supports bound properties, it is required to support the binding mechanism described earlier. This means that it must provide an addPropertyChangeListener() method for any client object that wants to receive bound property changes via the PropertyChangeListener interface. The same holds true for constrained properties. In that case, the Bean must provide an addVetoableChangeListener() method for any client object that wants to receive VetoableChangeEvent notifications via the VetoableChangeListener interface. But the Bean also has the option of providing specific registration methods for listeners to register for property change and vetoable change notifications for specific properties. There is no requirement to support these mechanisms, but they may be useful under some circumstances.

There is a design pattern for registering and unregistering event listeners for changes to specific bound properties. The method signatures are as follows:

```
public void add<PropertyName>Listener(PropertyChangeListener p);
public void remove<PropertyName>Listener(PropertyChangeListener p);
```

There is also a design pattern for registering and unregistering event listeners for vetoable change events for specific constrained properties. The method signatures are as follows:

```
public void add<PropertyName>Listener(VetoableChangeListener p);
public void remove<PropertyName>Listener(VetoableChangeListener p);
```

This is convenient if a source object supports many properties and you are only interested in one. It eliminates unwanted PropertyChangeEvent and VetoableChangeEvent notifications. If you're interested in changes for multiple properties, however, this technique probably doesn't add any value. All of the property changes will still be directed to your one and only implementation of the propertyChange() or vetoableChange() methods. If you wanted to direct various property change events to different methods, you could combine these patterns with the adapter technique described in Chapter 3, *Event Adapters*.

## A java.awt Example

The components provided by the java.awt package expose properties using the techniques just described. These user interface elements can be manipulated in the same way as any other object that conforms to the JavaBeans architecture. So let's create an applet that illustrates the concepts of bound and constrained properties.

Our applet will have a data member named primaryLabel which is an instance of class NumberLabel. A NumberLabel is a subclass of java.awt.Label that has a bound and constrained property named *Value*. The *Value* property is of type int, and the label always displays the contents of this property. We also have another instance of the NumberLabel class, named mirrorLabel, that will bind itself to the *Value* property of primaryLabel, and will keep its display consistent with it. There is one button to decrement the *Value* property of primaryLabel, and one to increment it; these button instances will be named decButton and incButton, respectively. Lastly, we will create an instance of class Constrainer, named cnstr, that constrains the *Value* property of primaryLabel to be between 10 and 20. A diagram of the interactions that will take place between the objects is shown in Figure 4-3.

Let's take a look at the code for the NumberLabel class first:

```
import java.applet.*;
import java.awt.*;
import java.awt.event.*;
import java.beans.*;
import BeansBook.util.*;
```

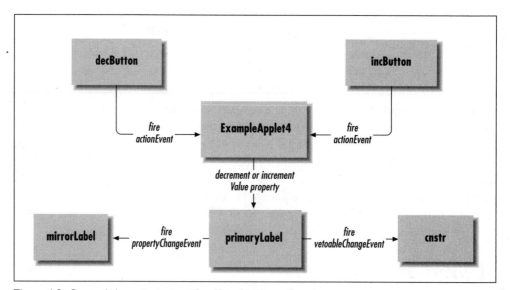

*Figure 4-3. Constraining a property with a VetoableChangeEvent*

```
// the NumberLabel class
class NumberLabel extends Label
        implements PropertyChangeListener
{
    // the support object for bound listeners
    protected PropertyChangeSupport boundSupport;

    // the support object for constrained listeners
    protected VetoableChangeSupport vetoSupport;

    // the implementation of the Value property
    protected int theValue = 15;

    // constructor
    public NumberLabel(String text)
    {
        // call the super class
        super(text);

        // construct the support objects
        boundSupport = new PropertyChangeSupport(this);
        vetoSupport = new VetoableChangeSupport(this);
    }

    // add a bound property listener
    public void addPropertyChangeListener(PropertyChangeListener l)
    {
```

```
        // defer to the support object
        boundSupport.addPropertyChangeListener(l);
    }

    // remove a bound property listener
    public void removePropertyChangeListener(PropertyChangeListener l)
    {
        // defer to the support object
        boundSupport.removePropertyChangeListener(l);
    }

    // add a constrained property listener
    public void addVetoableChangeListener(VetoableChangeListener l)
    {
        // defer to the support object
        vetoSupport.addVetoableChangeListener(l);
    }

    // remove a constrained property listener
    public void removeVetoableChangeListener(VetoableChangeListener l)
    {
        // defer to the support object
        vetoSupport.removeVetoableChangeListener(l);
    }

    // the get method for the Value property
    public int getValue()
    {
        return theValue;
    }

    // the set method for the Value property
    public void setValue(int newValue)
            throws PropertyVetoException
    {
        // fire the change to any constrained listeners
        vetoSupport.fireVetoableChange("Value", new Integer(theValue),
                                        new Integer(newValue));

        // no veto, so save the old value and then change it
        Integer oldVal = new Integer(theValue);
        theValue = newValue;
        setText(String.valueOf(theValue));
        repaint();

        // fire the change to any bound listeners
        boundSupport.firePropertyChange("Value", oldVal,
                                        new Integer(theValue));
    }
```

```
    // handle property change events from others
    public void propertyChange(PropertyChangeEvent evt)
    {
        // only interested in changes to Value properties
        if (evt.getPropertyName().equals("Value"))
        {
            // just change our own property
            Integer val = (Integer)evt.getNewValue();

            try
            {
                setValue(val.intValue());
            }
            catch (PropertyVetoException e)
            {
            }
        }
    }
}
```

The NumberLabel class extends java.awt.Label, a class for creating a static text
field. NumberLabel implements the java.beans.PropertyChangeListener interface because we will use one instance of the NumberLabel class to monitor the
*Value* property of another. Since NumberLabel supports a property named *Value*
that is both bound and constrained, we use an instance of java.beans.Property-
ChangeSupport as well as an instance of VetoableChangeSupport. The
implementation of the methods addPropertyChangeListener(), removeProper-
tyChangeListener(), addVetoableChangeListener(), and removeVetoable-
ChangeListener() all defer to their respective support objects.

Since the *Value* property is read/write, we implement a getValue() method as
well as a setValue() method. The latter declares that it can throw the
java.beans.PropertyVetoException because the *Value* property is constrained
as well as bound. The setValue() method first instructs the support object to fire
a VetoableChangeEvent for the *Value* property by calling the fireVeto-
ableChange() method. If the event is not vetoed, SetValue() stores the new
value, updates the label's text, and repaints. Finally, the other support object is
instructed to fire a PropertyChangeEvent by invoking the fireProperty-
Change() method.

The NumberLabel class also implements the propertyChange() method to handle
property changes from other objects. In this example, we know that a Number-
Label listens for property changes only from the other instance of NumberLabel.
We can therefore take a shortcut and simply have the NumberLabel set its own
*Value* property based on the new value of the PropertyChangeEvent that it
received. This is guaranteed to keep our two labels in sync. Of course, we first

check to make sure that it was the *Value* property that changed, and that we haven't received a notification about some other property.

Now let's take a look at the code for the `Constrainer` class:

```
class Constrainer implements VetoableChangeListener
{
    // handle the vetoable change event
    public void vetoableChange(PropertyChangeEvent evt)
            throws PropertyVetoException
    {
        // we constrain the value to between 10 and 20
        Integer val = (Integer)evt.getNewValue();
        if (val.intValue() < 10 || val.intValue() > 20)
        {
            throw new PropertyVetoException("Bad Value", evt);
        }
    }
}
```

The `Constrainer` class vetoes any property changes that attempt to change the *Value* property of a `NumberLabel` object to a value below 10 or above 20. The `vetoableChange()` method examines the new value and rejects it if it does not meet the criteria.

Now we can create an applet that ties all this together. The applet uses an instance of the class `BeansBook.util.GenericButtonAdapter` to route action events that occur when the two buttons are pressed. Here's what the code looks like:

```
public class ExampleApplet4 extends Applet
{
    // the button adapter for handling button action events
    protected GenericButtonAdapter adapter;

    // the decrement button
    protected Button decButton = new Button("<<");

    // the increment button
    protected Button incButton = new Button(">>");

    // the constrained label
    protected NumberLabel primaryLabel = new NumberLabel("*****");

    // the label that mirrors the primary label
    protected NumberLabel mirrorLabel = new NumberLabel("*****");

    // the constraining object
    protected Constrainer cnstr = new Constrainer();
```

```java
// the constructor
public ExampleApplet4()
{
}

// the applet init
public void init()
{
    // add the user interface elements
    add(decButton);
    add(incButton);
    add(primaryLabel);
    add(mirrorLabel);

    // register the constrainer with the primary label
    primaryLabel.addVetoableChangeListener(cnstr);

    // register the mirroring label with the primary label
    primaryLabel.addPropertyChangeListener(mirrorLabel);

    // setup the button adapter
    try
    {
        adapter = new GenericButtonAdapter(this);
        adapter.registerActionEventHandler(decButton,
                                    "handleDecrement");
        adapter.registerActionEventHandler(incButton,
                                    "handleIncrement");
    }
    catch (NoSuchMethodException e)
    {
    }
    catch (ClassNotFoundException e)
    {
    }

    // start the labels at different values
    try
    {
        primaryLabel.setValue(15);
        mirrorLabel.setValue(5);
    }
    catch (PropertyVetoException e)
    {
    }
}

// handle the decrement button push
public void handleDecrement(ActionEvent evt)
```

```
    {
        // get the current value and subtract 1
        int val = primaryLabel.getValue() - 1;

        // try to set the new value
        try
        {
            primaryLabel.setValue(val);
        }
        catch (PropertyVetoException e)
        {
        }
    }

    // handle the increment button push
    public void handleIncrement(ActionEvent evt)
    {
        // get the current value and add 1
        int val = primaryLabel.getValue() + 1;

        // try to set the new value
        try
        {
            primaryLabel.setValue(val);
        }
        catch (PropertyVetoException e)
        {
        }
    }
}
```

When the decrement button is pressed, the handleDecrement() method gets called. The *Value* property of the primary NumberLabel object is retrieved and its value is decremented and stored locally. Then handleDecrement() attempts to set the *Value* property to this new value. The PropertyVetoException must be caught in case the change is vetoed. When the increment button is pressed, the handleIncrement() method does the same thing, except that the value is incremented instead.

When the applet's init() method is called, the buttons and labels are added first. Next, the instance of the Constrainer class is registered as a listener for VetoableChange events from the primary NumberLabel object, and the other NumberLabel object (mirrorLabel) is registered to listen for PropertyChange events. The button adapter is set up to route action events, and the two labels are initialized with two different values. Figure 4-4 shows what the applet looks like when it first starts up. The components are labeled with the variable names to show where they appear on the applet.

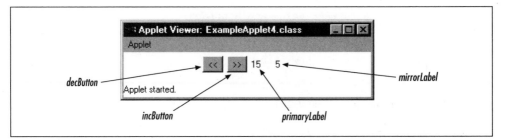

*Figure 4-4. An applet using a constrained property: initial state*

When the decrement (<<) and increment (>>) buttons are pressed, both labels update together. Press the buttons and watch how these two labels stay in sync by setting the *Value* property of one of them, while the other monitors those changes and updates its own *Value* property in response. Figure 4-5 shows an example.

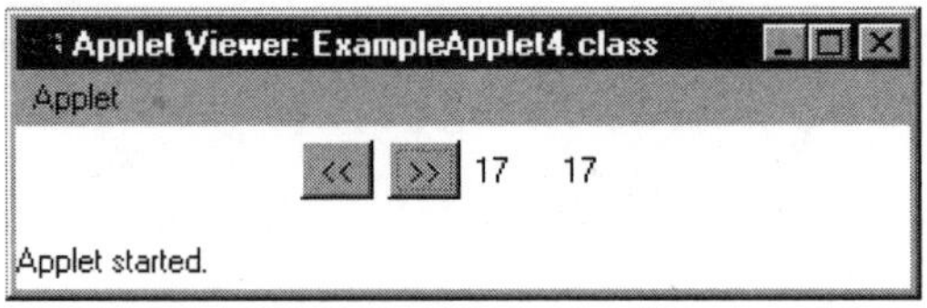

*Figure 4-5. An applet using a constrained property*

If you continue to press the increment button, the labels will eventually have values of 20. If you try to increment again, the Constrainer object vetoes the change. The result is that the *Value* properties of both labels remain at 20. The same is true if you decrement the *Value* properties to 10. If you continue decrementing, the Constrainer object again vetoes the change and the *Value* properties remain at 10.

# 5

# *Persistence*

Most components maintain information that defines their appearance and behavior. This information is known as the state of the object. Some of this information is represented by the object's properties. For instance, the font or color properties of a visual component are usually considered to be part of that object's state. The Thermometer class that we've been discussing in previous chapters has a *MinimumTemperature* property that is part of its state. There may also be internal data used by an object that is not exposed as properties, but plays a part in defining the behavior of the object nevertheless.

An applet or application may use one or more components, and these components will be configured to exhibit specific behavior. When the application is loaded, these components should automatically exhibit the prescribed behavior. This means that the state information of all of the components, as well as the application or applet itself, must be saved on a persistent storage medium so that it can be used to recreate the overall application state at run-time. Figure 5-1 shows that some portion of an application will be saved to, and subsequently restored from, persistent storage. An important aspect of application state is the definition of the components themselves: the persistent state of an application includes a description of the components being used, as well as their collective state.

The JavaBeans architecture uses the Java object serialization mechanisms for persistence. These mechanisms are designed to make it very easy for simple Beans to implement persistence, while at the same time providing the flexibility needed

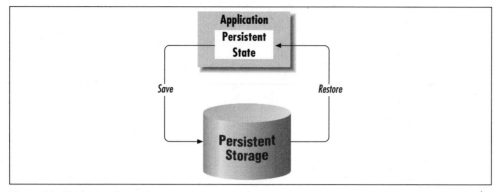

*Figure 5-1. Saving and restoring components*

by more complex Beans. We'll see shortly that under some circumstances it requires very little extra programming effort to implement persistence, but it can often require extra work and careful planning.

# Object Serialization

The java.io package provides a streaming mechanism for serializing the persistent state of objects. Any type of input or output stream can be used, which allows persistence streams to be stored on a variety of storage mediums. The most common form of this is a file stream, using an instance of class java.io.FileOutputStream to save the data and class java.io.FileInputStream to restore it.

Serialization can be broken down into streams and components. The stream is responsible for saving and restoring objects and primitive data types such as int and float. The components of serialization are those objects and data members that are saved and restored. The stream controls the process of saving objects by requesting that those objects write their own contents, and must contain enough information to reconstruct the object. The new instance should be of the same class or data type and should contain the same internal data values.

The object stream contains the methods for saving or restoring objects and primitive data types. The java.io package defines two interfaces for this purpose. The java.io.ObjectOutput interface, which is implemented by objects that can save other objects to the stream; and the java.io.ObjectInput interface, which is implemented by objects that can restore other objects from the stream. The java.io.ObjectOutputStream and java.io.ObjectInputStream classes implement the java.io.ObjectOutput and java.io.ObjectInput interfaces, respectively. These classes provide methods for saving and restoring objects, as well as for saving and restoring the primitive data types. Here are two code snippets that show how these classes are used:

```
// save a string and a double to the stream
String str = "Sample";
double d = 3.14;
FileOutputStream f = new FileOutputStream("Beans.tmp");
ObjectOutputStream s = new ObjectOutputStream(f);
s.writeObject(str);
s.writeDouble(d);
s.flush();

// restore the string and double
FileInputStream f = new FileInputStream("Beans.tmp");
ObjectInputStream s = new ObjectInputStream(f);
String str = (String)s.readObject();
double d = s.readDouble();
```

In the first example we create an instance of the java.lang.String class and an instance of the primitive type double. Next we create an instance of java.io.FileOutputStream, and use it to create an instance of java.io.ObjectOutputStream. We then call the writeObject() method on the stream to save the string object, and call the writeDouble() method to save the double. Lastly, we call flush() to commit everything in the stream to the file. The second example reconstructs the objects from the file. An instance of java.io.FileInputStream is created and used to create an instance of java.io.ObjectInputStream. Next, the readObject() method is called on the stream to restore the string. Because the readObject() method does not distinguish between classes, the returned object must be cast to the appropriate type. Next, we call the readDouble() method to restore the value of the double. What's not clear from the example is that there's no call to the constructor (explicit or implicit) of an object being read back from the stream.

The Java object serialization mechanism requests that an object read or write its own state. In order to handle these requests an object must implement either the java.io.Serializable interface or the java.io.Externalizable interface.

## *The java.io.Serializable Interface*

Objects that implement the java.io.Serializable interface can have their state saved and restored. This state includes data from all of the classes in the object's class hierarchy. So an object need not worry about the serialization of data from superclasses, as this is handled automatically.

The Serializable interface has no methods. It is used as a marker, indicating that the class is serializable. All subclasses of a class that implements this interface will also be serializable. So it is not necessary to declare that a class implements `java.io.Serializable` if one of its superclasses has already done so. The object serialization mechanism analyzes objects that implement `java.io.Serializable`, looking for data members to save or restore. By default, all non-static and non-transient data members will be serialized.

Let's take a look at a simple example. We create an applet that contains a single instance of `java.awt.Button`, which is serializable. The button's *Label* property is set by specifying it as a parameter of the constructor. In this case the string *Beans Book* is used. We also set the button's *Font* property, using a bold 36-point font. After adding the button to the applet, we serialize the button to file *Saver.tmp*. Figure 5-2 shows the applet, and its code is shown here:

```java
import java.applet.*;
import java.awt.*;
import java.io.*;

public class SimpleSaver extends Applet
{
    public void init()
    {
        Button b = new Button("Beans Book");
        b.setFont(new Font("System", Font.BOLD, 36));
        add(b);
        try
        {
            FileOutputStream f = new FileOutputStream("Saver.tmp");
            ObjectOutput s = new ObjectOutputStream(f);
            s.writeObject(b);
            s.flush();
        }
        catch (Exception e)
        {
            System.out.println(e);
        }
    }
}
```

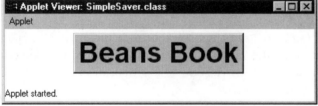

*Figure 5-2. An applet that saves and restores itself*

The next applet, SimpleReader, simply reads the serialized button object from file *Saver.tmp* and adds it to the applet. When this applet is run, the button appears with the properties that were established in the first example. You'll have to take it for granted that this applet creates the same display (Figure 5-2) as the previous one, SimpleSaver. The code for SimpleReader is shown next:

```
import java.applet.*;
import java.awt.*;
import java.io.*;

public class SimpleReader extends Applet
{
    public void init()
    {
        try
        {
            FileInputStream f = new FileInputStream("Saver.tmp");
            ObjectInput s = new ObjectInputStream(f);
            Button b =(Button)s.readObject();
            add(b);
        }
        catch (Exception e)
        {
            System.out.println(e);
        }
    }
}
```

While the model used for serialization is very simple, it has some drawbacks. First, it's not as simple as marking serializable classes with the Serializable interface. It is possible—common, in fact—for an object that can't be serialized to implement Serializable (either directly or by inheritance). Ultimately, serialization has to do with the data members of the class, not the methods it contains; after all, Serializable is an empty interface and doesn't require you to implement any methods. A class is serializable if, and only if, it has no members that aren't serializable—specifically: no non-static, non-transient members. By default, static and transient members are ignored when an object is serialized. Generally speaking, classes that belong to the standard Java distribution are serializable unless serializing an object of that class would be a security risk. The problem is that there are many standard classes that would present security risks if serialized—for example, a FileInputStream can't be serialized, because when it is deserialized at a later time (and possibly on a different machine), you have an object that references some file handle that may no longer be meaningful, or that may point to a different file than it did originally. You should make it a practice to check the class of any data members you add to a serializable class to make sure that those data members can be serialized also. Don't make any assumptions; just look it up in the documentation.

Stating that a class implements `Serializable` is essentially a promise that the class can be successfully saved and restored using the serialization mechanism. The problem is that any subclass of that class automatically implements `Serializable` via inheritance, even if it adds some non-serializable members. Java throws a `NotSerializableException` (from the `java.io` package) if you try to save or restore a non-serializable object. This probably isn't what you want to happen. When you are writing Beans (or any class that you may want to serialize), you have to think carefully about what the class contains, and you also have to think about how the class will be used. As we'll see, you can redesign almost any class so that it is serializable, but this redesign may have implications for the interface between your class and the rest of the world. Ultimately, that's the trick with object serialization. It's not as simple as marking a few classes `Serializable`; it has real implications for how you write code.

## Static Data Members

Static data members are not serialized automatically. Only the data associated with a specific instance of the class is serialized. If you want to serialize data stored in a static variable, you'll have to provide class-specific serialization. We'll look at the technique for doing so a little later.

Data members that are marked as `static final` are considered to be part of the class definition, so they don't have to be saved during serialization. In fact, it would be impossible to set their values during deserialization, since they are marked as `final`.

## Transient Data Members

Some data members may not be a part of the persistent state of the object. Classes may define data members for use as scratch variables, or to make some other part of their processing easier. It may be unnecessary, or even inappropriate, to serialize these data members. For instance, you might include some data members to keep run-time statistics on your object. These statistics may, for example, keep track of how many times a particular property is accessed. This is not the kind of data you want to serialize since it is not part of the persistent state of the object—you wouldn't want to restore that information when the object is reconstructed. These data members should be marked with the `transient` modifier. The standard object serialization mechanism will not save and restore data members that are marked as `transient`.

It is also necessary to use the transient modifier on data members that are instances of classes that are not serializable. As I mentioned above, a java.io.NotSerializableException will be thrown when an attempt is made to save or restore an instance of a class that is not serializable. If this happens, the serialization process won't complete. However, it's not as simple as marking a data member as transient. After all, this data may represent all or part of the state of the object. We'll examine this problem more closely a little later when we look at how the GenericButtonAdapter from an earlier chapter interacts with the serialization process.

## Implementing Serialization

Let's look at the following example:

```
public class SimpleExample implements java.io.Serializable
{
    protected int anInteger;
    protected float aFloat;
    protected java.awt.Button aButton;

    public SimpleExample()
    {
    }
}
```

The class SimpleExample contains three data members. The first two, anInteger and aFloat, are primitive data types. As we discussed earlier, all primitive data types are automatically serializable. The data member called aButton is an instance of type java.awt.Button. This is a subclass of java.awt.Component, which itself implements java.io.Serializable. So the SimpleExample class can be serialized without doing anything more than declaring that it implements the java.io.Serializable interface.

When an object is saved, its internal data members are saved along with any other objects that it refers to. The resulting serialized data contains information about the types and classes of the objects, as well as their values. There is enough information stored to be able to reconstruct the objects with their values at a later time, including any references to other objects. In some cases, one object can be referenced by more than one other object. The serialization mechanism keeps track of objects efficiently so that if multiple references to an object exist, the object is only stored once. This is important when the objects are reconstructed from the serialized data, ensuring that there is only one new instance of the object that is referenced by others. Let's look at an example.

```java
import java.io.*;

class WidgetA implements Serializable
{
   protected int val;

   public WidgetA()
   {
   }

   public void setValue(int value)
   {
      val = value;
   }

   public int getValue()
   {
      return val;
   }
}

class WidgetB implements Serializable
{
   protected int val;
   protected WidgetA AA;

   public WidgetB(WidgetA a)
   {
      AA = a;
   }

   public void setValue(int value)
   {
      val = value;
   }

   public int getValue()
   {
      return val;
   }
}

class Container implements Serializable
{
   protected int val;
   protected WidgetA a1;
   protected WidgetB b1;
```

```
    public Container()
    {
        a1 = new WidgetA();
        b1 = new WidgetB(a1);
    }

    public void setValue(int value)
    {
        val = value;
        a1.setValue(val * 2);
        b1.setValue(val * 3);
    }

    public int getValue()
    {
        return val;
    }

    public void dump()
    {
        System.out.println(val + ":" + a1.getValue() + ":" +
                           b1.getValue());
    }
}
```

The Container class has data members a1 and b1, which are instances of class
WidgetA and WidgetB, respectively. The Container class constructs the instance
of WidgetA, and then uses it as the parameter for constructing an instance of
WidgetB. The WidgetB class holds onto the reference to the instance of class
WidgetA in data member AA. So there is only one instance of class WidgetA in this
example, and it is referenced two times. All three of these classes expose a property named *Value*. Whenever the *Value* property of the Container object is
changed, it in turns changes the *Value* property of a1 and b1. The Container class
also contains a method called dump() which is used to print out its *Value* property,
along with the *Value* property of a1 and b1. An object graph for these relationships is shown in Figure 5-3.

It is important that the serialized data for this example include only one instance
of class WidgetA. When the objects are deserialized this single instance of class
WidgetA is recreated and referenced by the instance of the Container class in its
data member a1, and by the instance of class WidgetB in its data member AA.

Let's create an application to illustrate how this works. We create an application
called Example5 that contains an instance of Container named aContainer. This
application will take a command-line parameter, telling it whether to save or
restore the state of the data member aContainer. When the command-line parameter is *save*, the application creates an instance of Container, sets its *Value*

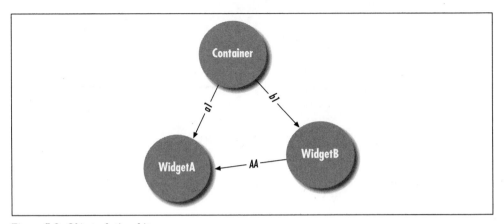

*Figure 5-3. Object relationships*

property to 13, and then serializes it to a file named *Example5.tmp*. When the
command-line parameter is *restore*, the application restores the instance of
`Container` by reading it from file *Example5.tmp*. In both cases the `dump()` method
is called to print the *Value* property of all of the objects. Here's the code for this
application:

```java
import java.io.*;

public class Example5
{
    // the application entry point
    public static void main(String[] args)
    {
        if (args[0].equals("save"))
        {
            Container c = new Container();
            c.setValue(13);
            try
            {
                FileOutputStream f = new FileOutputStream("Example5.tmp");
                ObjectOutputStream s = new ObjectOutputStream(f);
                s.writeObject(c);
                s.flush();
            }
            catch (Exception e)
            {
                System.out.println(e);
            }

            c.dump();
        }
```

```
        else if (args[0].equals("restore"))
        {
          try
          {
             FileInputStream f = new FileInputStream("Example5.tmp");
             ObjectInputStream s = new ObjectInputStream(f);
             Container c = (Container)s.readObject();
             c.dump();
          }
          catch (Exception e)
          {
             System.out.println(e);
          }
        }
      }
    }
```

Run the application with the following command:

```
java Example5 save
```

The application first creates an instance of class `Container`, and sets its *Value* property to 13. This object creates instances of `WidgetA` and `WidgetB`, and then sets their *Value* properties accordingly. Next an instance of `java.io.FileOutput-Stream` is created for the file named *Example5.tmp*, which is used to create an instance of `java.io.ObjectOutputStream`. This stream is used to write the instance of class `Container`. All of the objects that are reachable from that object are also written automatically. Finally, the `dump()` method of the `Container` object is invoked, resulting in the following output:

```
13:26:39
```

Now that we have serialized the objects to file *Example5.tmp*, let's reconstruct the objects by running the application again as follows:

```
java Example5 restore
```

First an instance of `java.io.FileInputStream` is created based on the file *Example5.tmp*. The `FileInputStream` is then used to create an instance of class `java.io.ObjectInputStream`. Next, the instance of `Container` is reconstructed by calling the `readObject()` method on the stream. After that, the `dump()` method is called on the `Container`, which prints the following in the console window:

```
13:26:39
```

# Class-Specific Serialization

Sometimes the data members that are marked as transient are an important part of the run-time state of the object. Consider a class that maintains an instance of a java.io.FileOutputStream, a class that cannot be serialized because it uses a file handle. It would be dangerous to save the handle because it is allocated at run-time, and the objects may be reconstructed on another system that uses a different scheme for allocating file handles. Also, if the file handle were to be saved it could be modified to resemble a handle that is not normally accessible. This would be a security violation, and could even result in unwanted or malicious behavior. Nevertheless, when the object is reconstructed, we would want to reestablish the instance of the java.io.FileOutputStream. We might handle this by saving the name of the file along with the current value of the seek offset.

It is possible to extend the default serialization behavior. Any class that implements java.io.Serializable can implement its own writeObject() and readObject() methods for this purpose.

If you want the serialization mechanism to ask your object to write its own data, it should provide a writeObject() method with the following signature:

```
private void writeObject(ObjectOutputStream stream)
            throws java.io.IOException;
```

If this method exists, the data members will not automatically be serialized. It is up to the writeObject() method to store the state of the object. However, it doesn't need to consider the state of any subclass or superclass data. That information will still be handled by the default serialization process. This means that you can store data that is not represented by data members. You can use write-Object() in order to add additional state information to the stream, including any relevant information about objects that are marked as transient. You should always call the defaultWriteObject() method of the java.io.ObjectOutput-Stream instance before you add any additional information. This is the method that implements default serialization of the non-static and non-transient data members of the object for the class being serialized. The same process is repeated for each class in an object's inheritance hierarchy. After you invoke default-WriteObject() on the stream, you are free to add anything else you want to that stream.

If you implement writeObject() to store the state of your object, then you'll need to implement readObject() so that you can be in control of the reconstruction of the object from the stream. The method signature for readObject() is as follows:

```
private void readObject(ObjectInputStream stream)
            throws java.io.IOException;
```

If the readObject() method exists, the default serialization of data members will not take place. Again, it is up to the readObject() method to reconstruct the state of the object. You should always call defaultReadObject() on the stream before reading back any additional data. Just like before, this method implements the default serialization of the non-static and non-transient data members of the object being reconstructed. The defaultReadObject() method implements the logic necessary to deal with class evolution, which is discussed later. You should also note that the defaultReadObject() method can throw a ClassNotFoundException. This will happen if the class of the object being restored is not available. Remember that the object may be restored on a different machine than the one that saved it, and that machine may have a very different set of classes available.

Let's make the WatchList class from the previous chapter serializable. We do this by declaring that the class implements java.io.Serializable. The class defines one data member, an instance of java.util.Vector, which is named stocks. The class java.util.Vector is itself serializable, and we are using it to store instances of java.lang.String, which is also serializable. The only required change to the WatchList class then is to declare that it implements the java.io.Serializable interface, as shown here:

```
public class WatchList implements java.io.Serializable
{
    // a vector that contains the actual stock names
    protected Vector stocks = new Vector();

    [ the rest of the WatchList code goes here ]
}
```

The same thing holds true for the Temperature, Thermometer, and Thermostat classes introduced in previous chapters. The only change required to allow these classes to participate in object serialization is to declare that each implements the java.io.Serializable interface. This is not to say that every subclass of a serializable class will itself be serializable. Implementing java.io.Serializable is only one part of the process. As we'll see shortly, it may require some effort to deal with the serialization of data members that are not themselves serializable.

## Walking the Class Hierarchy

When an object is serialized, the highest serializable class in its derivation hierarchy is located and serialized first. Then the hierarchy is walked, with each subclass being serialized in turn. In order to illustrate this, let's create an example with a three-level class hierarchy. Class C is a subclass of class B, which is a subclass of class A. Since class A implements java.io.Serializable, all of its subclasses are considered serializable as well. Again, this is due to the fact that all of its data members can be serialized. Each class implements the writeObject() and readObject() methods.

```java
class A implements java.io.Serializable
{
    protected int a;

    private void writeObject(ObjectOutputStream stream)
            throws java.io.IOException
    {
        System.out.println("writeObject called for class A");
        stream.defaultWriteObject();
    }

    private void readObject(ObjectInputStream stream)
            throws java.io.IOException
    {
        System.out.println("readObject called for class A");

        try
        {
            stream.defaultReadObject();
        }
        catch (ClassNotFoundException e)
        {
            throw new IOException();
        }
    }

    public A()
    {
    }
}

class B extends A
{
    protected int b;

    private void writeObject(ObjectOutputStream stream)
            throws java.io.IOException
    {
        System.out.println("writeObject called for class B");
        stream.defaultWriteObject();
    }

    private void readObject(ObjectInputStream stream)
            throws java.io.IOException
    {
        System.out.println("readObject called for class B");
```

```
        try
        {
            stream.defaultReadObject();
        }
        catch (ClassNotFoundException e)
        {
            throw new IOException();
        }
    }


    public B()
    {
        super();
    }
}

class C extends B
{
    protected int c;

    private void writeObject(ObjectOutputStream stream)
                throws java.io.IOException
    {
        System.out.println("writeObject called for class C");
        stream.defaultWriteObject();
    }

    private void readObject(ObjectInputStream stream)
                throws java.io.IOException
    {
        System.out.println("readObject called for class C");

        try
        {
            stream.defaultReadObject();
        }
        catch (ClassNotFoundException e)
        {
            throw new IOException();
        }
    }

    public C()
    {
        super();
    }
}
```

We can write a simple test to illustrate the order in which the class hierarchy is serialized. Let's create an application that creates an instance of class C, writes it to an instance of java.io.ObjectOutputStream, and then reads it back from an instance of java.io.ObjectInputStream. Note that we use ByteArray streams since we have no need to store anything to disk. The code for the application looks like this:

```java
import java.io.*;

public class Example7
{
    // the application entry point
    public static void main(String[] args)
    {
        // the byte array buffer
        byte[] buffer = null;

        // create an instance of class C
        C c = new C();
        try
        {
            ByteArrayOutputStream f = new ByteArrayOutputStream();
            ObjectOutputStream s = new ObjectOutputStream(f);
            s.writeObject(c);
            s.flush();
            buffer = f.toByteArray();
        }
        catch (Exception e)
        {
            System.out.println(e);
        }

        try
        {
            ByteArrayInputStream f = new ByteArrayInputStream(buffer);
            ObjectInputStream s = new ObjectInputStream(f);
            c = (C)s.readObject();
        }
        catch (Exception e)
        {
            System.out.println(e);
        }
    }
}
```

Now we can run this application, and during the writing and reading of the instance of class C, we will get output from the writeObject() and readObject()

methods of each class in the hierarchy. Run the application with the following command:

```
java Example7
```

When the application is run, an instance of class C is created, written to a stream, then read back. In doing so, the following output is generated to the console window:

```
writeObject called for class A
writeObject called for class B
writeObject called for class C
readObject called for class A
readObject called for class B
readObject called for class C
```

As you can see from the output, the serialization process walks up the class hierarchy to the highest-level superclass that implements java.io.Serializable, and then walks back down to serialize data from each class. The sequencing of output from class A to class B to class C shows this clearly.

Let's create a more complex example to illustrate the use of class-specific serialization. First, we define a class called ListeningPanel. This class extends java.awt.Panel, which itself extends java.awt.Container, and it contains three instances of java.awt.Button named b1, b2, and b3. The ListeningPanel uses a GenericButtonAdapter to listen for action events from the buttons and routes them to the methods called handleB1(), handleB2(), and handleB3(), respectively.

This example poses a problem with the use of the GenericButtonAdapter class because it isn't serializable. Furthermore, we can't trivially make the adapter serializable by adding implements Serializable to the class definition, because it contains a hash table that holds Method objects, and the Method class can't be serialized. We could mark the instance of GenericButtonAdapter within the ListeningPanel class as transient. Doing so would exclude the adapter from the process of serializing an instance of ListeningPanel. But the Listening-Panel class is not the only one that will have a reference to the GenericButtonAdapter instance. The adapter is the registered listener of action events for the buttons. These buttons are added to the panel using the add() method, and references to them are kept by the base java.awt.Container class. These relationships are shown in Figure 5-4.

When the ListeningPanel instance is serialized, the class hierarchy is walked upward. So when the data from the java.awt.Container class is serialized, the buttons are also serialized at that time. These buttons keep references to their action listeners, which in this case is an instance of the GenericButtonAdapter

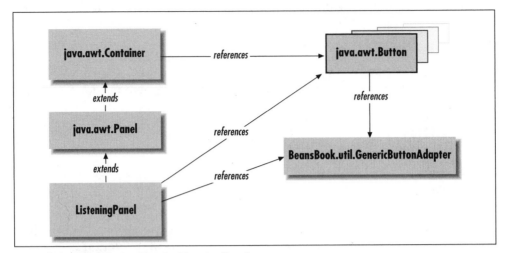

*Figure 5-4. Object relationships for ListeningPanel*

class. Since `GenericButtonAdapter` is not serializable, the process fails. It doesn't help us to mark the instance of the adapter within the `ListeningPanel` as transient, because that isn't the only reference to the adapter. So we need to find another solution.

Let's modify the `GenericButtonAdapter` class to be serializable. The first step is to declare that it implements the `java.io.Serializable` interface. However, declaring that the class is serializable isn't enough. As I said previously, the real issue here is that the hash table is holding references to instances of `java.lang.reflect.Method`, which are not serializable. We're going to have to do some extra work when the adapter is serialized and deserialized. We also have to mark the `java.util.Hashtable` data member, which is named `mappingTable`, as `transient`. This prevents Java from including the hash table when it serializes our adapter objects. However, this has significant implications for the design of our program—both for the `GenericButtonAdapter` class itself, and also the adapter's clients.

The original implementation of the `registerActionEventHandler()` method added the method mappings to the hash table and registered the adapter as an action event listener for the button. Since we can't serialize the hash table, we need to provide a way to rebuild the mappings as part of the deserialization process. Therefore, we need a method to add elements to the mappings—but we don't want to call the `addActionListener()` method on the button again, as this relationship already exists in the object stream being deserialized. To solve the problem, let's introduce a new method called `addMapping()`, which adds elements to `mappingTable`. Now the `registerActionEventHandler()` method invokes `addMapping()` and `addActionEventListener()` on the button. The `addMapping()` method allows us to recreate the method mappings during deserialization. But we still need a mechanism to create an empty instance of the hash table. This can be handled by the `addMapping()` method. When it gets called, we can check to see if the hash table has been created. If it hasn't, it can be created right there.

We need to implement `writeObject()` and `readObject()` so that we can save and restore the data that is held in the hash table. The `writeObject()` method invokes `defaultWriteObject()` on the stream to store the non-transient data members, but now we need to store enough information from `mappingTable` so that it can be reconstructed later. First we have to consider the case where `mappingTable` has not yet been constructed. In this case we store a count of 0 elements to the stream and return, since there isn't anything else to do. Otherwise, we need to make a clone of the hash table within a synchronized block to ensure that no mappings are added while we are serializing. We synchronize on `mappingTable` itself in order to prevent another thread from accessing the hash table. This is sufficient because all of the access routines on the `Hashtable` class are synchronized.

The first step is to save the number of elements in `mappingTable`. We call the `size()` method on the hash table to determine how many elements it has, and store this value in the stream by calling `writeInt()`. We need to iterate over the keys and values of the hash table, so we invoke the `keys()` and `elements()` methods to get instances of `java.util.Enumeration` for each. Now we can loop through the objects in the two enumerations together. We retrieve a `java.awt.Button` from one enumeration and store it to the stream using `writeObject()`. The other enumeration contains instances of `java.lang.reflect.Method`. This is the object that gives us a little trouble; we can't directly serialize an instance of `java.lang.reflect.Method`. But all we really need is the method name, because we can use our `addMapping()` method to reconstruct the method object later. We get the name of the method by invoking its `getName()` method, which returns an instance of `java.lang.String`. Finally, we pass the name to the stream using `writeObject()`.

For reconstructing the adapter during deserialization, we implement `readObject()`. The `defaultReadObject()` method is called on the stream to read the non-transient data members of the adapter. Next, the number of mappings are read from the stream by invoking the `readInt()` method. Finally we run a loop over the number of mappings to read back the stored instances of `java.awt.Button` and `java.lang.String`. For each pair of objects read from the stream, the `addMapping()` method is called in order to reconstruct the elements of `mappingTable`.

The most important aspect of this example is that it is possible to add additional data to a stream that can be used during deserialization to reconstruct objects that are not serializable. Here's the code for the modified GenericButtonAdapter class:

```
package BeansBook.util;

import java.awt.*;
import java.awt.event.*;
import java.lang.reflect.*;
import java.util.*;
import java.io.*;

public class GenericButtonAdapter
        implements ActionListener, // the adapter receives the events
                    Serializable
{
    // the target object
    protected Object theTarget;

    // the class of the target object
    protected Class theTargetClass;

    // the class array for the parameters used for
    // the target method
    protected final static Class paramClasses[] =
                    { java.awt.event.ActionEvent.class };

    // the mapping of source objects to callback methods
    protected transient Hashtable mappingTable;

    // constructor
    public GenericButtonAdapter(Object target)
    {
        theTarget = target;
        theTargetClass = target.getClass();
    }

    // add an action object to listen for, along with the
    // method to call on the target when the action event
    // is received
    public void registerActionEventHandler(Button b, String methodName)
                throws NoSuchMethodException
    {
        addMapping(b, methodName);
        b.addActionListener(this);
    }
```

```java
// add a method mapping
protected void addMapping(Button b, String methodName)
            throws NoSuchMethodException
{
   if (mappingTable == null)
   {
      mappingTable = new Hashtable();
   }

   Method m = theTargetClass.getMethod(methodName, paramClasses);
   mappingTable.put(b, m);
}

// implement the listener method
public void actionPerformed(ActionEvent evt)
{
   try
   {
      // invoke the registered method on the target
      Method m = (Method)mappingTable.get(evt.getSource());
      Object[] params = { evt };
      m.invoke(theTarget, params);
   }
   catch (InvocationTargetException e)
   {
      System.out.println(e);
   }
   catch (IllegalAccessException e)
   {
      System.out.println(e);
   }
}

// handle the writing of the object state
private void writeObject(ObjectOutputStream stream)
        throws IOException
{
   // use default serialization for the non-transient members
   stream.defaultWriteObject();

   // store the number of mappings
   int cnt = 0;

   if (mappingTable == null)
   {
      // there are no mappings, so store a 0 count and return
      stream.writeInt(cnt);
      return;
   }
```

```
    // get a clone of the mapping table
    Hashtable tempmapping;
    synchronized (mappingTable)
    {
        tempmapping = (Hashtable)mappingTable.clone();
    }

    cnt = tempmapping.size();
    stream.writeInt(cnt);

    // get the enumerations of the keys and values
    Enumeration keys = tempmapping.keys();
    Enumeration vals = tempmapping.elements();

    // store the keys and values
    for (int i = 0; i < cnt; i++)
    {
        // get the button and associated method
        Button b = (Button)keys.nextElement();
        Method m = (Method)vals.nextElement();

        // get the method name
        String name = m.getName();

        // store the button and method name
        stream.writeObject(b);
        stream.writeObject(name);
    }
}

// handle the reading of the object state
private void readObject(ObjectInputStream stream)
        throws IOException
{
    // use default serialization for the non-transient members
    try
    {
        stream.defaultReadObject();

        // get the number of mappings
        int cnt = stream.readInt();

        // read the keys and values for the mapping
        for (int i = 0; i < cnt; i++)
        {
            // read the button and method name
            Button b = (Button)stream.readObject();
            String name = (String)stream.readObject();
```

```
                    // add the mapping
                    addMapping(b, name);
                }
            }
        catch (Exception e)
        {
            throw new IOException();
        }
        }
    }
}
```

Now let's consider the ListeningPanel class. It contains three instances of java.awt.Button, and one instance of GenericButtonAdapter. The initialize() method creates the buttons and adds them to the panel. It also creates an instance of the adapter and then calls registerAction-EventHandler() to register the event handlers associated with each button.

The ListeningPanel class implements writeObject() for storing its state. This method invokes defaultWriteObject() to perform default serialization on the data members of the panel. Next, it creates an instance of java.lang.String and populates it with the concatenation of the button labels. The string is then written to the stream. This string will be retrieved during reconstruction as a sanity check. This is another example of saving additional data to the object stream.

The readObject() method is also implemented by ListeningPanel. The first thing it does is invoke defaultReadObject() to reconstruct the data members. Next it reads an instance of java.lang.String. This is the string that was written out previously as a sanity check on the serialization. A new sanity check string is created by concatenating the button labels, and it is compared to the string that was retrieved from the object stream. Here is the code for the ListeningPanel class:

```
import java.awt.*;
import java.awt.event.*;
import java.io.*;
import BeansBook.util.*;

public class ListeningPanel extends Panel
{
    // the buttons
    protected Button b1;
    protected Button b2;
    protected Button b3;

    // the button adapter
    protected GenericButtonAdapter adapter;
```

```java
// the constructor
public ListeningPanel()
{
}

// initialize the panel
public void initialize()
{
    // construct the buttons
    b1 = new Button("Button 1");
    b2 = new Button("Button 2");
    b3 = new Button("Button 3");

    // add the buttons to the panel
    add(b1);
    add(b2);
    add(b3);

    // setup the adapter
    try
    {
        adapter = new GenericButtonAdapter(this);
        adapter.registerActionEventHandler(b1, "handleB1");
        adapter.registerActionEventHandler(b2, "handleB2");
        adapter.registerActionEventHandler(b3, "handleB3");
    }
    catch (Exception e)
    {
    }
}

// handle click for b1
public void handleB1(ActionEvent evt)
{
    System.out.println(b1.getLabel() + " Clicked");
}

// handle click for b2
public void handleB2(ActionEvent evt)
{
    System.out.println(b2.getLabel() + " Clicked");
}

// handle click for b3
public void handleB3(ActionEvent evt)
{
    System.out.println(b3.getLabel() + " Clicked");
}
```

```java
    // handle the writing of the object state
    private void writeObject(ObjectOutputStream stream)
                throws java.io.IOException
    {
        // store the state of the buttons.
        stream.defaultWriteObject();

        // retrieve the labels of the buttons and store it
        // to use as a sanity check during readObject
        String sanity = b1.getLabel() + b2.getLabel() + b3.getLabel();
        stream.writeObject(sanity);
    }

    // handle the reading of the object state
    private void readObject(ObjectInputStream stream)
        throws java.io.IOException
    {
        try
        {
            // restore the buttons
            stream.defaultReadObject();

            // read back the sanity check string
            String sanity = (String)stream.readObject();

            // if the sanity check fails, throw an exception
            String check = b1.getLabel() + b2.getLabel() + b3.getLabel();
            if (!sanity.equals(check))
            {
                throw new IOException();
            }
        }
        catch (ClassNotFoundException e)
        {
            System.out.println(e);
        }
    }
}
```

Here's an application that uses an instance of `ListeningPanel`. The application creates an instance of `java.awt.Frame`, and then an instance of `ListeningPanel`, which gets added to the frame. The `init()` method is passed the command-line argument. If the argument is *save*, the panel is created and initialized, and the frame is sized and shown. Next, an instance of `java.io.ObjectOutputStream` is created for file *Example8.tmp*, and the panel is written to the stream. If the argument is *restore*, the panel is read from the stream and added to the frame, which is then sized and shown. When the buttons are clicked, a message is printed to the console window indicating which button was pressed. The code for the application is shown here:

```java
import java.awt.*;
import java.io.*;

public class Example8
{
    protected Frame fr;

    public void init(String cmd)
    {
        fr = new Frame("Example8");

        if (cmd.equals("save"))
        {
            ListeningPanel p = new ListeningPanel();
            p.initialize();
            fr.add(p);
            fr.setVisible(true);
            fr.reshape(100,100,300,100);
            fr.repaint();

            try
            {
                FileOutputStream f = new FileOutputStream("Example8.tmp");
                ObjectOutput s = new ObjectOutputStream(f);
                s.writeObject(p);
                s.flush();
            }
            catch (Exception e)
            {
                System.out.println(e);
            }
        }
        else if (cmd.equals("restore"))
        {
            try
            {
                FileInputStream f = new FileInputStream("Example8.tmp");
                ObjectInput s = new ObjectInputStream(f);
                ListeningPanel p = (ListeningPanel)s.readObject();
                fr.add(p);
                fr.setVisible(true);
                fr.reshape(100,100,300,100);
                fr.repaint();
            }
            catch (Exception e)
            {
```

```
            System.out.println(e);
        }
      }
    }

    public static void main(String[] args)
    {
        Example8 a = new Example8();
        a.init(args[0]);
    }
  }
```

This example illustrates that entire collections of objects can be serialized together. It also points out that it is important to understand where an object may be referenced from, and how that might impact the success or failure of the serialization process. The GenericButtonAdapter had to be modified so that it could be serialized. Figure 5-5 shows the window created by the application, regardless of whether it is run with the command java Example8 save  or the command java Example8 restore.

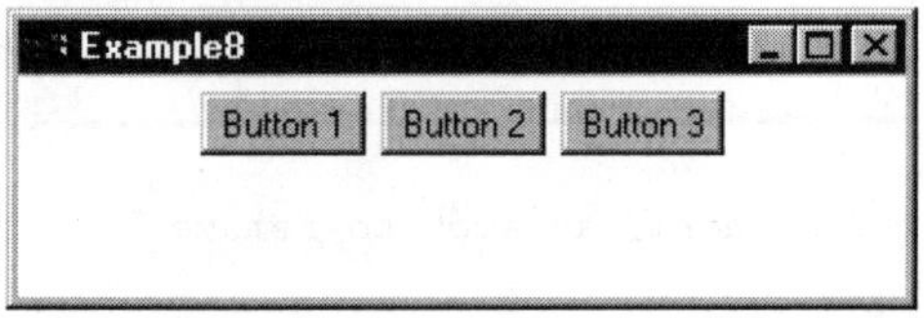

*Figure 5-5. Serialized program using the GenericButtonAdapter*

## Serializing Event Listeners

Event-source objects keep references to their target event listeners, either directly or indirectly through a support object. It's very important to recognize that these listeners may not be serializable. For instance, if you keep a Vector of event listeners, an attempt will be made to serialize the listeners when the Vector is serialized. One possible solution is to mark the collection of event listeners as transient. But we certainly don't want to ignore the listeners, as some or all of them may very well be serializable. The best we can do is to serialize those listeners that can be serialized, and skip the others. Let's look at a simple example class called SimpleTemperature that fires a TemperatureChangeEvent to its registered listeners. References to those listeners are kept in a Vector called listeners. Since we don't know if the elements of listeners are serializable, we mark listeners as transient. We won't actually be serializing listeners at all, only those elements of it that are serializable. We really don't even need to construct the Vector until an event listener is added, so we won't create it until it's needed. The code illustrating this is next.

```java
public class SimpleTemperature
{
   // collection of temperature change listeners
   protected transient Vector listeners = null;

   public synchronized void
   addTemperatureChangeListener(TemperatureChangeListener l)
   {
      // if the vector doesn't exist yet, create it now
      if (listeners == null)
      {
         listeners = new Vector();
      }

      // add the listener
      if (!listeners.contains(l))
      {
         listeners.addElement(l);
      }
   }

   public synchronized void
   removeTemperatureChangeListener(TemperatureChangeListener l)
   {
      // if we have a collection of listeners, attempt to remove
      // the specified listener
      if (listeners != null)
      {
         listeners.removeElement(l);
      }
   }

   private void writeObject(ObjectOutputStream stream)
            throws java.io.IOException
   {
      // perform default writing first
      stream.defaultWriteObject();

      // clone the vector in case one is added or removed
      Vector v = null;
      synchronized (this)
      {
         if (listeners != null)
         {
            v = (Vector)listeners.clone();
         }
      }

      // if we have a collection...
      if (v != null)
      {
```

```
            int cnt = v.size();
            for(int i = 0; i < cnt; i++)
            {
                // get the listener element from the collection
                TemperatureChangeListener l =
                        (TemperatureChangeListener)v.elementAt(i);

                // if the listener is serializable, write it to the stream
                if (l instanceof Serializable)
                {
                    stream.writeObject(l);
                }
            }
        }

        // a null object marks the end of the listeners
        stream.writeObject(null);
    }

    // handle the reading of the object state
    private void readObject(ObjectInputStream stream)
        throws java.io.IOException
    {
        try
        {
            stream.defaultReadObject();

            Object l;
            while(null != (l = stream.readObject()))
            {
                addTemperatureChangeListener((TemperatureChangeListener)l);
            }
        }
        catch (ClassNotFoundException e)
        {
            throw new IOException();
        }
    }
}
```

We have an addTemperatureChangeListener() method for registering event
listeners. This is where we create the listeners Vector if we don't have one yet.
There is also the corresponding removeTemperatureChangeListener() method,
where we must first check for the existence of the Vector before we attempt to
remove the listener element. Since we marked listeners as transient, we need
to implement our own readObject() and writeObject() methods to serialize
the event listeners.

The first thing we do in `writeObject()` is call `defaultWriteObject()` on the stream to write any non-transient data members. Before we start looking at the elements of the `Vector`, we need to clone it within a synchronized block to ensure that none get added or removed while we're looping through the collection. Now we can check each element of the collection to see if it can be serialized. First the element is cast to `TemperatureChangeListener`, and then the `instanceof` operator is used to see if the element implements `Serializable`. If it does, we write it to the stream; if not, we just skip it. This simple process writes only the serializable listeners to the stream. After every element of `listeners` is checked, we write a `null` to the stream to mark the end of the list of event listeners. This technique is used because we don't know how many serializable event listeners we have until we reach the end.

We start the `readObject()` method by calling `defaultReadObject()` on the stream to read back any non-transient data members. Now all we have to do is start reading objects back from the stream using `readObject()`. For each object, we cast it to `TemperatureChangeListener`, and then we pass it to the `addTempera-tureChangeListener()` method. This will also take care of creating an instance of the `Vector` the first time it is called. The loop continues until we reach the `null` that we wrote to the stream, marking the end of the list.

If you are using one of the support classes, such as `java.beans.PropertyChange-Support`, you can go ahead and allow the object to be serialized automatically. The event listener support classes in the `java.beans` package use the same technique to ensure that the serializable event listeners are saved to the stream.

## *Versioning*

Serialization of objects to persistent storage presents a potential problem with class version mismatches. This is because the class itself is not serialized with the object. Instead, an instance of `java.io.ObjectStreamClass` that describes the class of the object is serialized. The `java.io.ObjectStreamClass` contains the class name and a version identifier for the serialized object. This allows the local version of the class to evolve independently of the serialized data.

It is possible that when an object is deserialized, the class available to the virtual machine is not the same as the one that originally serialized the object. (Remember that serialization stores the data needed to reconstruct the class, but doesn't store the class's Java byte code.) As classes evolve, some of the changes that are made will be compatible with earlier versions of the class, and some will not. Generally, compatible changes are those that do not render the serialized data unusable by an earlier version of the class. For instance, adding or removing a method would be a compatible change, since this does not impact the useful-ness of the serialized data. The fact that the newer class contains a new method is not relevant to the older version of the class. On the other hand, changing the superclass of a class is not a compatible change because this clearly renders the serialized data useless. After all, the data that was serialized for the old base class can't possibly be useful to the new one.

The versioning mechanism tries to identify classes that are compatible with the serialized data, not classes that necessarily have compatible interfaces. This scheme is not time-ordered, meaning that compatibility doesn't imply that serialized data can only be compatible with newer classes. In practice, this would be far too limiting, since the class that is deserializing the data could be either older or newer than the one that serialized it. If we always required that the deserializing class were newer than or the same as the class that serialized the data, we would never be able to deserialize objects using classes that are older than the one that serialized the object. You simply can't guarantee that the classes used by the objects stored in a persistence stream will be updated on every system that might use the stream before it is deserialized. With this scheme there is at least a chance that the classes available are good enough to do something useful with the deserialized data.

Sometimes, a compatible change may still lead to undesirable or unacceptable behavior. Imagine that you modified a class to include a new data member. This is considered to be a compatible change. If the original class was serialized without a value for that field, a default value will be provided when the stream is deserialized to the newer version of the class. But the default value may not be appropriate. For example, if the proper operation of an object is dependent upon a data member of type int having a value of either 1 or 2, what would happen if the default value of 0 was assigned during the deserialization process? This is certainly something to consider when upgrading an existing class. This can be handled inside of the readObject() method; and the section "Object Validation" later in this chapter discusses another technique for validating the state of an object during deserialization.

In general, a compatible version of a class is one that can make use of the data serialized by another version. This versioning scheme isn't really making any promises about the interfaces that are available on the class, as that is already being handled by the class itself.

## Stream Unique Identifiers

Compatible changes, such as the addition of a method, result in a class definition that is different from the original. If we tried to deserialize an object whose class evolved this way, a java.io.InvalidClassException would be thrown, because the new class version is considered to be incompatible with the previous version that serialized the object. Let's try it. Add the following method to the `GenericButtonAdapter` class:

```
public void doNothing()
{
}
```

Now run the previous example with the *restore* command-line argument:

```
java Example8 restore
```

Since the objects were originally serialized with a previous version of `GenericButtonAdapter`, the following message appears on the console window:

```
java.io.InvalidClassException: BeansBook.util.GenericButtonAdapter;
Local class not compatible
```

By default, the virtual machine considers any change to the class incompatible. But certainly there is nothing incompatible about the addition of the `doNothing()` method. To tell the virtual machine that nothing significant has changed, you can mark the class with an identifier that indicates the earliest compatible version of the class. This is known as a *Stream Unique Identifier,* or SUID. The program *serialver* is provided as part of the JDK to allow you to generate the SUID for any class that supports serialization. Before we continue, remember to remove the `doNothing()` method from the `GenericButtonAdapter` class and recompile it. Now, run *serialver* on the `Generic ButtonAdapter` class:

```
serialver BeansBook.util.GenericButtonAdapter
```

The program will respond as follows:

```
BeansBook.util.GenericButtonAdapter:
static final long serialVersionUID = 6291086927484045907L;
```

---

*NOTE*  The *serialver* program can also be run with the *-show* command-line argument. This brings up a graphical interface that allows you to specify a fully qualified class name and get back an SUID that can be copied and pasted into your code. The interface for *serialver* is shown in Figure 5-6.

---

This static data member named `serialVersionUID` can be included directly in any new version of the `GenericButtonAdapter` class that implements a compatible change. This SUID will be used to determine that the serialized data is compatible with the new version of the class during deserialization. Add this static data member to the `GenericAdapterClass` code, and then add back the `doNothing()` method and recompile. Now when you run the command `java Example8 restore`, the deserialization process will accept the data as compatible.

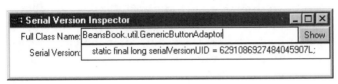

*Figure 5-6. Graphical interface to serialver*

The SUID is generated by computing a hash value based on the class definition. The SUID of the serialized data is compared to that of the local class definition in order to determine whether the classes are compatible. You might be thinking that the serialVersionUID is too hard for a human being to keep track of, and so why not just use version numbers such as 1, 2, etc. Again, it's important to remember that the SUID is used by the serialization process to determine if the data stored in the object stream can be used by the class available on the virtual machine. If your design requires that the object stream only be deserialized by classes that are newer than the one that serialized the stream, you can certainly implement your own version management scheme by storing the version information as part of the object's persistent state. You can easily check this information within the readObject() method, and do whatever you deem appropriate if the version information is not acceptable. This could even be handled by object validation, which is described in the next section.

Whenever you evolve a serializable class, you may need to update the serialVersionUID static data member to reflect the compatible versions of the class. Whenever you update a class, you should be thinking about how the change affects earlier versions of the class. Two questions need to be addressed: How will older versions of this class deal with serialized data from this new version? How will this new version handle serialized data from older versions? If you believe that the new class is compatible, you want the serialVersionUID to reflect that. You can skip this for the initial version of the class, but it's probably good practice to include it right from the start so that it doesn't get overlooked in the future.

## *Object Validation*

Sometimes, an object will be serialized successfully and still be left in an invalid state. It may be desirable to perform some validation of one or more objects before the readObject() method of the java.io.ObjectInputStream returns the object to the caller. This validation can use any criteria that is appropriate for the class. For instance, let's consider one of the compatible class changes mentioned earlier. If a data member is added that is an int and should have a value of either 1 or 2, we may want to perform validation in case the object was serialized from an earlier version of the class that does not contain the data member. During the validation phase, we might determine that the rest of the

state of the object would be considered valid as long as we set this data member to
1. This determination might depend upon the state of other objects that are referenced. This is why the validation methods are called only after the entire object
graph has been restored. Any object-specific validation that does not depend on
the state of the entire object graph could be handled within the readObject()
method of the specific class.

The interface java.io.ObjectInputValidation is implemented by an object
that wants to participate in the validation of an object during deserialization. This
interface contains one method, with the following signature:

```
public void validateObject()
                throws InvalidObjectException;
```

In order to perform object validation, the registerValidation() method must
be invoked on the input stream. This method takes two parameters: the first identifies an object that implements the java.io.ObjectValidation interface; the
second is an integer value which specifies a priority. There can be multiple validation objects registered, and they will be called in priority order (beginning with
priority 1) after the object graph has been restored. This registration can only be
made from inside the readObject() method of a serializable object. An object
can perform its own validation by passing itself into the registerValidation()
method, or some other object can be used for this purpose.

Let's update the ListeningPanel class to perform its own validation. Before we
make any changes, we run *serialver* to determine the SUID. Enter the following on
the command line, making sure you are in the directory where the Listening-
Panel class is located:

```
serialver ListeningPanel
```

This results in the following output:

```
ListeningPanel: static final long
                serialVersionUID = 5150576658460927998L;
```

We add this data member to the class so that the new class is recognized as being
compatible with the previous version. We also declare that ListeningPanel implements the interface java.io.ObjectInputValidation, and we add the
validateObject() method. The addition of this method is one of the reasons
that the SUID is required. The validation criteria we use for the ListeningPanel
class is to ensure that all three buttons were reconstructed. This is a trivial
example of validation, used only to illustrate that the validation method is free to
use any criteria it chooses. In most cases the validation criteria will be much more
complex, and involve the state and relationships of multiple objects. The sanity
check string that is checked inside the readObject() method is another example
of object validation. That check is an example of validation before the entire

graph has been reconstructed. We also need to call to the `registerValidation()` method on the `java.io.ObjectInputStream` object from inside the `readObject()` method. Here's what the affected code looks like:

```
public class ListeningPanel extends Panel
        implements ObjectInputValidation
{
    protected static final long serialVersionUID = 5150576658460927998L;

    [ the rest of the existing code goes here ]

    // handle the reading of the object state
    private void readObject(ObjectInputStream stream)
        throws java.io.IOException
    {
        try
        {
            // restore the buttons
            stream.defaultReadObject();

            // register for object validation with priority 1
            stream.registerValidation(this, 1);

            // read back the sanity check string
            String sanity = (String)stream.readObject();

            // if the sanity check fails, throw an exception
            String check = b1.getLabel() + b2.getLabel() + b3.getLabel();
            if (!sanity.equals(check))
            {
                throw new IOException();
            }
        }
        catch (ClassNotFoundException e)
        {
            System.out.println(e);
        }
    }

    public void validateObject()
                throws InvalidObjectException
    {
        if (b1 == null || b2 == null || b3 == null)
        {
            throw new InvalidObjectException("Null Button Encountered");
        }
    }
}
```

After recompiling the ListeningPanel class, you can once again run the application with the *restore* command-line argument. If the validation criteria had not been met, the following would have been printed to the console window:

```
java.io.InvalidObjectException: Null Button Encountered
```

# *The java.io.Externalizable Interface*

Objects that implement the java.io.Externalizable interface can also have their state saved and restored. When an object is encountered during the serialization process, it is examined to see if it implements java.io.Serializable. If it doesn't, it is examined to see if it implements java.io.Externalizable. Externalizable objects are in complete control of their own serialization. There is no default mechanism for saving or restoring their state. The object's writeExternal() method is called when the object is being saved, and its readExternal() method is called when it is being restored.

The class hierarchy will not be walked for objects that implement java.io. Externalizable. It is up to the object to make sure that data from any superclasses gets serialized since it isn't handled automatically. Versioning is also the responsibility of the object itself. The object serialization mechanism reads and writes the class definition of the object, and then turns the rest of the process over to the object.

Let's look at an example with a three-level hierarchy, similar to the example used previously. Class CC is a subclass of class BB, which is a subclass of class AA. Since class AA implements java.io.Externalizable, all of its subclasses are externalizable as well. Each class implements the writeExternal() and readExternal() methods. The code for these classes is shown here:

```
class AA implements java.io.Externalizable
{
    protected int a = 0;

    public void writeExternal(ObjectOutput stream)
            throws java.io.IOException
    {
        System.out.println("writeExternal called for class AA");
        stream.writeInt(a);
    }

    public void readExternal(ObjectInput stream)
            throws java.io.IOException
    {
        System.out.println("readExternal called for class AA");
        a = stream.readInt();
    }
```

```java
    public AA()
    {
    }
}


class BB extends AA
{
    protected int b = 0;

    public void writeExternal(ObjectOutput stream)
                throws java.io.IOException
    {
       super.writeExternal(stream);
       System.out.println("writeExternal called for class BB");
       stream.writeInt(b);
    }

    public void readExternal(ObjectInput stream)
                throws java.io.IOException
    {
       super.readExternal(stream);
       System.out.println("readExternal called for class BB");
       b = stream.readInt();
    }

    public BB()
    {
       super();
    }
}


class CC extends BB
{
    protected int c = 0;

    public void writeExternal(ObjectOutput stream)
                throws java.io.IOException
    {
       super.writeExternal(stream);
       System.out.println("writeExternal called for class CC");
       stream.writeInt(c);
    }

    public void readExternal(ObjectInput stream)
                throws java.io.IOException
    {
       super.readExternal(stream);
       System.out.println("readExternal called for class CC");
       c = stream.readInt();
    }
```

```
    public CC()
    {
        super();
    }
}
```

In classes BB and CC, the readExternal() and writeExternal() methods invoke their superclass versions by calling super.readExternal() and super.writeExternal(), respectively. This is to ensure that superclass data is serialized, since this is not handled automatically. The superclass's method is called before the data is read or written so that we can emulate the order of serialization that occurs when the java.io.Serializable interface is implemented. However, you're not required to use this order. The order in which data is serialized for externalizable objects is up to the implementor.

Now let's create an application that creates an instance of class CC, writes it to a java.io.ObjectOutputStream, and then reads it back from a java.io.ObjectInputStream. The code for the application looks like this:

```
public class Example9
{
    // the application entry point
    public static void main(String[] args)
    {
        // create an instance of class CC
        CC c = new CC();
        try
        {
            FileOutputStream f = new FileOutputStream("Example9.tmp");
            ObjectOutputStream s = new ObjectOutputStream(f);
            s.writeObject(c);
            s.flush();
        }
        catch (Exception e)
        {
            System.out.println(e);
        }

        try
        {
            FileInputStream f = new FileInputStream("Example9.tmp");
            ObjectInputStream s = new ObjectInputStream(f);
            c = (CC)s.readObject();
        }
        catch (Exception e)
        {
            System.out.println(e);
        }
```

```
        }
    }
```

Now we can run the application. When it is writing or reading the instance of class CC, we get output from the `writeExternal()` and `readExternal()` methods of each class in the hierarchy. Run the application with the following command:

```
    java Example9
```

When the application is run, an instance of class CC is created, written to a stream, then read back. In doing so, the following output is generated:

```
    writeExternal called for class AA
    writeExternal called for class BB
    writeExternal called for class CC
    readExternal called for class AA
    readExternal called for class BB
    readExternal called for class CC
```

The only difference between the code for Example9 and Example7, shown earlier, is the use of class CC instead of class C. This points out that the code that controls serialization and deserialization doesn't need to concern itself with whether an object implements `java.io.Serializable` or `java.io.Externalizable`. When a collection of objects is serialized, it is certainly possible that some of those objects will implement one of these interfaces and some the other. An object stream can contain both types of objects at the same time.

## *Instantiating Serialized Objects*

So far, we've used the new operator to create instances of Beans. But there is another way to instantiate Beans that is more flexible and often preferable. The class `java.beans.Beans` contains a static method named `instantiate()` that can be used to create an instance of a Bean. This method takes two parameters: a class loader and a string containing the desired Bean's fully qualified class name. If null is used for the first parameter, `instantiate()` uses the default class loader. `instantiate()` first looks for a "pickled" bean, which is nothing more than an object stream file that contains an instance of the serialized state of the Bean class. If it finds such a file, `instantiate()` creates the new instance directly from that file, without calling the Bean's constructor. If `instantiate()` cannot find a serialized file, it uses the new operator to create the new instance in the customary way: by calling the Bean's default constructor. Therefore, in order for `instantiate()` to work, the class must provide a constructor that takes no parameters (i.e., a default constructor)—the `instantiate()` method does not allow you to provide any parameters with which to call the constructor.

To find the pickled bean, `instantiate()` converts the fully qualified class name into a filename by using the package hierarchy as a file hierarchy, and then adding the *.ser* file extension. For example, a fully qualified class name of `Beans-Book.Simulator.Thermostat` will be converted into the filename *BeansBook/Simulator/Thermostat.ser*. If that file exists in the class path, it will be used to deserialize the object; `instantiate()` gets the Bean's class from the pickled file, and uses it to look up an appropriate class file, if one is needed. If it can't find a pickled file, `instantiate()` looks for a class file matching the Bean's name (in this case, *Beans-Book/Simulator/Thermostat.class*), and instantiates the object using the default constructor.

It's important to note that you don't have to give the *.ser* file the same name as the *.class* file. In fact, you probably would never give a pickled Bean the same name as its class, since the whole point is to store customized versions of the class using object serialization. This means that you can provide a file that contains an object's default state without hard-coding the state into the class. You can have a single class file that corresponds to many pre-customized pickled Beans.

Let's create a simple Bean to illustrate the pickling process. The class is nothing more than a repackaging of the `java.awt.Button` class, placed in the `Beans-Book.util` package in order to illustrate this technique. We call this class `PickleButton`, because we'll be providing a pickled state for it shortly. The code for the `PickleButton` class is shown below:

```
package BeansBook.util;

public class PickleButton extends java.awt.Button
{
    public PickleButton()
    {
        super("Pickle Button");
    }
}
```

We can create an instance of `PickleButton` as follows:

```
import java.beans.*;
import BeansBook.util.*;

try
{
    PickleButton p = (PickleButton)Beans.instantiate(null,
                                    "BeansBook.util.PickleButton");
}
catch (Exception e)
{
}
```

This technique results in a call to the empty constructor for the `PickleButton` class because we have not provided a pickled file for the object yet. The following applet creates a pickled version of the `PickleButton` class, and then instantiates it so that you can see what it looks like. The code should look familiar, as it uses the standard technique for serializing an object. We set the font property to a bold, 36-point font, and the label property will be set to the string *Sour Pickle*.

```java
import java.applet.*;
import java.awt.*;
import java.io.*;
import BeansBook.util.*;

public class PickleSaver extends Applet
{
    public void init()
    {
        // create an instance of PickleButton
        PickleButton b = new PickleButton();

        // set the properties
        Font ft = new Font("System", Font.BOLD, 36);
        b.setFont(ft);
        b.setLabel("Sour Pickle");

        // serialize the pickle button
        try
        {
            FileOutputStream f = new FileOutputStream("PickleButton.ser");
            ObjectOutputStream s = new ObjectOutputStream(f);
            s.writeObject(b);
            s.flush();
        }
        catch (Exception e)
        {
            System.out.println(e);
        }
        add(b);
    }
}
```

The file *PickleButton.ser* must be placed into the same directory as the *PickleButton.class* file. Now we can write an applet that instantiates the button:

```java
import java.applet.*;
import java.beans.*;
import BeansBook.util.*;
```

```java
public class PickleUser extends Applet
{
    public void init()
    {
        try
        {
            PickleButton p = (PickleButton)Beans.instantiate(null,
                                    "BeansBook.util.PickleButton");
            add(p);
        }
        catch (Exception e)
        {
        }
    }
}
```

Figure 5-7 shows what the applet looks like when it can't find the *.ser* file and loads the button directly from the class file; Figure 5-8 shows what the applet looks like when it finds the pickled file.

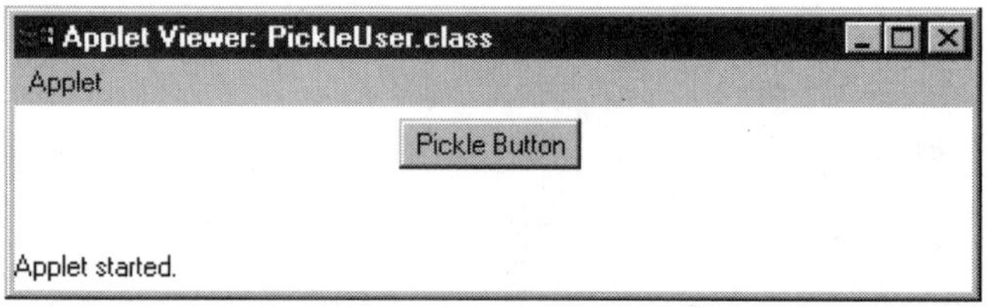

*Figure 5-7. Using instantiate() to load from a class file*

*Figure 5-8. Using instantiate() to load from a pickled file*

I said earlier that it was somewhat unusual to use the same name for the pickled file and the class file. In this case, I used the same name to make the search process clear: `instantiate()` looks for a pickle first, then a class file. The real power of pickling comes when you give serialized classes unique names. In real life, you wouldn't bother writing a program to instantiate a Bean, modify its properties, and save the pickled Bean; you'd use a development tool to modify the properties and save the pickles with little effort. In later chapters, I'll copy *Pickle-Button.ser* to *SourPickle.ser*, allowing us to refer to the serialized Bean as

SourPickle. We could rewrite the applet to use *SourPickle.ser,* the only change to the code would be in the call to the Beans.instantiate() method:

```
PickleButton p = (PickleButton)Beans.instantiate(null,
                                "BeansBook.util.SourPickle");
```

The new applet produces the same display as Figure 5-8.

# 6

In this chapter:
- *The jar Program*
- *The Manifest*
- *Using JAR Files with HTML*
- *Using JAR Files on the CLASSPATH*
- *An Alternative to the jar Program*

# JAR Files

Version 1.1 of the JDK introduced the Java Archive (or JAR) file. JAR file archives can contain any number of files, and they can provide compression based upon the ZIP format. JAR files can be used for packaging related class files, serialized Beans, and other resources. This scheme allows multiple Beans to be packaged in a single JAR file, providing a convenient way to share common class files and resources. Optionally, a JAR file may contain a manifest describing its contents.

We'll be taking advantage of JAR files in later chapters to bundle Beans and their related support classes. Although this is the preferred way of packaging Beans, there is another reason to make use of JAR files. As we'll discuss later in the section "Using JAR Files with HTML," JAR files can also be used to improve the download performance of Java applets that are retrieved from the Web using HTTP.

## The jar Program

The *jar* program is provided as part of the JDK. It can be used to create JAR files, extract some or all of their contained elements, and list their contents. The *jar* program is executed from the command-line prompt. Its usage is:

```
jar {ctx}[vfmOM] [jar-file] [manifest-file] files ...
```

One, and only one, of the required command-line options (*c*, *t*, or *x*) can be selected at a time. The rest of the options can be combined or omitted as needed. All of the command-line options for the *jar* program are described in Table 6-1.

The optional *jar-file* argument is used to specify the name of the archive file. This argument should be specified when the command-line option *f* is used. There is no required naming convention for JAR files. They can use any naming style, and use any file extension supported by the native operating system. However, the tools that use JAR files are free to mandate their own naming conventions. For instance, the BeanBox program described in Chapter 7, *The BeanBox Tool*, requires that JAR files use a file extension of *.jar*.

The optional *manifest-file* argument is used to specify the name of a file that contains the manifest information to be used for the archive. The *manifest-file* should be specified when the command-line option *m* is used. The contents of a manifest file are described later in the section "The Manifest."

*Table 6-1. jar Command Options*

| Option | Description |
| --- | --- |
| c | Create a new archive file. |
| t | List the table of contents for the archive file. |
| x | Extract the named files from the archive. If no filenames are specified, all files are extracted. |
| v | Generate verbose output. |
| f | Specify the archive filename following the options. If this option is not used, standard in and standard out are used. |
| m | Include manifest information from the specified manifest file. |
| 0 | Do not use compression. |
| M | Do not create a manifest file for the archive entries. |

The files to be archived are specified following all of the command-line arguments. Multiple files can be separated by whitespace, and you can use any appropriate wildcard characters as well. When directory names are used, they will be followed recursively, and all files that are found will be added to the archive. Note that file names are relative to the directory from which you run the *jar* program. You can specify either full or relative pathnames for files. The *jar* program allows you to use either the forward slash or the backslash (/ or \) in path names, so you don't have to worry about operating system differences.

You can't remove an entry from, or add an entry to, an existing JAR file. Each time you want to change the contents of the JAR file you have to recreate the entire file. This is inconvenient, but it's not going to stop you from accomplishing your task.

Suppose you wanted to create a JAR file called *MyStuff.jar* that contained the file *MyBean.class*. You would first go to the directory that contained *MyBean.class*. Then you would execute the following command:

```
jar cf MyStuff.jar MyBean.class
```

This command says that a new archive is to be created with the name *MyStuff.jar*, and that the file *MyBean.class* is to be included.

Let's look at another example. We create an archive named *BeansBook.jar* that contains the `GenericButtonAdapter` class from the `BeansBook.util` package. We go to the directory that contains the *BeansBook* package directory, and execute the following command:

```
jar cvf BeansBook.jar BeansBook/util/GenericButtonAdapter.class
```

This command says that we are creating a new archive named *BeansBook.jar*, which contains the *BeansBook/util/GenericButtonAdapter.class* file, and that the *jar* program should produce some verbose output when it creates the archive. The resulting output looks like this:

```
adding: BeansBook/util/GenericButtonAdapter.class in=2999 out=1507
deflated 49.0%
```

This tells us that the *BeansBook/util/GenericButtonAdapter.class* file was added to the archive and that its size was deflated by 49% due to compression. Now let's examine the contents of the archive by executing the following command:

```
jar tvf BeansBook.jar
```

This command says that we want to list the table of contents of the archive file named *BeansBook.jar*. The program then produces the following output:

```
179 Sat Feb 15 16:27:04 EST 1997 META-INF/MANIFEST.MF
2999 Sat Feb 08 14:33:18 EST 1997
BeansBook/util/GenericButtonAdapter.class
```

The resulting verbose output shows that the archive contains a file named *manifest.mf* in directory *META-INF*. This is the manifest file for the archive. The JAR file also contains the file *BeansBook/util/GenericButtonAdapter.class*. This listing also includes the original size of each element along with its time stamp.

## *The Manifest*

The *jar* program automatically generates a manifest when the archive is created (unless you specify the *M* option). The manifest is always named *manifest.mf* and placed into a directory named *META-INF*, and is made up of one or more sections, each of which describes an entry in the archive. Sections in the manifest are separated by a blank line.

Each section in the manifest contains a series of attribute/value pairs. These pairs are used to specify various attributes of the contents of the archive. The entries in the manifest take the form *attribute: value*, where the attribute is immediately followed by a colon and whitespace, and then the value. The first section in the archive is used to identify the manifest version used by the archive. The name of the attribute is *Manifest-Version*. The only version currently supported is 1.0, so the first section of the manifest looks like this: `Manifest-Version: 1.0`

The version section is followed by sections that describe the elements contained in the archive. Each section contains an attribute called *Name* that identifies the name of the archived element. The *jar* program also produces some hash values for the archived element. Each of these values is entered into the manifest. The `Digest-Algorithms` attribute specifies one or more hash algorithms used to generate hash values for the element. This is followed by attributes for each of the algorithms, with the associated hash value.

To get a better idea of what these entries look like, let's extract the manifest from the *BeansBook.jar* archive we just created, using the following command:

```
jar xf BeansBook.jar META-INF
```

This will extract everything in the archive from the directory *META-INF*, which includes the manifest file *manifest.mf.* If the *META-INF* directory does not already exist, it will be created when the manifest is extracted. The contents of the manifest look like this:

```
Manifest-Version: 1.0

Name: BeansBook/util/GenericButtonAdapter.class
Digest-Algorithms: MD5 SHA
MD5-Digest: wuX4KYNI+D3QYBTtNn6wdA==
SHA-Digest: R8cIwi1GSAgAdwAdrxb9AX1SBV8=
```

The first line of the manifest identifies the manifest version used. The *Name* attribute identifies the entry as *BeansBook/util/GenericButtonAdapter.class*, the fully qualified pathname of the class file in the archive. Notice that I've used the forward slash in the pathname. The slash character used here is not dependent upon the operating system; you always use "/". The `Digest-Algorithms` attribute identifies the two algorithms used by the *jar* program to produce hash values for the entry. The next two, `MD5-Digest` and `SHA-Digest`, are used for the actual hash values that were generated when the archive was created.

For Beans, we use an attribute name called `Java-Bean` that specifies whether a particular entry in the archive is a Bean. If so, its value will be `True`; if not, its value will be `False`. Neither the JAR file nor the manifest are interested in the *Java-Bean* attribute.* Tools that read a JAR file looking for Beans use this attribute. You are free to define other attribute/value pairs in the manifest, assuming that there is some other piece of software that is looking for these entries. The only ones that are currently expected are `Name`, `Java-Bean`, `Digest-Algorithms`, and the related `XXX-Digest` entries for the algorithms listed.

---

\* The Java-Bean attribute begs the question "What is a Bean?" Virtually anything can be a Bean: a Bean is just a class that exposes its features in a certain way. For that matter, nothing requires a Bean to expose any features, though it's not clear what such a Bean would be good for. Fundamentally, the decision about which classes are Beans is up to you.

## Specifying a Manifest File

The *jar* program allows you to specify manifest information for the archive. You don't have to specify manifest information for every entry in the archive, or even specify all of the attributes for each entry. *jar* uses the information you provide in a manifest file, and generates information for the rest of the entries for you. You do, however, need to create entries in the manifest if you want to include attribute/value pairs other than the defaults (name and hash entries). We need to provide explicit manifest entries in order to identify any Beans in our JAR file by using the Java-Bean attribute with a value of True. For clarity, I create entries for classes that are Beans, as well as those that aren't. When you are creating your JAR files, remember to include all of the class files, not just those that implement your Beans. My own rule is to include every class and resource file for the packages in the archive. Remember that you aren't limited to class files; you can also include images, audio files, and any other resource files your package needs. Take care not to forget any support classes—in particular, any class files that are generated automatically by the compiler (for example, class files for inner classes).

Let's create a new version of the *BeansBook.jar* file; this time we'll include four entries. In addition to the BeansBook.util.GenericButtonAdapter class, we include the BeansBook.util.PickleButton class from the previous chapter along with the file that contains its pickled state (*BeansBook/util/SourPickle.ser*), as well as the PickleUser applet class. Let's create a manifest file named *Beans-Book.mf* for these entries. Note that sections for individual elements of the archive are separated by blank lines. The file should contain the following:

```
Manifest-Version: 1.0

Name: BeansBook/util/GenericButtonAdapter.class
Java-Bean: False

Name: BeansBook/util/PickleButton.class
Java-Bean: True

Name: BeansBook/util/SourPickle.ser
Java-Bean: True

Name: PickleUser.class
Java-Bean: False
```

Now let's create the archive file by entering the following commands (typed on one very long line):

```
jar cfm BeansBook.jar BeansBook.mf
    BeansBook/util/GenericButtonAdapter.class
    BeansBook/util/PickleButton.class BeansBook/util/PickleButton.ser
    PickleUser.class
```

Now let's take a look at the manifest that was created. Extract the manifest the same way we did before, using the command `jar xf BeansBook.jar META-INF`. The contents of the *manifest.mf* file in the *META-INF* directory contains the following:

```
Manifest-Version: 1.0

Name: BeansBook/util/GenericButtonAdapter.class
Java-Bean: False
Digest-Algorithms: MD5 SHA
MD5-Digest: wuX4KYNI+D3QYBTtNn6wdA==
SHA-Digest: R8cIwi1GSAgAdwAdrxb9AXlSBV8=

Name: BeansBook/util/PickleButton.class
Java-Bean: True
Digest-Algorithms: MD5 SHA
MD5-Digest: epcJZvqx0WgXP6X1BCpaNg==
SHA-Digest: 8V1b4pD5cEt7CuWsdaqiBdiB19Q=

Name: BeansBook/util/SourPickle.ser
Java-Bean: True
Digest-Algorithms: MD5 SHA
MD5-Digest: kyblfan921nF3DQxWYVa8Q==
SHA-Digest: JXzZA7MrSX6rkX+D/8q6BTIINlg=

Name: PickleUser.class
Java-Bean: False
Digest-Algorithms: MD5 SHA
MD5-Digest: E9im1ojFyQFoND1z3nYn4Q==
SHA-Digest: 7pusBfP5YWDlVVcbyTfnT+G5+eQ=
```

As you can see, the information from the manifest file that we supplied is included along with the hash values generated by the *jar* program. This manifest information can be used by programming environments to determine if there are any Beans contained in the archive, and their fully qualified names.

## Using JAR Files with HTML

Since JAR files allow us to package a collection of files into one, and to compress the archive, they offer the opportunity to improve the download performance of applets that are retrieved from the Web via HTTP transactions. Basically, we can download the entire archive file in a single HTTP transaction. This reduces the number of trips we must make over the network to get all of the classes and associated files needed for an applet. Without an archive, multiple HTTP transactions may be required to download the required class files. There is also a performance boost because the archive can be compressed, reducing the download time.

## The ARCHIVES Attribute

The ARCHIVES attribute is used in the HTML file to indicate that an archive file is used. The filename is relative to the location of the HTML page. Let's look at the HTML file we used for running the PickleUser applet from the previous chapter:

```
<APPLET
  ARCHIVE="BeansBook.jar"
  CODE=PickleUser.class
  WIDTH=350
  HEIGHT=125>
</APPLET>
```

The ARCHIVES attribute specifies that the *BeansBook.jar* archive file should be downloaded. Class files will be searched for in the specified archive first. If the class is not found in the archive, then the normal mechanism of searching the server and local file system will be used. Notice that the CODE attribute is still used to specify the starting class for the applet.

When you run this HTML file with *appletviewer*, the PickleUser class will be loaded from the archive. The applet instantiates a pickled version of the Beans-Book.util.PickleButton class, which is found inside the archive as *BeansBook/util/SourPickle.ser*. If you look back at the applet code at the end of Chapter 5, *Persistence*, you'll notice that the class loader for Beans-Book.util.PickleButton can be used when instantiating the pickled version of the class. This step may be necessary when the Bean is being loaded from an archive, since the class loader is actually what tells the Beans.instantiate() method where to find the pickled class file.

It is possible to specify more than one archive file using the ARCHIVES attribute. In this case, archive filenames are separated by a comma. Imagine that in the previous example we wanted to include another archive file named *Another.jar*. The ARCHIVES attribute in the HTML file would look like the following:

```
ARCHIVE="BeansBook.jar, Another.jar"
```

In this case, both the *BeansBook.jar* and *Another.jar* archives will be downloaded. When a class file is searched for, both of these archives would be searched before falling back on the standard mechanism.

# Using JAR Files on the CLASSPATH

My class path is configured to look in the *classes.zip* file provided by the JDK, followed by the root directory of the packages that I am developing. The CLASS-PATH environment variable looks as follows:

```
CLASSPATH=c:\jdk1.1\lib\classes.zip;c:\java\projects
```

We can include the JAR file on the class path the same way any other path is put there. For example, if I wanted to keep all of the packages developed for this book in the *BeansBook.jar* file instead of keeping them in separate files, I could modify my CLASSPATH variable to look as follows:

```
CLASSPATH=c:\jdk1.1\lib\classes.zip;c:\java\projects\BeansBook.jar
```

Now the HTML file for running the PickleUser applet can be restored to its original content by removing the ARCHIVES tag. In this case the PickleUser and BeansBook.util.PickleButton classes will be loaded from the *BeansBook.jar* file because it is part of the class path.

This technique works just fine as long as the JAR file is not compressed. (You can create a JAR file without compression using the 0 command-line option). If you want to put a compressed JAR file on the class path, it must contain all entries for every subdirectory involved. If you want a compressed JAR file to contain *Beans-Book/Simulator/Thermostat.class*, the JAR file needs entries for the following:

- *BeansBook/*
- *BeansBook/Simulator*
- *BeansBook/Simulator/Thermostat.class*

## Archive Signing

JAR files also support archive signing using digital signatures. Although this topic is beyond the scope of this book, you should be aware of the *javakey* program that is provided with the JDK. This program can be used to create digital keys and certificates, as well as to sign a JAR file digitally. A security manager can grant additional privileges to classes with an appropriate signature. You should go to the JDK documentation for more information on this subject.

## An Alternative to the jar Program

The *jar* program that comes with the JDK certainly does its job, but it definitely has some drawbacks. As your JAR files grow larger, it's probably going to become a nuisance that you can't add or delete entries individually, and having to deal with a separate manifest file is an inconsistency waiting to happen. Finally, in the world of graphical user interfaces, the *jar* program leaves you wishing for more.

The people at The Open Group have created a visual JAR file tool called *MoaJar* that addresses the drawbacks I just discussed. You can download *MoaJar* from their web site at *http://www.opengroup.org/RI/DMO/moajar/index.html*. The Open Group is making *MoaJar* freely available, so I highly recommend taking a look. The source code even comes with it, and you are permitted to develop a commercial product from it as long as you include their copyright.

*MoaJar* has a few added features that make it well worth the effort of downloading it from the Web:

- Add, remove, extract, or rename a file in the JAR

- Edit the name/value attributes in the JAR manifest

- Create a serialized object from any class in the JAR or on the CLASSPATH

- Edit the properties of a serialized object in the JAR

Figure 6-1 shows what the *MoaJar* user interface looks like. A list box contains all of the entries in the JAR file. When you select one, the edit area below the list allows you to edit the manifest contents—you can add, delete, or modify attribute/value pairs associated with the entry. *MoaJar* also allows you to instantiate a Bean, customize it, and save it as a new entry. This is a convenient way of creating pickled (serialized) versions of your Beans.

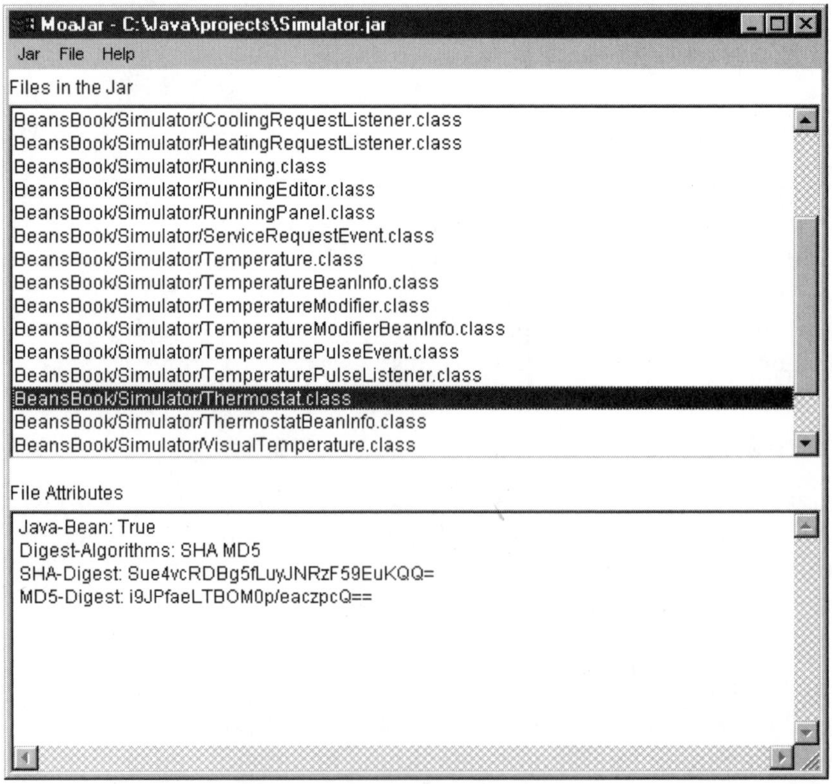

*Figure 6-1. The MoaJar utility*

# 7

# *The BeanBox Tool*

The BeanBox tool is a sample Bean container that comes with the Beans Development Kit (BDK). It allows you to test the functionality of your Beans, including properties, events, and serialization. BeanBox is not an application development tool, nor does it try to be one. It is designed to be a simple testing tool, and it serves this purpose well enough.

You should keep in mind that the user interface and features of BeanBox are not intended to be a guideline for application tools to follow. Commercial development tools that work with Beans are free to use any preferred mechanisms for assembling components into applications. In fact, those mechanisms are what help differentiate one tool from another.

This chapter doesn't try to cover every aspect of BeanBox. We'll just look at some of the features that will be helpful in testing your work. BeanBox allows you to select Beans from a palette and drop them onto a form. It provides a property sheet for setting the values of a Bean's properties, and it allows you to connect event sources and event targets by visually associating them. BeanBox also lets you save the entire state of your form by serializing all of the Beans; you can subsequently reload the form and its constituent Beans.

## *Running BeanBox*

The *beanbox* directory in your BDK installation contains two command scripts for running BeanBox. The first one, *run.bat*, is for running BeanBox on Windows NT and Windows 95. The other, *run.sh*, is for running it on a UNIX system. When you execute the appropriate command, either run or run.sh, BeanBox presents three separate windows. The first one is a toolbox of the Beans that are available. The second is the main window. This contains the form that Beans are dropped onto, as well as some menus for connecting Beans and reporting on them. The last window is the property sheet. This window allows you to edit the properties of the currently selected Bean.

Figure 7-1 shows the BeanBox toolbox. Each available Bean is listed by name. The Beans that expose an icon have it shown just to the left of the name. Note that Beans are not required to expose an icon, in which case this space is left empty. We'll be talking about associating an icon with a bean in a later chapter.

*Figure 7-1. The BeanBox toolbox*

To select a Bean to be dropped onto the main form window, just click on it. The cursor will change to a crosshair, indicating that you can drop the Bean on the form by clicking on the spot where you want it placed. There is no visual indication of which Bean you have selected to drop, and there is no way to cancel out of placement mode if you decide not to drop the Bean on the form. You can, of course, remove the Bean from the form if you really didn't want to put it there. We'll get to this shortly.

Figure 7-2 shows the main form window of BeanBox, before any Beans have been added to it. This window, like the others, can be resized by dragging the edges or corners. The menu bar contains three dropdown menus, *File, Edit,* and *View,* which are used for manipulating the contents of BeanBox. We'll address some of the items on these menus as we go along.

*Figure 7-2. The BeanBox main window*

Figure 7-3 shows the property sheet. This window will change its contents to reflect the editable properties of the currently selected Bean. The BeanBox form itself has some properties that are shown when there is no Bean selected.

*Figure 7-3. The BeanBox property sheet*

# *Dropping Beans on BeanBox*

Let's add a Bean to the BeanBox form. Select the *ExplicitButton* Bean from the toolbox and then click on the spot on the form where you want to place it. When a Bean is added to the form it is shown with a hatched border around it. This border indicates that the Bean is selected. Figure 7-4 shows the BeanBox form with an instance of the *ExplicitButton* currently selected. You can also use this border to move the Bean around on the form, or to resize it if the Bean supports that operation. When you want to select a Bean on the form you usually have to click just outside it, where the hatched border would be. Since the border isn't shown for unselected Beans, you'll have to guess where it is (just around the perimeter of the Bean). Some Beans allow you to select them by clicking anywhere within their border, but most do not. This is a bit of a nuisance, but you'll get the hang of it.

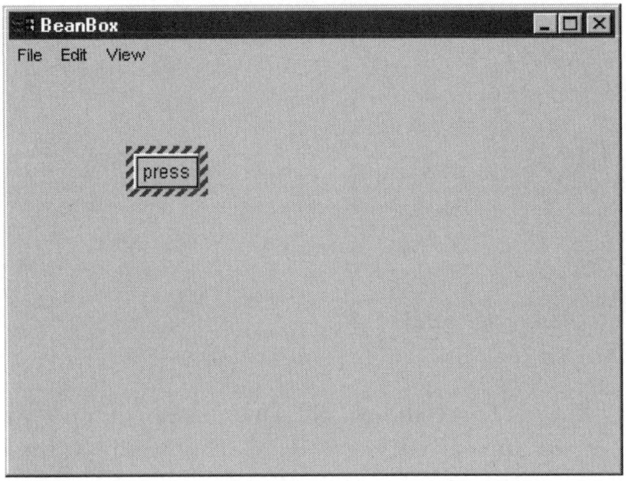

*Figure 7-4. A button in BeanBox*

You can remove the selected Bean from the form by selecting *Cut* from the *Edit* menu. When the Bean is removed, no other Bean on the form is selected. In some cases you may be able to remove the currently selected Bean from the form by pressing the *DEL* key. This doesn't seem to work all the time, particularly for Beans that react to keyboard events. The safe bet here is to use the menu.

## Editing a Bean's Properties

The editable properties for the currently selected Bean are shown on the property sheet. Each property is shown with its name and associated property editor. Some editors allow you to interact directly, while others launch a separate editor window for the property. The editor that is provided is specific to the data type of the property. For instance, a string property editor allows you to edit the value by entering the new string. A color property editor paints its area of the display with the selected color. When you click on the color editor, a dialog box appears that allows you to enter a color according to an RGB triple, or by selecting from a list of predefined color names.

When the instance of the *ExplicitButton* Bean is selected, the property sheet shows its editable properties as shown in Figure 7-5. Edit the label property for the button so that it contains the string *Start*. As you edit the property, the changes are reflected immediately on the button.

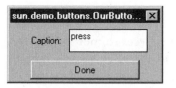

*Figure 7-5. The button's editable properties*

You should play around a little with the various property editors to see how they work. In a later chapter, we will create our own custom property editors. The size of the property sheet will grow and shrink as needed to accommodate the number of editable properties for the selected Bean. Not all properties will be shown in the property sheet—read-only properties are not presented, since they cannot be changed, except by the Bean itself.

Some Beans may also provide a customizer. This is a separate user interface that allows you to configure the properties and behaviors of the Bean. This customizer may allow you to edit various aspects of the Bean that are not represented specifically as properties. They can also provide a more guided approach to configuring complex aspects of the Bean's behavior. If the selected Bean provides a customizer, the *Edit* menu will contain an entry called *Customize* that launches it. Figure 7-6 shows the customizer for the *ExplicitButton* Bean. This is a simple customizer that allows you to change the caption of the Bean.

![customizer dialog]

*Figure 7-6. A simple customizer*

Customizers are frequently used with Beans that require more elaborate configuration. The customizer provides a user interface that makes it easier to configure complicated aspects of the Bean. The *JDBC SELECT* Bean provides a more complex customizer, which is shown in Figure 7-7. We'll be building our own Bean customizer in a later chapter.

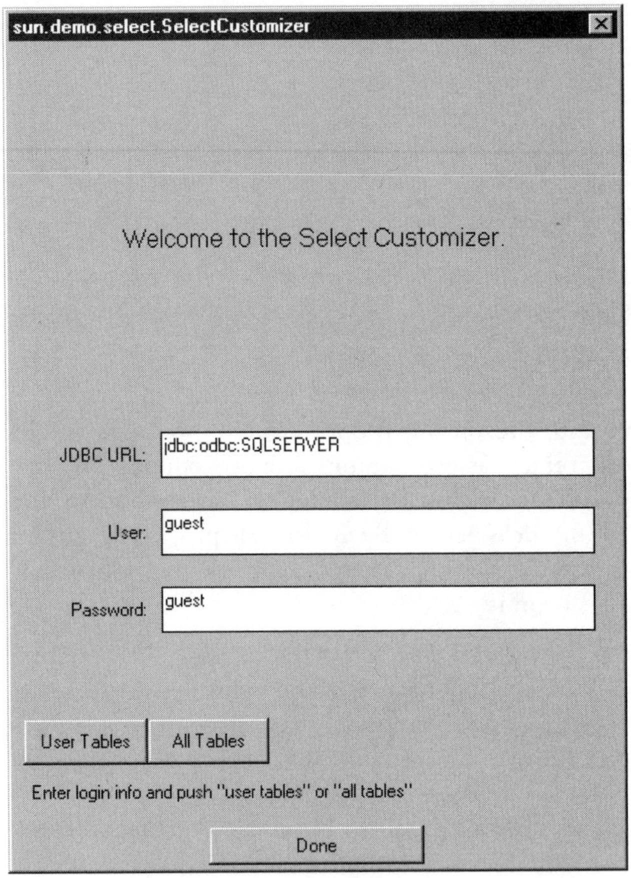

*Figure 7-7. Customizer for the JDBC SELECT Bean*

# *Hooking Up Beans*

Beans are hooked up to each other by matching event sources to methods on the target Bean. The BeanBox does not hook event sources directly to event targets. Instead, BeanBox generates Java code for a specialized adapter. This allows BeanBox to match event sources to target methods that are not necessarily designed specifically for handling that event. For instance, we already know that we could match an `actionEvent` source Bean with one that implements the `ActionEventListener` interface through its `actionPerformed()` method. But BeanBox uses a more flexible approach. It allows you to map the action event to a variety of target methods. The custom adapter code that is generated handles the specifics. We'll look at the Java code for a hookup adapter a little later.

Let's look at some examples. Drop two instances of the *ExplicitButton* Bean onto the form, along with an instance of *Juggler*. Change the label property of the

Beans named *ExplicitButton* so that one of them is *Start* and the other is *Stop*. The *Juggler* Bean is an animation Bean that shows the Java mascot juggling some coffee beans. The animation can be started and stopped by invoking the Bean's `start-Juggling()` and `stopJuggling()` methods, respectively. We use the buttons to invoke these methods. We hook up various events and methods of these Beans to examine the way BeanBox works, as well as the adapter code that it generates. Figure 7-8 shows what the BeanBox form looks like with the Beans that we dropped on it.

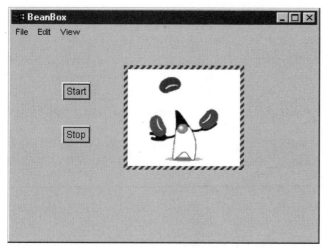

*Figure 7-8. Hooking up Beans*

Now we want to use the *Stop* button to stop the animation running in the *Juggler* Bean. The first step is to select the *Stop* button. Then select the *Edit* menu on the BeanBox window. It contains a cascading menu entry named *Events*. This menu will contain entries for all of the event interfaces that this object can fire events to. Each of these is also a cascading menu that contains the individual events that can be fired. For the *Stop* button, we want to select the *actionPerformed* event from the *button push* menu. Now when you move the mouse cursor around the BeanBox form, you will see a rubber banding line being tracked from the *Stop* button to the mouse cursor. This indicates that you should select a Bean to be the target of the *actionPerformed* event. Select the *Juggler* Bean, since this is the Bean we want to manipulate when the *Stop* button is pressed. When you do so, a dialog box appears that allows you to select the method that you want to invoke on the *Juggler* Bean when the *Stop* button is pressed. Figure 7-9 shows what this dialog looks like.

Since we want to stop the animation when the button is pressed, select `stopJuggling` from the list and press *OK*. The dialog will tell you that the adapter is being generated and compiled. When the dialog disappears, the adapter is completed.

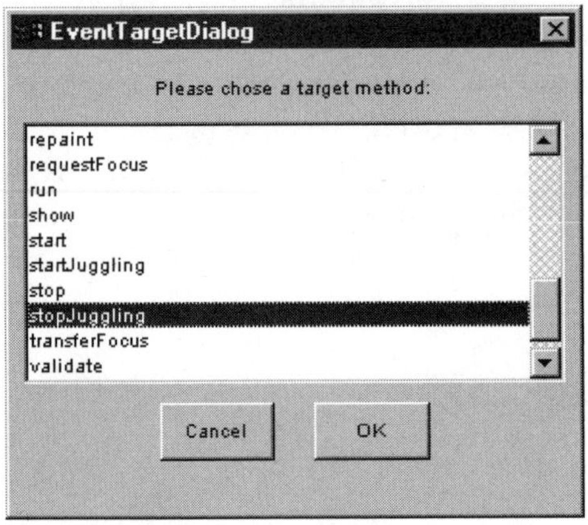

*Figure 7-9. Targets for an event*

Adapter files are always placed into the *tmp* directory under the *beanbox* directory where BeanBox was launched. The name of the adapter is a special unique name generated by BeanBox. Let's look at the Java code for the adapter that was just created when we wired the two components together.

```
// Automatically generated event hookup file.

package tmp.sun.beanbox;

public class ___Hookup_140a4964da implements
java.awt.event.ActionListener, java.io.Serializable {

    public void setTarget(sunw.demo.juggler.Juggler t) {
        target = t;
    }

    public void actionPerformed(java.awt.event.ActionEvent arg0) {
        target.stopJuggling();
    }

    private sunw.demo.juggler.Juggler target;
}
```

Notice that the adapter's constructor takes an instance of the *Juggler* Bean's class as a parameter. This is stored in a private data member named `target`. The BeanBox registers the adapter as an action event listener with the button. When the button is pressed, the event is sent to the adapter. The `actionPerformed()` handler method of the adapter calls the `stopJuggling()` method on the target `Juggler` class, which will stop the animation. Go back to the BeanBox now and press the *Stop* button. The Java mascot stops juggling the coffee beans. You can go ahead and take the same approach for the *Start* button. In this case, choose the startJuggling method on the Juggler Bean as the target method. After the adapter is compiled, you can press the *Start* button to start the animation.

# Saving and Restoring the BeanBox Form

Now that you have created a running BeanBox application, you can save it to be restored later. BeanBox uses Java object serialization to accomplish this. Go to the *File* menu on the main BeanBox window and select *Save*. A dialog box appears that allows you to specify the file to save the application to; specify a filename and press the *Save* button. The file you specified now contains an object stream for the BeanBox form and all of the Beans you added to it, including the hookup adapters that were generated.

To restore the application you created, first go to the *File* menu and select *Clear*. This will remove all Beans from the BeanBox. Next, go to the *File* menu and select *Load*. A dialog box will appear, allowing you to choose the file in which you stored your BeanBox application; select your file and press the *Open* button. The Beans are reconstructed in the same state they were in when you saved them. You can verify this by pressing the *Start* and *Stop* buttons to ensure that they still start and stop the *Juggler* animation.

# Adding Your Own Beans to BeanBox

BeanBox uses JAR files to specify the Beans that it can use. The Beans directory of your BDK installation contains a subdirectory named *jars*. This directory contains the JAR files for the Beans that are used by BeanBox. All you need to do to add your Bean to BeanBox is to package it up in a JAR file and place it into the *jars* directory. BeanBox can work with either compressed or uncompressed JAR files.

If, for some reason, you don't want to put your JAR file into the *jars* directory, you can load them at run-time by using the *File* menu and selecting *LoadJar*. This results in a dialog box that you can use to browse the file system for the JAR file that contains the Beans you want to load.

Let's add the *BeansBook.jar* archive file from the previous chapter to the *jars* directory. This archive contains the BeansBook.util.PickleButton Bean class, along with its serialized state in file *BeansBook/util/SourPickle.ser*.

## Using Your Beans in BeanBox

You use your Beans in BeanBox in exactly the same way that you use the Beans that were provided by the BDK. After the *BeansBook.jar* file is included in the *jars* directory, the *PickleButton* and *SourPickle* Beans will be available in the BeanBox toolbox, as shown in Figure 7-10.

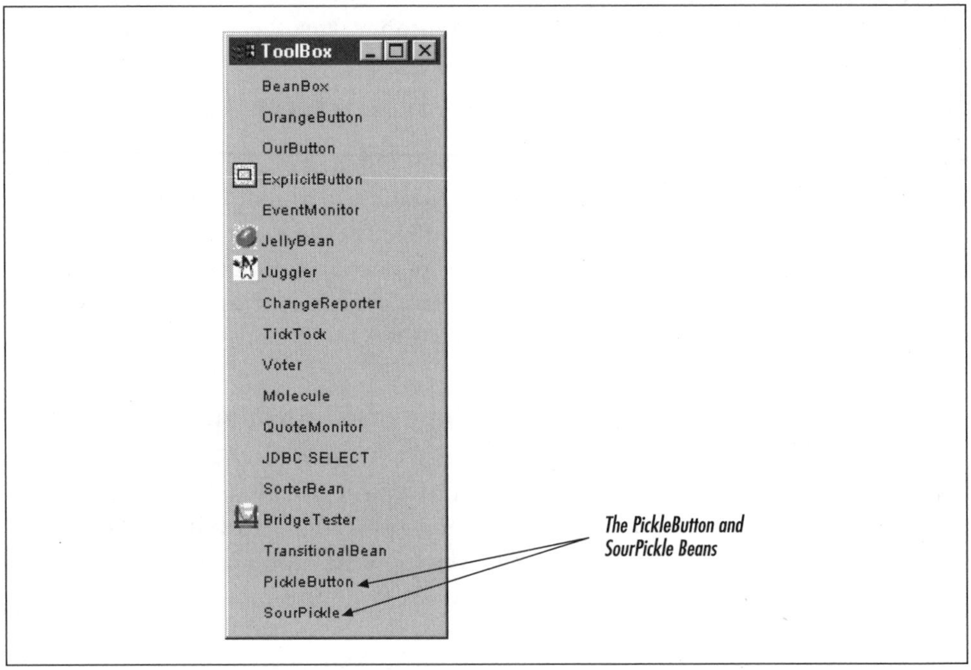

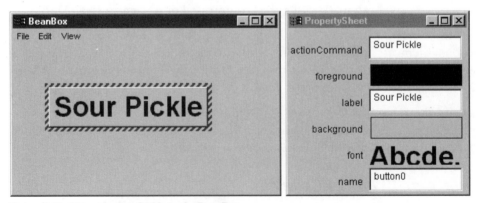

The PickleButton and
SourPickle Beans

*Figure 7-10. The Toolbox with our own Beans added*

If you want to use the *SourPickle* or *PickleButton* Bean on the BeanBox form, just select it and drop it on the form the same way you would any other Bean in the tool box. Figure 7-11 shows the BeanBox with an instance of the *SourPickle,* along with the property sheet showing its editable properties.

*Figure 7-11. Using the SourPickle in the BeanBox*

# 8

# *Putting It All Together*

We've managed to cover all of the basic concepts necessary for developing Java-Beans components. Before we get into the more advanced topics, however, it would be worthwhile to look at a larger example than those we've done previously. This will give us the opportunity to apply everything we've done to this point, and to see how some of the concepts and techniques play together.

In many of the previous examples, we've used objects that related to a temperature control simulator, such as a thermostat and a temperature source. In this chapter, we build the entire simulator. This includes all of the Beans and support classes, as well as a JAR file and a sample applet. We'll add on to the code developed here as new topics are introduced later in the book.

## *Defining the Temperature Control Simulator*

Before we start writing code, it would be a good idea to define what we want to build. Let's specify some simple requirements for the simulator. We want the system to exhibit the following characteristics and behaviors:

- The simulator will monitor and alter the ambient temperature of the system.

- There must be a mechanism for raising and lowering the temperature according to a desired value.

- There must be a way to view the ambient temperature of the system in either Celsius or Fahrenheit.

- The entire simulation must be serializable.

The next step is to interpret the requirements. Our interpretation will lead to the identification of the major components of the system, which we'll implement as Beans.

## The Temperature Object

The core to the simulator is the temperature object. It is used to represent the ambient temperature of the system at any given moment. The rest of the major components of the simulator either monitor or modify the value of the temperature object. We know that we're going to need a way to expose the value of the temperature object, and we'll also need a way for other objects to tell the temperature object to alter its value. It's probably not important to have any visible aspect to the temperature object. We're going to expose the value of the temperature, and rely on some other object to show it to the user.

## The Thermostat Object

The thermostat serves multiple functions in the system. First, it displays the ambient temperature of the system to the user. Remember that the requirements state that the temperature must be displayable in both Celsius and Fahrenheit. The thermostat will have the ability to convert between formats in order to satisfy this requirement.

The simulator also needs a way for the user to change the temperature of the system. The thermostat provides a way for the user to specify the desired temperature. Again, we allow this new temperature to be specified in either Celsius or Fahrenheit.

The thermostat is the object that knows the ambient temperature of the system, as well as the desired temperature set by the user. This means that the thermostat also knows if the ambient temperature of the system needs to be changed.

## The Heating and Cooling Objects

These are the elements of the system that are used to alter the ambient temperature. Each of these objects operate at a specific temperature. When they are running, they can send out pulses that indicate their operating temperature. These pulses are sent out at a specified time interval. They have no concept of when they should be running and when they should not. Instead, they rely on other objects to tell them when to turn themselves on and off.

## Significant Events

We've identified the major components of the simulator. In order for these components to do anything useful, however, they need a way to send information to each other. The simulator is a dynamic system, where the objects react to events, and generate other events themselves. The next step is to figure out the kinds of events that the various objects would be interested in, as well as the events they would generate.

As I mentioned earlier, the thermostat knows when there is a difference between the ambient temperature and the desired temperature. When this condition exists, the thermostat will request either a cooling or heating device to start running. Likewise, when the thermostat recognizes that there is no longer a mismatch between the ambient and desired temperatures, it will inform the heating or cooling device that its services are no longer needed.

When the heating and cooling devices are operating, they send out temperature pulses at regular intervals. These events are interesting to the temperature object, because this is the mechanism that will be used to alter the value of the ambient temperature. In turn, the thermostat is interested in knowing when the temperature object changes the value of the ambient temperature, so it can display the temperature, and determine if the services of heating or cooling devices are required.

There is a circular flow to these events. The thermostat changes its desired temperature, which causes either a heating or cooling device to start, which causes the temperature to change, which causes the thermostat to change its display and compare it to the desired temperature. Eventually, this temperature change will cause the thermostat to shut down the heating or cooling devices. Figure 8-1 shows these relationships.

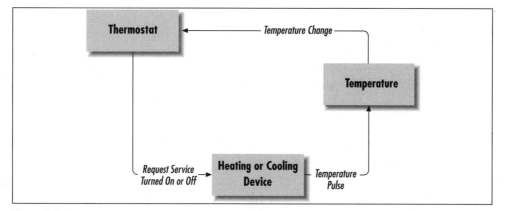

*Figure 8-1. A temperature control system*

# Building the Simulator

Let's start building the classes that make up the simulator. We start with the event classes first since they have no dependencies on other classes in the system. After that, we'll develop the interfaces used to listen for the various events. We'll finish up with the objects that throw and catch the events in the system. All of the classes will be part of the BeansBook.Simulator package.

## Temperature Pulse Events

A temperature pulse event is used to coax a temperature object to alter its value. The pulse contains the temperature value that the source object would like the temperature object to synch up with. First, let's create a class and call it TemperaturePulseEvent. This is the event object that will be passed as a parameter when the temperature pulse event is fired. The code for the class looks like this:

```java
package BeansBook.Simulator;

// class definition for the temperature pulse event
public class TemperaturePulseEvent
        extends java.util.EventObject
{
    // the pulse temperature
    protected double theTemp;

    // constructor
    public TemperaturePulseEvent(Object source, double t)
    {
        // pass the source to the superclass
        super(source);

        // save the temperature
        theTemp = t;
    }

    // return the pulse temperature
    public double getPulseTemperature()
    {
        return theTemp;
    }
}
```

As with all event objects, TemperaturePulseEvent extends java.util.EventObject. The variable theTemp stores the value of the temperature pulse. The constructor takes two parameters, named source and t. source is used to specify the object that is generating the event. This object is saved by calling super(), the superclass constructor that takes the source object as a parameter. The second parameter, t, is used to specify the value of the pulse. This value is stored in the variable theTemp.

When this object is received by the event listener, the getPulseTemperature() method can be used to determine the pulse temperature for the associated event. This method simply returns theTemp, which is the variable that contains the value of the temperature pulse.

In order to listen for temperature pulse events, an object will have to implement the TemperaturePulseListener interface. This interface extends the base class java.util.EventListener, which is required for all event-listener interfaces. The interface defines a single method called temperaturePulse(); this is the method that will be invoked on the listener when the event is fired. An instance of TemperaturePulseEvent is passed as the parameter to temperaturePulse(). The code for the interface is shown below:

```
package BeansBook.Simulator;

// interface for temperature pulse listener
public interface TemperaturePulseListener
        extends java.util.EventListener
{
    // event-handler method for temperature pulse
    public void temperaturePulse(TemperaturePulseEvent evt);
}
```

## Service Request Events

A service request event tells a device to turn itself on or off. We create a class called ServiceRequestEvent for this purpose. This is the event object that will be passed as a parameter when the service request event is fired. Here is the code for the class:

```
package BeansBook.Simulator;

// the service request event class
public class ServiceRequestEvent
        extends java.util.EventObject
{
    // true if the request is to start the service
    protected boolean bStart;

    // constructor
    public ServiceRequestEvent(Object source, boolean start)
    {
        // call the superclass constructor
        super(source);
```

```
        // save the value of the start flag
        bStart = start;
    }

    // determine if the request is to start the service
    public boolean isStart()
    {
        // return the start value
        return bStart;
    }
}
```

The implementation of this class is similar to the `TemperaturePulseEvent` class. Again, it extends `java.util.EventObject`. There is a `boolean` variable called `bStart` that is used to specify whether the request is to start the device or to stop it. Like before, the source object of the event is passed as a parameter, along with a `boolean` value, which indicates if this is a request to start the device or not. The superclass constructor, `super()`, is called to save the source object, and the request type is stored in the `bStart` class variable. The object that receives the event can determine if the request is to start the device by calling the `isStart()` method, which simply returns the value of the `bStart` variable.

When the thermostat discovers that there is a mismatch between the desired temperature and the ambient temperature in the system, it will fire an event-requesting service from a heating or cooling device. We could provide a single service-request listener interface that could be implemented by either type of device, but this would mean that cooling devices would always receive service requests that are meant for heating devices, and vice versa. Instead, let's create specific interfaces for heating and cooling devices. This way, when heat is required, only heating devices will be informed, and when cooling is required, only cooling devices will be informed. This approach still allows us to pass instances of `ServiceRequestEvent`, regardless of which type of service is needed.

The `HeatingRequestListener` interface is implemented by objects that provide heating service, while the `CoolingRequestListener` interface is implemented by objects that provide cooling services. Again, as with all event-listener interfaces, both `HeatingRequestListener` and `CoolingRequestListener` extend the base Java class `java.io.EventListener`. These interfaces each define a single method for handling the event, named `heatingRequest()` and `coolingRequest()`, respectively. Both of these methods take an instance of `ServiceRequestEvent` as the sole parameter. The code for these interfaces is shown here:

```
package BeansBook.Simulator;

// the interface definition for heating request listeners
public interface HeatingRequestListener
        extends java.util.EventListener
```

```
{
    // the heating request event handler
    public void heatingRequest(ServiceRequestEvent evt);
}

// the interface definition for cooling request listeners
public interface CoolingRequestListener
        extends java.util.EventListener
{
    // the cooling request event handler
    public void coolingRequest(ServiceRequestEvent evt);
}
```

## Property Change Events

The `TemperaturePulseEvent` and `ServiceRequestEvent` classes are needed because they convey information that is known only at the time the event is fired. The information is not stored as a property of the source object of the event.

There are circumstances where we can use a bound property instead of creating a custom event. An example, which we'll look at more closely a little later, is the value of the `Temperature` object. In that case, we will make use of a property change event to relate changes to the value of the `Temperature` object. An instance of `java.beans.PropertyChangeEvent` will be passed as a parameter whenever a property change event is fired.

We also have an opportunity to use a constrained property. We know that the user will be able to specify the desired temperature of the system, but there are limits to what the system can accommodate. If the user specified a desired temperature that is higher than the operating temperature of the heating device, it could never be achieved. If we make the desired temperature a constrained property, we could give objects such as the heating device a chance to veto the change, thereby ensuring that the user can never input an unachievable desired temperature. Whenever a vetoable change event is fired, an instance of `java.bean.Veto-ableChangeEvent` will be passed as a parameter. We'll cover this in detail when we talk about the thermostat, as well as the heating and cooling objects.

## Temperature

The core to this system, as I mentioned earlier, is the object that represents the ambient temperature. The `Temperature` class is used to implement this function. The code for the rest of the classes in the simulator tends to be longer than those we've dealt with before. Instead of dumping all of it on you at once, I'll intersperse the discussion with the code—this way the description won't be too far away from the code it addresses.

The `Temperature` class implements `TemperaturePulseListener` for handling temperature pulse events from heating and cooling devices. It also implements `java.io.Serializable`, marking it as a serializable object:

```
package BeansBook.Simulator;

import java.beans.*;

// the temperature bean class definition
public class Temperature
    implements TemperaturePulseListener,  // listens for temp pulses
               java.io.Serializable       // declare Serializable
```

The `boundSupport` variable is an instance of `java.beans.PropertyChangeSupport`, a class that implements the functions necessary to support bound property listeners and event firing. This makes it easier for the `Temperature` class to support property change listeners. There is also a variable named `theTemperature`, of type `double`. `theTemperature` stores the current value of the `Temperature` property, which defaults to a value of 22 degrees Celsius. The `boundSupport` variable is allocated inside the constructor.

```
{
    // support object for bound property listeners
    protected PropertyChangeSupport boundSupport;

    // the current temperature
    protected double theTemperature = 22.0;

    // constructor
    public Temperature()
    {
        // construct the support object
        boundSupport = new PropertyChangeSupport(this);
    }
```

The `addPropertyChangeListener()` and `removePropertyChangeListener()` methods are used to add and remove property change listeners for the bound properties of the `Temperature` class. These methods simply defer to the associated methods on the `boundSupport` variable.

```
    // add a property change listener
    public void addPropertyChangeListener(PropertyChangeListener l)
    {
        // defer to the support object
        boundSupport.addPropertyChangeListener(l);
    }

    // remove a property change listener
    public void removePropertyChangeListener(PropertyChangeListener l)
```

```
    {
        // defer to the support object
        boundSupport.removePropertyChangeListener(l);
    }
```

There is a single read/write property named Temperature, so we provide getTemperature() and setTemperature() methods. The getTemperature() method simply returns the value stored in the variable theTemperature. The setTemperature() method is a little more interesting. The first thing it does is check the new value against the current one. If there is no change, the method returns without doing anything else. Otherwise this method prepares to fire a property change event. The current value of theTemperature is used to create an instance of Double holding the old value for the event, then theTemperature is assigned the new value, which was passed in as parameter t. Remember that bound properties should change their value before firing a property change event. The last thing setTemperature() has to do is to invoke firePropertyChange() on boundSupport. This method fires the property change event to all of the property change listeners that are registered. We pass the string *Temperature* as the first parameter to identify the name of the property that has changed. The next two parameters are used for the old and new values of the property. These parameters must be instances of java.lang.Object or its subclasses, which is why we use instances of Double.

```
    // get the value of the Temperature property
    public double getTemperature()
    {
        return theTemperature;
    }

    // set the value of the Temperature property
    public void setTemperature(double t)
    {
        // don't bother if the value didn't change
        if (t == theTemperature)
            return;

        // save the old value
        Double old = new Double(theTemperature);

        // save the new value
        theTemperature = t;

        // fire the property change event
        boundSupport.firePropertyChange("Temperature",
                                old, new Double(t));
    }
```

The `temperaturePulse()` method is used to handle temperature pulse events. Even though the *Temperature* property is read/write, we don't want external objects to make drastic changes to its value. Temperature changes occur gradually over time, not instantly, which is why the `Temperature` object takes temperature pulses. This allows it to make changes to its *Temperature* property gradually by bringing the temperature 1 degree closer to the pulse temperature each time a pulse is received. We're going to need to compare the pulse temperature with the value of the *Temperature* property, so we call `getPulseTemperature()` on the evt parameter and `getTemperature()` on ourselves to get their respective values. If the pulse temperature is greater than or less than the current temperature by more than 1.0 degree, we call our own `setTemperature()` method to set its new value.

```
// handle a temperature pulse event
public void temperaturePulse(TemperaturePulseEvent evt)
{
    // get the pulse temperature
    double p = evt.getPulseTemperature();

    // get the current temp
    double c = getTemperature();

    // if the pulse is greater than the current temperature
    if (p > c)
    {
        // only change if the difference is more than 1
        if ((p - c) >= 1.0)
        {
            // add 1 to the current temperature
            setTemperature(c + 1.0);
        }
    }
    else if (p < c) // pulse less than the current temperature
    {
        // only change if the difference is more than 1
        if ((c - p) >= 1.0)
        {
            // subtract 1 from the current temperature
            setTemperature(c - 1.0);
        }
    }
}
```

The `Temperature` class works with temperatures in degrees Celsius. The temperature pulses it receives, as well as the property changes it fires, are all in Celsius too.

## *Coolers and Boilers*

Coolers and boilers are objects that operate at a consistent temperature, and fire temperature pulses at regular intervals while they are running. If they are not running, no pulses are delivered. It seems that a cooler and a boiler are just about the same thing in the context of this simulator. They operate at different temperatures, and they probably have different display characteristics, but otherwise, they provide the same functionality.

Let's create a base class called TemperatureModifier for both of these kinds of objects. This class will handle all of the details of running the object, displaying it, and firing the temperature pulses. Later, we'll create subclasses of Temperature-Modifier for the cooler and boiler objects. Actually, this class should never be instantiated by itself. It is designed to be subclassed, so we mark it as abstract.

In order to provide a visual aspect for coolers and boilers, TemperatureModifier extends the java.awt.Label class. As we'll see shortly, this class provides enough display flexibility for the subclasses to display their operating state. This class also implements java.lang.Runnable. We implement Runnable because we want to use separate threads for our cooling and heating equipment. Temperature modifiers send out temperature pulses at regular intervals. We implement this feature within the run() method of this class, which is called by the thread when it is started. This class implicitly declares that it is serializable because the base class java.awt.Label is itself serializable.

```
package BeansBook.Simulator;

import java.awt.*;
import java.beans.*;
import java.io.*;
import java.util.*;

// class definition for the temperature modifier
public abstract class TemperatureModifier extends Label
                implements Runnable
```

The variable thrd is an instance of java.lang.Thread. As previously mentioned, this thread will send temperature pulses to registered listeners. thrd is marked as transient because threads are not serializable. We'll have to get the thread up and running again when the object is deserialized. The listener variable is an instance of TemperaturePulseListener, which holds a reference to the object that is receiving temperature pulse events from this object. Note that we are only keeping track of one listener. This means that instances of TemperatureModifier are unicast event sources for temperature pulse events. The variable listener is marked as transient because we don't know if the registered event listener is

serializable. We will have to deal with this in the `writeObject()` and `readOb-`
`ject()` methods.

The `boolean` variable `running` keeps track of whether this object is operating.
Temperature pulses will be delivered only when `running` is set to `true`. If pulses
are being fired, they will be delivered to the event listener at the interval specified
by the `rate` variable. The interval represents the number of milliseconds between
pulses.

Subclasses of `TemperatureModifier` have a different visual presentation
depending on whether or not they are running. The strings `onText` and `offText`
hold the text for the label when the object is on and off, respectively. The label's
background color changes with the running state of the object; the `Color` variables `onColor` and `offColor` hold the colors we choose for each state. The
variable `temp` stores the temperature at which the object is operating; its value is
used when the object fires temperature pulses.

```
{
    // a thread to send temperature pulses
    protected transient Thread thrd;

    // the temperature pulse listener
    protected transient TemperaturePulseListener listener = null;

    // the running state
    protected boolean running = false;

    // the rate (in msecs) that pulses are generated
    protected int rate = 1000;

    // the text to use when running
    protected String onText;

    // the text to use when not running
    protected String offText;

    // the color to use when running
    protected Color onColor;

    // the color to use when not running
    protected Color offColor;

    // the pulse temperature
    protected double temp;
```

The constructor takes five parameters to configure its operation: the operating
temperature, the "on" string, the "off" string, and the colors to use for the "on"
and "off" states. The `offT` parameter is passed as a parameter to `super()`, the

superclass constructor. This specifies the initial string to use in the label, which in this case represents the string to use when the object is not running. Next, the operating temperature is stored to temp.

The strings and colors for the on and off states of the object are stored, and the background color is set by calling the setBackground() method. We want the text to be centered in the label, so we call setAlignment(Label.CENTER).

Finally, we call the startThread() method to get the thread running. This method creates an instance of java.lang.Thread in variable thrd, and calls its start() method to get it running.

```
public TemperatureModifier(double tmp, String onT, String offT,
                          Color onC, Color offC)
{
    // start the label out with the text for not running
    super(offT);

    // save the operating temperature
    temp = tmp;

    // save the various text and color values
    onText = onT;
    offText = offT;
    onColor = onC;
    offColor = offC;
    setBackground(offColor);

    // set text alignment to center
    setAlignment(Label.CENTER);

    // start the pulse thread
    startThread();
}

// start the pulse thread
private void startThread()
{
    // create and start the pulse thread
    thrd = new Thread(this);
    thrd.start();
}
```

The writeObject() and readObject() methods are implemented so that we can handle serialization ourselves. We need these methods because we have a transient thread object that needs to be reconstructed when the object is deserialized, and we have a transient listener that may be serializable. The writeObject() method calls defaultWriteObject() on the output stream first. Since we've

already marked the thread variable thrd as transient, we don't need to worry
about it here. Next we check to see if there is a temperature pulse listener. If
there is, and it is serializable, then we write it to the stream. Otherwise, we write
null to the stream. Once again, we get a copy of listener first within a synchronized block in case the event listener is unregistered while we are serializing. The
readObject() method calls defaultReadObject() on the input stream to deserialize all of the non-transient data members. Next we read back the temperature
pulse listener and pass it to the addTemperaturePulseListener() method. This
still leaves us without a running thread, which is why we then call startThread()
to create a new instance of java.lang.Thread and get it running.

```java
// write the state of the object
private void writeObject(ObjectOutputStream stream)
        throws IOException
{
    // defer to the default process
    stream.defaultWriteObject();

    // get a copy
    TemperaturePulseListener lstnr = null;
    synchronized (this)
    {
        lstnr = listener;
    }

    boolean bWriteNull = (lstnr == null);
    if (!bWriteNull)
    {
        // is it serializable?
        if (lstnr instanceof Serializable)
        {
            stream.writeObject(lstnr);
        }
        else
        {
            // write a null to the stream
            bWriteNull = true;
        }
    }

    // should we write a null?
    if (bWriteNull)
    {
        stream.writeObject(null);
    }
}
```

```
// read the state of the object
private void readObject(ObjectInputStream stream)
        throws IOException
{
   try
   {
      // defer to the default process
      stream.defaultReadObject();

      // read back the listener
      Object obj = stream.readObject();
      addTemperaturePulseListener((TemperaturePulseListener)obj);

      // start the pulse thread
      startThread();
   }
   catch (Exception e)
   {
      System.out.println(e);
   }
}
```

Temperature modifiers objects have two read/write properties named *Rate* and *Running*. The *Rate* property specifies the rate at which temperature pulses are fired. It is implemented by the setRate() and getRate() methods, which in turn set and get the value of the rate variable. The *Running* property specifies whether the object is running or firing temperature pulses. The setRunning() method sets the value of the *Running* property. Again, if the value is not changing, the method returns without doing anything. Otherwise, the value of the running variable is updated, and the setText() and setBackground() methods are called with the appropriate string and color values. The isRunning() method returns the value of the *Running* property. Remember that this is an alternative naming convention that can be used in place of, or in addition to, a method named getRunning(), which I chose not to implement.

```
// set the value of the Rate property
public void setRate(int r)
{
   rate = r;
}

// get the value of the Rate property
public int getRate()
{
   return rate;
}
```

```
      // set the value of the Running property
      public synchronized void setRunning(boolean b)
      {
          // don't bother if there is no change
          if (running == b)
          {
              return;
          }

          // save the new value
          running = b;

          // set the appropriate label text and background color
          if (running)
          {
              setText(onText);
              setBackground(onColor);
          }
          else
          {
              setText(offText);
              setBackground(offColor);
          }
      }

      // get the value of the Running property
      public boolean isRunning()
      {
          return running;
      }
```

The addTemperaturePulseListener() and removeTemperaturePulseLis-
tener() methods register and unregister an object that listens for temperature
pulse events. As mentioned earlier, I decided to make this object a unicast event
source for temperature pulses. There is a good reason for this. Think about an air
conditioner that is trying to cool one room in your house. This is equivalent to a
single cooler firing pulses to a single Temperature object in our simulator. If you
try to cool two rooms with the same air conditioner, each room would get half the
amount of cooling. There are two ways that we could implement this. One way
would have been to stagger the pulses when there was more than one listener,
where each listener would receive pulses in round-robin fashion, producing the
effect of less cooling over a period of time. The way I handled it was to say that the
object could offer its services to only one listening object at a time, which is represented by the unicast event source. If you have multiple Temperature objects to
cool you'll need a cooler object for each. Therefore, the addTempera-
turePulseListener() method may throw a TooManyListeners exception. The

`removeTemperaturePulseListener()` method only removes the specified listener if it is the one that is currently registered.

```
// add a unicast temperature pulse listener
public synchronized void
addTemperaturePulseListener(TemperaturePulseListener l)
                                    throws TooManyListenersException
{
    // if there is already a listener, throw an exception
    if (listener != null)
    {
        throw new TooManyListenersException();
    }

    // store the listener
    listener = l;
}

// remove the unicast temperature pulse listener
public synchronized void
removeTemperaturePulseListener(TemperaturePulseListener l)
{
    // make sure this is the listener we have
    if (listener == l)
    {
        listener = null;
    }
}
```

The `run()` method is called by the thread referenced by `thrd` when it is first started. This method just loops forever, sleeping for the amount of time specified by the `rate` variable. When the thread wakes up, it looks to see if there is a listening object and if the `running` variable is set to `true`. If both of these conditions are met, the `temperaturePulse()` method on the listening object is invoked with an instance of `TemperaturePulseEvent` as a parameter.

```
// the run method for the pulse thread
public void run()
{
    // loop forever
    while(true)
    {
        try
        {
            // sleep for the time specified by rate
            thrd.sleep(rate);

            // if there is a listener and the service is running, then
            //  send the pulse event
```

```
                    if (listener != null && running)
                    {
                       listener.temperaturePulse(new
                                         TemperaturePulseEvent(this, temp));
                    }
                 }
                 catch (Exception e)
                 {
                 }
              }
           }
        }
```

Now that we have a base class for any temperature modifier object, let's create class Cooler to act as an air conditioner. Besides extending TemperatureModifier, this class implements CoolingRequestListener so that it can respond to requests for cooling service. It also implements VetoableChangeListener because the Cooler must ensure that the user does not specify a desired temperature below a value that is achievable. We'll see later that the Thermostat will fire a VetoableChangeEvent when the user changes the desired temperature. This gives objects like the Cooler an opportunity to validate the change and veto it if it cannot be achieved.

The constructor calls the super class constructor, super(), to pass the configuration information required by the TemperatureModifier class. The Cooler operates at 0 degrees Celsius. This means that it fires temperature pulses of 0 degrees at the default rate of 1000 milliseconds. When the Cooler is running, it displays the string *COOLER ON* with a cyan background. When it isn't running, it displays *COOLER OFF* with a yellow background.

```
   package BeansBook.Simulator;

   import java.awt.*;
   import java.beans.*;

   // the Cooler bean class definition
   public class Cooler extends TemperatureModifier
       implements CoolingRequestListener, VetoableChangeListener
   {
      // constructor
      public Cooler()
      {
         // a cooler is a temperature modifier that operates at
         // 0 degrees celsius
         super(0.0, "COOLER ON", "COOLER OFF",
                 Color.cyan, Color.yellow);
      }
```

The coolingRequest() method is called when a service request event is fired. The event object is an instance of ServiceRequestEvent, which provides a method called isStart() to determine if the event is a request to start or stop the service from running. The result of this method call is passed to the setRunning() method provided by the base class, which sets the value of the *Running* property.

```
// handle a cooling request event
public void coolingRequest(ServiceRequestEvent evt)
{
    // set the Running property based on the value returned
    // by the isStart method from the event
    setRunning(evt.isStart());
}
```

The vetoableChange() method is called before the value of a constrained property is changed by the source. The Cooler is only interested in changes made to a *ComfortTemperature* property. This is the property that will be set by the Thermostat when the user changes the desired temperature. Since the Cooler operates at 0 degrees Celsius, it knows that it can never achieve a temperature less than that. If the proposed new value of the *ComfortTemperature* property is less than 0, a PropertyVetoException is thrown.

```
// handle a vetoable change event
public void vetoableChange(PropertyChangeEvent evt)
        throws PropertyVetoException
{
    // only interested in ComfortTemperature
    if (evt.getPropertyName().equals("ComfortTemperature"))
    {
        // get the proposed temperature
        Double d = (Double)evt.getNewValue();

        // veto a temperature under 0 degrees Celsius
        if (d.doubleValue() < 0.0)
        {
            throw new
            PropertyVetoException("Invalid Comfort Temperature", evt);
        }
    }
}
```

The Boiler class is the heating device in our simulator. It is almost identical to the Cooler, except that it operates at 100 degrees Celsius and it listens for heating request events. If you take a look at the code, you'll see the relevant differences between the Cooler and Boiler classes, so I won't bother to describe them.

```java
// the Boiler bean class definition
public class Boiler extends TemperatureModifier
    implements HeatingRequestListener,    // listens for heating requests
               VetoableChangeListener     // vetoes property changes
{
    // constructor
    public Boiler()
    {
        // a boiler is a temperature modifier that operates at
        // 100 degrees celsius
        super(100.0, "BOILER ON", "BOILER OFF",
                Color.red, Color.yellow);
    }

    // handle a heating request event
    public void heatingRequest(ServiceRequestEvent evt)
    {
        // set the Running property based on the value returned
        // by the isStart() method from the event
        setRunning(evt.isStart());
    }

    // handle a vetoable change event
    public void vetoableChange(PropertyChangeEvent evt)
            throws PropertyVetoException
    {
        // only interested in ComfortTemperature
        if (evt.getPropertyName().equals("ComfortTemperature"))
        {
            // get the proposed temperature
            Double d = (Double)evt.getNewValue();

            // veto a temperature over 100 degrees Celsius
            if (d.doubleValue() > 100.0)
            {
                throw new
                  PropertyVetoException("Invalid Comfort Temperature", evt);
            }
        }
    }
}
```

## The Thermostat

The thermostat controls the overall operation of the simulator. It allows the user to specify the desired temperature, and it decides when to turn the heating and cooling devices on and off. This is the only object in the simulator that has any kind of interesting user interface. So before we get into the code, let's think about how the object will be used so that we can make some user interface decisions.

We know that the thermostat displays the current temperature, so we need to provide some kind of a display label. The requirements statement at the beginning of the chapter said that the temperature should be displayable in both Celsius and Fahrenheit. Let's use a dropdown list for specifying the temperature units.

The thermostat also has to provide a mechanism for the user to specify the desired temperature. We can share the same display area that we use for the current temperature for this purpose. We need a mechanism for the user to switch the display mode between the two temperatures. This can also be done with a dropdown list, allowing for new display choices in the future. The last thing we need to do is to provide a way for the user to change the desired temperature. Let's just provide an increment and decrement button for this purpose. This will allow the user to change the desired temperature one degree at a time. These buttons should not be available when the current temperature of the system is being displayed.

The basic layout of the thermostat user interface is shown in Figure 8-2. The center display area is used to display either the current system temperature or the desired temperature, depending on the selection in the dropdown list below the display area. If the desired temperature is being displayed, the buttons to the left and right of the main display are used to decrement or increment the desired temperature. The dropdown list above the main display area is used to select the units to use for displaying temperature, either Celsius or Fahrenheit.

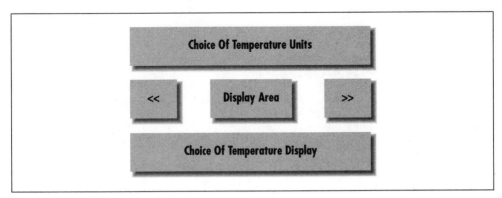

*Figure 8-2. Design for the thermostat's user interface*

The Thermostat class is similar to a form, in that it is a collection of various other user interface components. For this reason we extend the java.awt.Panel class, which is useful for this purpose. We also need to implement a number of interfaces. The `PropertyChangeListener` is used so that the `Thermostat` can listen for changes to the *Temperature* property of the `Temperature` object. The `ActionListener` interface is needed so that the pushbutton events from the increment and decrement buttons can be handled. Likewise, the `ItemListener` interface handles the item events from the dropdown lists.

```java
package BeansBook.Simulator;

import java.awt.*;
import java.awt.event.*;
import java.beans.*;
import java.util.*;
import java.io.*;

// the Thermostat bean class definition
public class Thermostat extends Panel   // subclasses Panel
    implements PropertyChangeListener,  // property changes
                ActionListener,          // action events from buttons
                ItemListener             // item events choice controls
```

The variables `unitsChoice` and `displayChoice` are instances of `java.awt.Choice`. They allow the user to select the temperature display units and which temperature (ambient or desired) they are displaying, respectively. We use two instances of `java.awt.Button`, `decButton` and `incButton`, which let the user decrement or increment the value of the desired temperature. The `display-Label`, an instance of `java.awt.Label`, is used to display the selected temperature to the user.

```java
{
    // the choice control for display units
    protected Choice unitsChoice;

    // the choice control for displaying ambient or
    //  comfort level temperature
    protected Choice displayChoice;

    // button for decrementing comfort level temperature
    protected Button decButton;

    // button for incrementing comfort level temperature
    protected Button incButton;

    // label for displaying temperatures
    protected Label  displayLabel;
```

The `bNeedsCooling` and `bNeedsHeating` variables are instances of `boolean`, used to keep track of whether cooling or heating services are needed. Next we have two variables of type `double`: `comfortTemp`, used to keep track of the desired comfort temperature; and `ambientTemp`, used to keep track of the *Temperature* property value of the associated Temperature object. This is needed because the only communication between the Temperature and Thermostat objects is via a property change event. The Thermostat doesn't actually store a reference to the Temperature object, so it has no way to query it for the value of its *Temperature* property.

We need to keep track of which temperature we are displaying; for this, we use the boolean variable bShowingAmbient. We keep track of the units being used for temperature display using the bShowingCelsius variable.

```
// flags for the NeedsCooling and NeedsHeating state
protected boolean bNeedsCooling = false;
protected boolean bNeedsHeating = false;

// the comfort level temperature
protected double comfortTemp = 22.0;

// the ambient temperature from the temperature source
protected double ambientTemp;

// flag indicating if ambient temperature is being displayed
protected boolean bShowingAmbient = true;

// flag indicating if Celsius units are being displayed
protected boolean bShowingCelsius = true;
```

The property named *ComfortTemperature* is constrained so that heating and cooling devices can veto unachievable temperatures. We use an instance of VetoableChangeSupport called vetoSupport to handle the registration and firing of a vetoable change event. We also keep vectors of objects registered as listeners for cooling and heating requests. These vectors are named coolingListeners and heatingListeners. Note that these vectors are marked as transient, because we can't guarantee that all of the registered listeners will be serializable. We'll handle the serializing and deserializing of these collections in the writeObject() and readObject() methods.

```
// support for the constrained properties
protected VetoableChangeSupport vetoSupport;

// cooling and heating request listeners
protected transient Vector coolingListeners;
protected transient Vector heatingListeners;
```

Let's take a close look at the constructor. This is where all of the parts of the thermostat get created. After the super class constructor is called the vetoSupport object is created. Based on Figure 8-2, the ideal layout is a border layout. The java.awt.BorderLayout class allows us to place components onto the form in either the north, south, east, west, or center positions. This coincides exactly with

the constituent parts of the `Thermostat` class, so we call `setLayout()` to install a
`BorderLayout` layout manager

Next we create all of the components. `displayLabel` is created with a string of
asterisks as its content, so that the object is initialized with enough space to display
temperatures. We use asterisks because we don't yet know what temperature to
display, but we want to make sure that there will be enough room to display any
reasonable temperature.

```
// constructor
public Thermostat()
{
    // call superclass constructor
    super();

    // create the support object for constrained properties
    vetoSupport = new VetoableChangeSupport(this);

    // use a border layout for the constituents
    setLayout(new BorderLayout());

    // create the constituents
    unitsChoice = new Choice();
    displayChoice = new Choice();
    decButton = new Button("<<");
    incButton = new Button(">>");
    displayLabel = new Label("**********");
```

We want to handle action events from the increment and decrement buttons, so
we call `addActionListener()` on `decButton` and `incButton`, specifying `this` as
the listening object. We also need to know when the user changes the temperature units and display selection. The `displayChoice` and `unitsChoice` fire item
events, so we call their `addItemListener()` methods, again specifying `this` as the
listening object.

The increment and decrement buttons are only used when the desired comfort
temperature is being displayed, which is not the default configuration when the
object is first created. To stop the user from interacting with these buttons when
the ambient temperature is displayed, we call their `setEnabled()` method with a
parameter of `false`.

```
    // register as action listener for the buttons
    decButton.addActionListener(this);
    incButton.addActionListener(this);

    // register as item listener for the choice controls
    displayChoice.addItemListener(this);
    unitsChoice.addItemListener(this);
```

```
            // disable the comfort temperature buttons
            decButton.setEnabled(false);
            incButton.setEnabled(false);
```

Now that the user interface components have been created, they have to be added to the panel. This is done by calling the add() method, specifying the component and position for each. Note that the displayLabel is positioned at center.

We want the temperature display to center its text, so we call setAlignment() on the displayLabel with a parameter of Label.CENTER. Now we need to add the choices to unitsChoice and displayChoice. We do this by calling their add() method with the appropriate strings as parameters.

```
            // add the constituents in their appropriate locations
            add(unitsChoice, BorderLayout.NORTH);
            add(displayChoice, BorderLayout.SOUTH);
            add(decButton, BorderLayout.WEST);
            add(incButton, BorderLayout.EAST);
            add(displayLabel, BorderLayout.CENTER);

            // use center alignment for the temperature display
            displayLabel.setAlignment(Label.CENTER);

            // add the units to the choice control
            unitsChoice.add("Celsius");
            unitsChoice.add("Fahrenheit");

            // add the display types to the choice control
            displayChoice.add("Ambient");
            displayChoice.add("Comfort");
        }
```

When the actionPerformed() method is invoked, it means that either the decrement or increment button was pressed. Although this seems trivial, there is actually quite a bit of logic involved. Remember that temperatures in the simulator are stored in degrees Celsius, but the user may be viewing temperatures in Fahrenheit. When the user presses the increment or decrement button, the desired comfort temperature should be incremented or decremented by one degree of the units that are being displayed—meaning that we have to do some conversions when the temperature is being displayed in Fahrenheit. We also have to deal with the fact that temperatures may have a fractional part, but we're only displaying temperatures as whole numbers. This means that we might have to perform some rounding of temperature values, particularly when a change to the desired comfort temperature is vetoed. Imagine that comfortTemp is 99.5 degrees Celsius, and the user presses the increment button. The Boiler class is going to veto the change because it is operating at 100 degrees; it can't ever achieve a temperature of 100.5 degrees. But, there is still room to change the value of comfortTemp to 100 degrees. This is an instance when we would round the value. The same thing happens when you attempt to drop below the lowest temperature that can be achieved by the Cooler. In order to handle rounding in a uniform manner, we set up some information in the tempDelta and roundingDelta variables based on which button was pressed. The rest of the code is then the same for either button.

```
// handle an action event
public void actionPerformed(ActionEvent evt)
{
    // change in temperature
    double tempDelta;

    // delta value for rounding
    double roundingDelta;

    // it was the decrement button
    if (evt.getSource() == decButton)
    {
        // reduce temp by 1
        tempDelta = -1.0;

        // delta is 0 for rounding down
        roundingDelta = 0.0;
    }
    else // it was the increment button
    {
        // increase temp by 1
        tempDelta = 1.0;

        // delta is 1 for rounding up
        roundingDelta = 1.0;
    }
```

Since *ComfortTemperature* is a constrained property, we have to use a temporary variable to store its value until we validate the change with the vetoable change listeners. If we're showing the current desired comfort temperature in Fahrenheit, we have to convert the temperature from Celsius, add the delta, and then convert back. Next we use the comfortTemp variable to create an instance of Double called old. This is the old value that we'll use to fire the vetoable change event.

We call the fireVetoableChange() method on the vetoSupport object. If the PropertyChangeException is not thrown, we can go ahead and make the change. If the change was vetoed, we have an opportunity to round the value and try one more time. If, however, there is no chance to make a change (because there is no fractional part of the new temperature) we just return. If there is a fractional part, we round the value and try again. If this change isn't vetoed, we assign the result to comfortTemp.

```java
// the new proposed comfort temperature
double newValue;

// displaying temperatures in Celsius
if (bShowingCelsius)
{
   // just add the delta
   newValue = comfortTemp + tempDelta;
}
else // displaying in Fahrenheit
{
   // convert to Fahrenheit, add the delta, and convert back
   double t = 32.0 + ((comfortTemp * 9.0) / 5.0);
   t += tempDelta;
   newValue = (t - 32.0) * 5.0 / 9.0;
}

// the old value object for firing the vetoable change event
Double old = new Double(comfortTemp);
try
{
   // fire the event
   vetoSupport.fireVetoableChange("ComfortTemperature", old, new
                      Double(newValue));

   // if we get this far we can make the change
   synchronized (this)
   {
      comfortTemp = newValue;
   }
}
catch (PropertyVetoException e)
{
   // the change was vetoed by a listening object, but
   // if we have a fractional part, we could try rounding the
   // value to use a whole number
   double wholePart = (double)old.longValue();
   if ((old.doubleValue() - wholePart) == 0.0)
   {
      // we can't make a change
      return;
   }

   // attempt to alter the comfort temperature using the whole
   // part of the old value and the rounding delta
   newValue = wholePart + roundingDelta;
```

```
try
{
   // fire the event
   vetoSupport.fireVetoableChange("ComfortTemperature", old,
                     new Double(newValue));
}
catch (PropertyVetoException ee)
{
   // we couldn't make this change either
   return;
}

// we can go ahead and change it now
synchronized (this)
{
   comfortTemp = wholePart + roundingDelta;
}
}
```

Now that we have a new comfort temperature, we can call the setNeeds-Cooling() and setNeedsHeating() methods. The parameters for these methods are computed by comparing ambientTemp to comfortTemp, determining if there is a difference and if that difference is greater than 1 degree. After that we just call displayTemp() to redisplay the comfort temperature. This method first determines which temperature is being displayed, and stores its value in the temporary variable t. The value is then converted if the temperature is being displayed in Fahrenheit. Finally, the integer value of the temperature is converted into a string and used as a parameter to the setText() method on displayLabel, which displays the new value on the screen.

```
   // set the needs cooling and needs heating states, comparing
   // the ambient and comfort level temperatures
   setNeedsCooling(ambientTemp - comfortTemp) >= 1.0);
   setNeedsHeating(comfortTemp - ambientTemp) >= 1.0);

   // redisplay the temperature
   displayTemp();
}

// display the temperature
protected void displayTemp()
{
   // temporary temperature value
   double t;
   if (bShowingAmbient)
   {
```

```
            // use the ambient temperature
            t = ambientTemp;
        }
        else
        {
            // use the comfort level temperature
            t = comfortTemp;
        }

        // if not using Celsius, convert to Fahrenheit
        if (!bShowingCelsius)
        {
            t = 32.0 + ((t * 9.0) / 5.0);
        }

        // display whole number part of the temperature
        Double d = new Double(t);
        displayLabel.setText(new Long(d.longValue()).toString());
    }
```

Whenever the user changes the selection in one of the Choice controls, the item-
StateChanged() method will be invoked. Actually, this method is called whenever
the state of an item in the Choice control changes, so we have to check to see if it
is really the event we're looking for. If the source of the event is displayChoice
and the state change is ItemEvent.SELECTED, then we know the user just changed
which temperature should be displayed.

The first step is to call the getItem() method to get the string value of the
selected item. If the string is *Comfort,* then the user wants to display the desired
comfort temperature; we set the bShowingAmbient variable to false, enable both
buttons by calling setEnabled(true) on them, and then call displayTemp() to
redisplay the temperature. If the string is *Ambient,* we set the bShowingAmbient
variable to true, call setEnable(false) on the buttons, and again redisplay the
temperature by calling the displayTemp() method.

If the event wasn't from the displayChoice, we check to see if it was an
ItemEvent.SELECTED event from the unitsChoice control. If so, we go through
essentially the same process as we did for the displayChoice event, this time
setting the bShowingCelsius variable to true or false depending on the
selected item, and then calling displayTemp() to redisplay the temperature.

```
    // handle item state change events
    public void itemStateChanged(ItemEvent evt)
    {
        if (evt.getSource() == displayChoice &&
            evt.getStateChange() == ItemEvent.SELECTED)
        {
            // determine the newly selected item string
```

```
        String sel = (String)evt.getItem();
        if (sel.equals("Comfort"))
        {
            // showing comfort level, not ambient
            bShowingAmbient = false;

            // enable comfort level buttons
            decButton.setEnabled(true);
            incButton.setEnabled(true);

            // display the temperature
            displayTemp();
        }
        else if (sel.equals("Ambient"))
        {
            // showing ambient temperature
            bShowingAmbient = true;

            // disable the comfort level buttons
            decButton.setEnabled(false);
            incButton.setEnabled(false);

            // display the temperature
            displayTemp();
        }
    }

    else if (evt.getSource() == unitsChoice &&
            evt.getStateChange() == ItemEvent.SELECTED)
    {
        // determine the newly selected item string
        String sel = (String)evt.getItem();
        if (sel.equals("Celsius"))
        {
            // showing Celsius
            bShowingCelsius = true;

            // display the temperature
            displayTemp();
        }
        else if (sel.equals("Fahrenheit"))
        {
            // showing Fahrenheit, not Celsius
            bShowingCelsius = false;

            // display the temperature
            displayTemp();
        }
    }
}
```

The addHeatingRequestListener() method is used to register a heating request listener for heating request events. First, we allocate heatingListeners, if that has not happened yet. Next, we add the specified listener to heatingListeners by calling its addElement() method, making sure that the listener is not already registered. The removeHeatingRequestListener() method unregisters a heating request listener. We check that heatingListeners is not null, and then we call removeElement(). We go through exactly the same procedure for cooling request listeners, using the methods addCoolingRequestListener() and removeCoolingRequestListener().

```
// add a heating request listener
public synchronized void
addHeatingRequestListener(HeatingRequestListener l)
{
    // add a listener if it is not already registered
    if (heatingListeners == null)
    {
        heatingListeners = new Vector();
    }

    if (!heatingListeners.contains(l))
    {
        heatingListeners.addElement(l);
    }
}

// remove the heating request listener
public synchronized void
removeHeatingRequestListener(HeatingRequestListener l)
{
    // remove it if it is registered
    if (heatingListeners != null)
    {
        heatingListeners.removeElement(l);
    }
}

// add a cooling request listener
public synchronized void
addCoolingRequestListener(CoolingRequestListener l)
{
    // add a listener if it is not already registered
    if (coolingListeners == null)
    {
        coolingListeners = new Vector();
    }

    if (!coolingListeners.contains(l))
```

```
        {
            coolingListeners.addElement(l);
        }
    }

    // remove the cooling request listener
    public synchronized void
    removeCoolingRequestListener(CoolingRequestListener l)
    {
        // remove it if it is registered
        if (coolingListeners != null)
        {
            coolingListeners.removeElement(l);
        }
    }
```

The value of the *ComfortTemperature* property can be retrieved by calling the getComfortTemperature() method. This property is read-only, which is why we don't provide a setComfortTemperature() method. The only way to change this property is to press either the increment or the decrement button on the Thermostat user interface.

```
    // return the comfort temperature
    public synchronized double getComfortTemperature()
    {
        return comfortTemp;
    }
```

The bNeedsCooling variable is used to maintain the internal state of the Thermostat that indicates whether the system is in need of cooling services. We don't want to expose this as a property because the Thermostat is the only object that can make this determination. The setNeedsCooling() method is used to set the value of the bNeedsCooling variable. Note that this is a private method, to ensure that it can't be called by another object and that it can't be mistaken as the pattern for a write-only property.

As we've done many times before, we simply return if the new value is the same as the old value. If not, we save the new value in bNeedsCooling, and then use it to create an instance of ServiceRequestEvent. At this point we check to see if coolingListeners has been allocated. If it hasn't, there are no listeners and we just return. Now we make a copy of the coolingListeners vector into temporary variable v. This is done inside a synchronized block, ensuring that none of the listeners can unregister themselves while we are firing events; now we can loop through the elements of the temporary vector. For each element, we cast it to type CoolingRequestListener, and invoke its coolingRequest() method.

The bNeedsHeating variable is handled in exactly the same way, using the setNeedsHeating() method.

```java
// set the needs cooling state
private void setNeedsCooling(boolean b)
{
   // do nothing if there is no change
   if (b == bNeedsCooling)
   {
      return;
   }

   bNeedsCooling = b;

   // nothing else to do if collection isn't allocated yet
   if (coolingListeners == null)
   {
      return;
   }

   // fire the cooling service request
   ServiceRequestEvent evt = new ServiceRequestEvent(this,
                                        bNeedsCooling);

   // make a copy of the listener object vector so that it cannot
   // be changed while we are firing events
   Vector v;
   synchronized(this)
   {
      v = (Vector) coolingListeners.clone();
   }

   // fire the event to all listeners
   int cnt = v.size();
   for (int i = 0; i < cnt; i++)
   {
      CoolingRequestListener client =
         (CoolingRequestListener)v.elementAt(i);
      client.coolingRequest(evt);
   }
}

// set the needs heating state
private void setNeedsHeating(boolean b)
{
   // do nothing if there is no change
   if (b == bNeedsHeating)
   {
      return;
   }
```

```
        bNeedsHeating = b;

        // nothing else to do if collection isn't allocated yet
        if (heatingListeners == null)
        {
            return;
        }

        // fire the heating service request
        ServiceRequestEvent evt = new ServiceRequestEvent(this,
                                                  bNeedsHeating);

        // make a copy of the listener object vector so that it cannot
        // be changed while we are firing events
        Vector v;
        synchronized(this)
        {
            v = (Vector) heatingListeners.clone();
        }

        // fire the event to all listeners
        int cnt = v.size();
        for (int i = 0; i < cnt; i++)
        {
            HeatingRequestListener client =
                (HeatingRequestListener)v.elementAt(i);
            client.heatingRequest(evt);
        }
    }
```

The addVetoableChangeListener() and removeVetoableChangeListener()
methods are used to register and unregister listeners for vetoable change events
by deferring to the corresponding methods on vetoSupport. These listeners are
given the opportunity to veto changes to the constrained property
*ComfortTemperature*.

```
    // add vetoable change listener
    public void addVetoableChangeListener(VetoableChangeListener l)
    {
        vetoSupport.addVetoableChangeListener(l);
    }

    // remove vetoable change listener
    public void removeVetoableChangeListener(VetoableChangeListener l)
    {
        vetoSupport.removeVetoableChangeListener(l);
    }
```

The Thermostat listens for changes to a *Temperature* property on a Temperature
object. Whenever the propertyChange() method is called, we first check to see

that the property name is *Temperature*. If it is, we extract the new value of the property by calling the getNewValue() method on the event object and casting it to type Double. Next we get the value from the object by calling the doubleValue() method, and we assign it to the ambientTemp variable. At this point we can set the values of the bNeedsCooling and bNeedsHeating variables by calling the setNeedsCooling() and setNeedsHeating() methods. In each case, we compute the new value by comparing the value of ambientTemp and comfortTemp, and by checking to see if their difference is greater than 1 degree. The last step is to call displayTemp() to redisplay the temperature.

```
// handle a property change from another source
public void propertyChange(PropertyChangeEvent evt)
{
    // check for a Temperature property change
    if (evt.getPropertyName().equals("Temperature"))
    {
        // modify the ambient temperature
        Double d = (Double)evt.getNewValue();
        ambientTemp = d.doubleValue();

        // update the bNeedsCooling and bNeedsHeating variables
        setNeedsCooling(ambientTemp - comfortTemp) >= 1.0);
        setNeedsHeating(comfortTemp - ambientTemp) >= 1.0);

        // display the temperature
        displayTemp();
    }
}
```

We made heatingListeners and coolingListeners transient because we aren't sure that the registered listeners will all be serializable. We deal with this issue by implementing writeObject() and readObject() methods, where we will serialize and deserialize those listeners that are actually serializable. The first thing we do in writeObject() is call defaultWriteObject() on the stream so that the rest of the data members get stored automatically. Now we deal with the registered cooling request listeners. We will store all of the registered listeners that are serializable, followed by a null to mark the end of the list.

As long as coolingListeners is not null, we have some work to do. The first step is to clone coolingListeners within a synchronized block so that the registered elements can't change while we're looping through the collection. Each element in the loop is cast to CoolingRequestListener, and then the instanceof operator is used to determine if the element is serializable. If it is, we write it to the stream; otherwise, we skip it. We finish off with null to mark the end of the list. The same process is used to serialize the elements of heatingListeners.

```java
private void writeObject(ObjectOutputStream stream)
        throws java.io.IOException
{
    // perform default writing first
    stream.defaultWriteObject();

    // if we have allocated coolingListeners
    if (coolingListeners != null)
    {
        // clone the vector in case one is added or removed
        Vector v = null;
        synchronized (this)
        {
            v = (Vector) coolingListeners.clone();
        }

        int cnt = v.size();
        for(int i = 0; i < cnt; i++)
        {
            // get the listener element from the collection
            CoolingRequestListener l =
                (CoolingRequestListener)v.elementAt(i);

            // if the listener is serializable, write it to the stream
            if (l instanceof Serializable)
            {
                stream.writeObject(l);
            }
        }
    }

    // a null object marks the end of the cooling request listeners
    stream.writeObject(null);

    // if we have allocated heatingListeners
    if (heatingListeners != null)
    {
        // clone the vector in case one is added or removed
        Vector v = null;
        synchronized (this)
        {
            v = (Vector) heatingListeners.clone();
        }

        int cnt = v.size();
        for(int i = 0; i < cnt; i++)
```

```
        {
            // get the listener element from the collection
            HeatingRequestListener l =
                (HeatingRequestListener)v.elementAt(i);

            // if the listener is serializable, write it to the stream
            if (l instanceof Serializable)
            {
                stream.writeObject(l);
            }
        }
    }

    // a null object marks the end of the heating request listeners
    stream.writeObject(null);
}
```

The readObject() method recovers any registered heating and cooling request
listeners that were stored by the writeObject() method. The defaultReadObject() method is invoked on the stream to read back the rest of the data
members. To read back the cooling request listeners, we keep calling readObject() on the stream until a null is encountered, marking the end of the list.
Each object is cast to CoolingRequestListener and passed as a parameter to the
addCoolingRequestListener() method. We use another similar loop to get back
the heating request listeners.

```
    // handle the reading of the object state
    private void readObject(ObjectInputStream stream)
        throws java.io.IOException
{
    try
    {
        stream.defaultReadObject();

        Object l;

        // get the cooling request listeners
        while(null != (l = stream.readObject()))
        {
            addCoolingRequestListener((CoolingRequestListener)l);
        }

        // get the heating request listeners
        while(null != (l = s.readObject()))
        {
            addHeatingRequestListener((HeatingRequestListener)l);
        }
    }
```

```
        catch (ClassNotFoundException e)
        {
            throw new IOException();
        }
    }
}
```

# *A Sample Simulator Applet*

Let's create a sample applet class called SimulatorSample that uses the Beans we created for the simulator. The applet will create instances of Temperature, Thermostat, Boiler, and Cooler, and make the required connections so that they work together. This is a pretty simple process. All of the work is done in the applet's init() method. Everything else is handled by the objects themselves.

```
import java.applet.*;
import java.awt.*;
import BeansBook.Simulator.*;
import java.beans.*;

// the SimulatorSample applet class
public class SimulatorSample extends Applet
{
    // the applet init method
    public void init()
    {
```

The applet uses a simple flow layout, which is set up by calling the setLayout() method. Next, the simulator Beans are created by calling their default constructors. The three visual Beans are then added to the applet by passing each as a parameter to the applet's add() method.

```
        // use a flow layout, with components centered, and a 20 pixel
        // separation between components
        setLayout(new FlowLayout(FlowLayout.CENTER, 20, 20));

        // create a temperature
        Temperature t = new Temperature();

        // create a thermostat
        Thermostat th = new Thermostat();

        // create a cooler
        Cooler c = new Cooler();

        // create a boiler
        Boiler b = new Boiler();
```

```
// add the thermostat, cooler, and boiler to the applet
add(th);
add(c);
add(b);
```

Now that all of the objects have been created, we need to wire them up. The Thermostat monitors changes to the Temperature object's *Temperature* property by listening for property change events, so we call the addPropertyChangeListener() method, passing the instance of Thermostat as a parameter. The Cooler and Boiler objects each listen for the appropriate service request events. This is done by passing these objects to the addCoolingRequestListener() and addHeatingRequestListener() methods on the Thermostat object. The Cooler and Boiler are also used to constrain the *ComfortTemperature* property of the Thermostat, so we pass them to its addVetoableChangeListener() method.

```
// make the thermostat a property change listener of the
// temperature object
t.addPropertyChangeListener(th);

// make the cooler a cooling request listener of the
// thermostat object
th.addCoolingRequestListener(c);

// make the boiler a heating request listener of the
// thermostat object
th.addHeatingRequestListener(b);

// make the boiler and cooler vetoable change listeners
// of the thermostat object
th.addVetoableChangeListener(b);
th.addVetoableChangeListener(c);
```

The last step in wiring up the objects is to make the Temperature object listen for temperature pulse events from the Cooler and Boiler. This is accomplished by passing the Temperature object to the addTemperaturePulseListener() method of the Boiler and Cooler objects. Now we can put the system into motion. The default value of the thermostat's *ComfortTemperature* property is 22 degrees. To get things moving, we set the *Temperature* property of the Temperature object to 0 degrees by calling its setTemperature() method. This causes the Temperature object to fire a property change event to the Thermostat, which in turn causes it to fire a heating request event to the Boiler. This causes the Boiler to start firing temperature pulses to the Temperature object, and so on.

```
try
{
    // make the temperature object a temperature pulse listener
    // of the cooler and boiler objects
    c.addTemperaturePulseListener(t);
```

```
            b.addTemperaturePulseListener(t);
        }
        catch (java.util.TooManyListenersException e)
        {
        }

        // start the temperature object at 0 degrees
        t.setTemperature(0);
    }
}
```

Figure 8-3 shows what the `SimulatorSample` applet looks like after the `Boiler` has fired eight temperature pulses to the `Temperature` object. The `Thermostat` is showing ambient temperature in Celsius, which is why it shows 8 degrees. You should see the `Boiler` with a red background until the ambient temperature display reaches 22 degrees, at which time the `Thermostat` will shut the `Boiler` down.

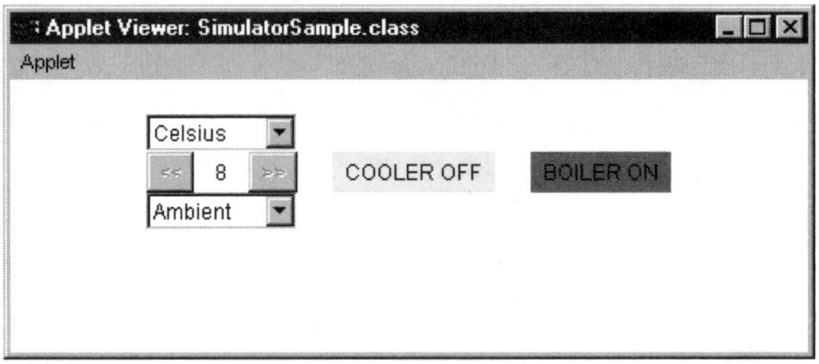

*Figure 8-3. The simulator in operation*

Go ahead and play around with the `Thermostat`. You can switch between Celsius and Fahrenheit, and you can change the display to show either the ambient or comfort level temperature. You can also either lower or raise the comfort level temperature by pressing the decrement (<<) or increment (>>) buttons, which will cause either the `Cooler` or `Boiler` to run until the comfort level temperature is reached. You should also notice that you can't specify a comfort level temperature below 0 degrees or above 100 degrees Celsius. This is because the `Cooler` or `Boiler` objects will veto those changes.

## *Creating a JAR File*

Let's package up the simulator classes in a JAR file. This will allow us to distribute the entire package in one unit, as well as to test the Beans using BeanBox. The first step is to create a manifest file called *Simulator.mf*, naming each class and specifying whether or not they are Beans. Marking a class as a Bean is meant to indicate that it qualifies as an object that exposes events, methods, and properties, and that it is a useful object in its own right. The listener interfaces and the event objects are useful, but they provide no useful function by themselves. The TemperatureModifier isn't marked as a Bean; it is the abstract base class for the Cooler and Boiler Beans, and so can never be instantiated by itself. The manifest file looks as follows:

```
Manifest-Version: 1.0

Name: BeansBook/Simulator/Boiler.class
Java-Bean: True

Name: BeansBook/Simulator/Cooler.class
Java-Bean: True

Name: BeansBook/Simulator/CoolingRequestListener.class
Java-Bean: False

Name: BeansBook/Simulator/HeatingRequestListener.class
Java-Bean: False

Name: BeansBook/Simulator/ServiceRequestEvent.class
Java-Bean: False

Name: BeansBook/Simulator/Temperature.class
Java-Bean: True

Name: BeansBook/Simulator/TemperatureModifier.class
Java-Bean: False

Name: BeansBook/Simulator/TemperaturePulseEvent.class
Java-Bean: False

Name: BeansBook/Simulator/TemperaturePulseListener.class
Java-Bean: False

Name: BeansBook/Simulator/Thermostat.class
Java-Bean: True
```

Note that only the Boiler, Cooler, Temperature, and Thermostat classes are marked as Beans. The other classes are there to support the Beans. The *Simulator.mf* file should be in the directory above the *BeansBook* directory, along with the *SimulatorSample.class* file for the applet. Remember that the *.class* files are in the *BeansBook/Simulator* directory. Now we can create the JAR file by invoking the following command on the command line:

```
jar cvfm Simulator.jar Simulator.mf BeansBook/Simulator/*.class
```

# Recreating the Sample Using BeanBox

In order to make the simulator Beans available to BeanBox, put a copy of *Simulator.jar* in the *jars* directory of your BDK installation (you could also leave it where it is and load it into BeanBox using the *LoadJar* entry of the *File* menu). Now start BeanBox and its toolbox window will show the simulator Beans, as shown in Figure 8-4.

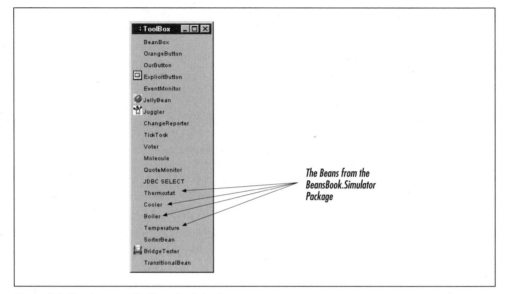

*Figure 8-4. Our Beans in the BeanBox's toolbox*

Now go ahead and add one instance of each simulator Bean to the form. Remember that *Temperature* is an invisible Bean, so make sure that you've got your BeanBox set to show invisible Beans. After you add the Beans, your form will look something like Figure 8-5. It doesn't matter where you place the Beans. I tried to put them in the same position as they were in the SimulatorSample applet, but it really doesn't matter where you put them.

Now we have to make the appropriate connections to wire things together. Let's start by selecting the Temperature object. We want to connect its property change events to the *Thermostat*, so go to the *Edit* menu and select the *propertyChange* event. Remember that this is done by following the cascading *Event* menu all the way to *propertyChange*. Now pull the rubber-band line over to the edge of the *Thermostat* and click on it. This will bring up the *EventTargetDialog* window as shown in Figure 8-6. Now select the propertyChange() method and press the *OK* button. BeanBox will generate and compile an appropriate adapter.

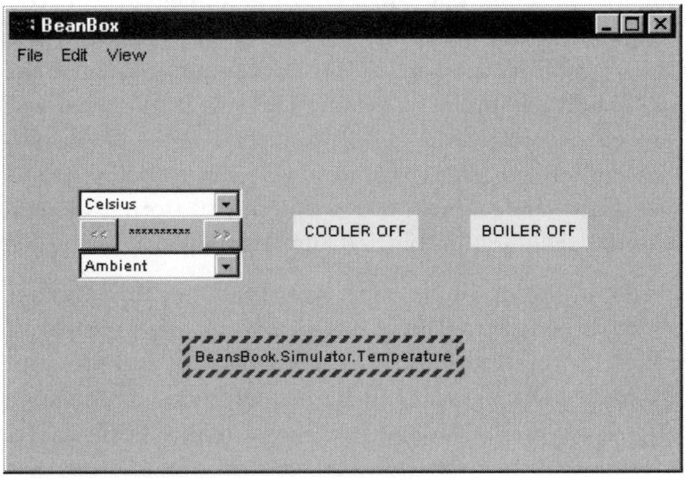

*Figure 8-5. Building the simulator in the BeanBox*

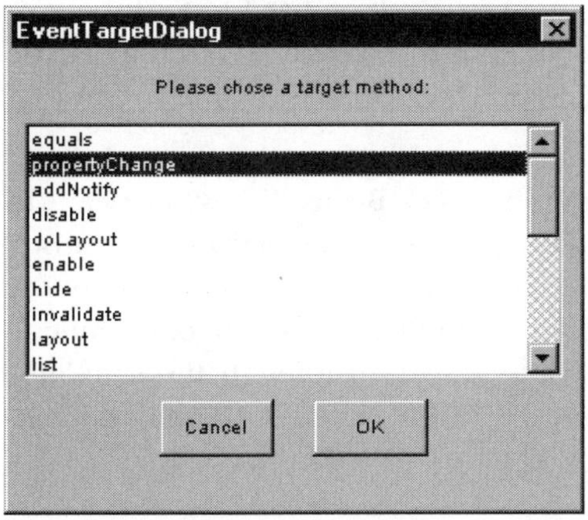

*Figure 8-6. Wiring the Temperature object to the Thermostat*

I'm going to forego the pictures at this point, since you already know how to use BeanBox. Let me just mention all of the connections you should make, and then I'll leave it up to you to play around with the simulator. You'll need to connect the `temperaturePulse` event from both the `Boiler` and `Cooler` objects to the `temperaturePulse()` method of the `Temperature` object. You should connect the `heatingRequest` event from the `Thermostat` to the `heatingRequest()` method on the `Boiler`, and the `coolingRequest` event to the `coolingRequest()` method on the `Cooler`. The last step is to connect the `vetoableChange` event from the `Thermostat` to the `vetoableChange()` methods of both the `Cooler` and `Boiler` objects. You should also select each of the simulator Beans and look at the property editors provided by the BeanBox property sheet.

Now you can use the simulator the same way you would the applet version. You can even save and restore the BeanBox form because all of the classes in the `BeanBox.Simulator` package properly support object serialization. Remember that support for serialization didn't happen magically. Each Bean was analyzed carefully to determine if any extra work was involved in making the class serializable. In some cases we had to implement our own `readObject()` and `writeObject()` methods to properly deal with the saving and restoring of data members that could not be serialized and deserialized automatically.

There's an important point about the examples that were created in this chapter. The components that I chose to include were just my preferences for creating a small, understandable example. There are endless combinations of components, resulting in endless application variations that can be created with components; that's the whole idea of a component architecture. You might want to try connecting the simulator Beans in other ways, just to see how they behave. For instance, you can add another boiler to the sample, wiring it to the thermostat and temperature objects the same way the first boiler was wired. The result will be that when the thermostat makes a heating request it will be fired to both boilers. In turn, the two boilers will start firing temperature pulses to the temperature object, resulting in the desired comfort temperature specified by the thermostat being reached in half the time.

You can also experiment with combining the simulator Beans with other Beans in BeanBox. Try putting an instance of the *ChangeReporter* Bean onto the BeanBox form, and wire the property change event from the *Temperature* Bean to the `reportChange` method. Now when you run the simulator, the current temperature of the system will be shown in the *ChangeReporter*. Although the simulator Beans are designed to work with each other, you can use them with other components as well.

# Introspection

When Beans are used by a visual development tool, they have to expose their properties, methods, and events. This allows both the tool and the user to manipulate the Bean's appearance and behavior. We've already seen this when we used BeanBox to work with the simulator Beans: BeanBox allowed us to change property values for the Beans, and to connect event sources with event targets. We didn't have to write any extra code to tell BeanBox about the Bean's properties and events. Instead, it relied on the Java reflection mechanism to gather this information. We've actually been providing all of the necessary information all along by following the design patterns for properties and events when we wrote the code for the Beans. For instance, all of the Beans we've created so far have used `getPropertyName()` and `setPropertyName()` methods for their properties. Remember that this is the pattern for coding a read/write property. Using these patterns allows the Java reflection mechanism to analyze the code and determine that there is a property called *PropertyName*.

Sometimes the information that we provide implicitly using design patterns is not enough, and sometimes the reflection mechanism exposes more information than we want exposed. Of course, the reflection mechanism also forces us to follow design patterns that may not make sense all of the time. Finally, we sometimes want to expose information about our Beans that can't be represented by the standard design patterns. An example of this, which we'll examine a little later, is providing a graphic icon for a Bean that can be used by a visual development tool.

## The BeanInfo Interface

Introspection is a mechanism for providing information about a Bean explicitly. This is done by creating a class that exists specifically to describe the Bean. This class implements the `java.beans.BeanInfo` interface, which specifies a set of methods that can be used to gather various pieces of information about a Bean. The methods defined by this interface are shown in Table 9-1. We'll look at each one more closely throughout this chapter.

*Table 9-1. Methods of the BeanInfo Interface*

| Method | Description |
| --- | --- |
| `getAdditionalBeanInfo()` | Returns any additional BeanInfo objects that are relevant to the associated Bean. |
| `getBeanDescriptor()` | Returns the Bean descriptor object. |
| `getDefaultEventIndex()` | Returns the default event index. |
| `getDefaultPropertyIndex()` | Returns the default property index. |
| `getEventSetDescriptors()` | Returns the event set descriptors. |
| `getIcon()` | Returns the specified icon for the Bean. |
| `getMethodDescriptors()` | Returns the method descriptors. |
| `getPropertyDescriptors()` | Returns the property descriptors. |

Unlike the reflection mechanism, which analyzes the Bean itself to discover the Bean's properties, methods, and events, with introspection a Bean relies on a meta-object to provide information on its behalf. There are both benefits and drawbacks to this approach. It is certainly a good idea to separate the Bean from its BeanInfo object, because visual development tools are probably the only ones interested in the introspection information. There's no need for a Bean to carry this baggage around with it all the time; in some cases the BeanInfo baggage might be larger than the Bean itself. It also means that the Bean itself doesn't have to implement any extra methods, or perform any additional functions, just to provide information. Separating a Bean from information about the Bean might also be beneficial when we want to ship our Beans as run-time–only objects. As Beans become more popular, developers will have to look for ways to license their work to others. If you design your Beans in a way that requires the associated BeanInfo object in order to get the introspection information, then you can ensure that a run-time–only distribution cannot (easily) be used in a design-time environment. You could do this by taking care *not* to follow the design patterns for methods, events, and properties. This would ensure that the BeanInfo object is needed in order to get introspection information for the Bean, allowing you to distribute your work as part of end-user applications without worrying that the Bean could be used again in a visual development tool without your approval. For approved development licenses, you would include the BeanInfo class in the distribution.

The BeanInfo class uses a design pattern of its own. The name of the class is formed by adding the string *BeanInfo* to the Bean's class name. If you have a Bean class named `Xyz`, its BeanInfo class must be named `XyzBeanInfo`. Normally, the BeanInfo class will be part of the same package as the Bean class it describes, but this is not a firm requirement. When a BeanInfo class is being located, the package path for the associated Bean class is searched first; so for the Bean `Package.Xyz`, the class `Package.XyzBeanInfo` is looked for first. If this class is not found, the `XyzBeanInfo` class will be searched for in the packages specified by the BeanInfo package search path. To access and modify the BeanInfo search path, call the `getBeanInfoSearchPath()` and `setBeanInfoSearchPath()` methods of the `java.beans.Instrospector` class.

The downside to this approach is that there is a tight coupling between a Bean and its BeanInfo object. The Bean developer is responsible for maintaining this relationship. Since BeanInfo is a completely separate class, we face the problems that exist when one of these classes evolves without the other. For example, when the properties of the Bean are updated you must also update the BeanInfo class to represent the change. Another problem is that there is no explicit relationship between the Bean and its BeanInfo class. We're relying on a design pattern to create an implied relationship between a Bean and its meta-object. My preference would be to ask the Bean itself to give me back an instance of its BeanInfo class.

One way that the JavaBeans architecture could have addressed this problem would have been to ask Beans to implement a method called `getBeanInfo()` that would return their associated BeanInfo object. This means that you could name your BeanInfo class anything you like, because the Bean itself would be responsible for returning an instance of the object to you. The BeanInfo class would not even have to be public. The `getBeanInfo()` method would return an instance of the interface `java.beans.BeanInfo`, not a specific class. The reflection mechanism could then be used to determine whether the `getBeanInfo()` method is implemented. We don't want to require every Bean to implement the `getBean-Info()` method even if it doesn't have an associated BeanInfo object.

Enough of alternative designs; back to reality. At first glance it appears that you'll have to implement the entire `java.beans.BeanInfo` interface even if you have a very simple Bean that only requires a few of the different descriptors. Actually, each of the methods in the interface are free to return `null`, indicating that the caller should use low-level reflection to gather the information. To make it easier to implement simple BeanInfo classes, the class `java.beans.SimpleBeanInfo` implements all of the interfaces of the `java.beans.BeanInfo` interface. Each method denies any knowledge of the associated data, suggesting that reflection should be used. You can derive your own BeanInfo classes by extending `java.beans.SimpleBeanInfo`, overriding those methods that return the information that you want to explicitly specify.

Another important aspect of providing explicit introspection information is information about base classes. If low-level reflection is used to analyze a Bean, all of its base classes (superclasses) are also analyzed by walking upwards through the class hierarchy. Each base class is analyzed in turn. The information gathered while analyzing a particular class is considered to be definitive. This means that if property information is found in a base class and that has already been discovered in a subclass, the subclass information takes precedence. For example, let's say class A has a read-only property called *Value*, and class B extends class A and implements the public methods `getValue()` and `setValue()`. The information in class B takes precedence over the information in class A, so any Bean based on class B will have a read/write property called *Value*, while the *Value* property of a Bean based on class A will be read-only.

It's easy to get confused about the relationship between information provided by BeanInfo and information that's available through reflection. If a Bean provides explicit information about one kind of feature in a BeanInfo object, the base classes won't be examined for information about that feature; the information in the BeanInfo is definitive. For example, if you provide explicit information about your Bean's events, the Bean and its superclasses won't be examined for further information about events. Thus, your BeanInfo must provide all of the information about events. If your Bean uses four events, BeanInfo must describe all four; you can't describe one, and assume that the others will be discovered by reflection or by looking at a base class. Likewise, if you provide BeanInfo information about some of your Bean's methods, you must provide information about all of its methods. In this respect, BeanInfo is an "all or nothing" thing. However, don't take this too far. Providing explicit information about events doesn't mean that you have to provide explicit information about methods or any other types of features. This sounds complicated, but it isn't if you think about how your Bean-Info object extends the `SimpleBeanInfo` class. If your BeanInfo object implements `getMethodDescriptors()`, it must provide descriptors for all the methods you want to expose. If you don't implement `getMethodDescriptors()`, you inherit the default implementation from `SimpleBeanInfo`, which returns `null`, which tells the caller to use reflection to find out about methods, starting with your Bean and continuing up the inheritance hierarchy.

This procedure may be desirable in most cases, but certainly not in every case. In some situations, you may want to provide information about a Bean's superclasses. Later we'll discuss how to provide additional BeanInfo objects that expose properties from superclasses.

## The Feature Descriptor

The aspects of a Bean that can be described by introspection can be thought of as the Bean's features. All features have certain basic information in common, such as a name and a description. The `java.beans.FeatureDescriptor` class provides this basic information, and is the base class for most of the introspection classes. So before we get into the specific feature classes, let's take a look at the common features that are available to all of the specific descriptors.

Every feature has a name. Depending on the type of feature, the name has different meanings. The name of a property is simply the text string that identifies it. The name of a method is just the name with which the method was declared, the same name that is used to invoke it. The `setName()` and `getName()` methods of the `FeatureDescriptor` interface are used to set and get the name, respectively. Some features may also have a display name, which is a more "friendly" name used when building displays. For example, the name of `BeansBook.Simulator.Thermostat` is simply *Thermostat*. If, however, we wanted a development tool to display a more useful name, we could define its display name as *Simulated Thermostat*. The `setDisplayName()` and `getDisplayName()` methods are used for this purpose. If no display name is set, the `getDisplayName()` method defers to the `getName()` method, thereby ensuring that something is available for display. Finally, a feature can have a short description that provides some descriptive text to describe the feature. Development tools might use this text to provide even more information to the end user. We might want to provide a description of the `Thermostat` object that says: *The thermostat for the BeansBook simulator.* The methods for manipulating this string are `setShortDescription()` and `getShortDescription()`. If no text is provided for the description, `getShortDescription()` defers to `getDisplayName()`, and so on. So, as you can see, the display name and short description strings are totally optional.

Features can also be marked as intended for expert users or for use by development tools only. The `setExpert()` and `isExpert()` methods are used to mark and query a feature for its expert status. Tool vendors are free to interpret the expert status of a feature as they see fit. Some may choose to display an expert feature, while others may hide it, and still others may provide a mechanism to toggle between expert and non-expert modes. Features that are intended for use by development tools only are considered "hidden," and shouldn't be displayed to the user. The methods for setting and querying this characteristic are `setHidden()` and `isHidden()`.

There is also a mechanism for providing additional information about a feature beyond the information defined by the `FeatureDescriptor` interface. Feature descriptors can hold a collection of attribute/value pairs. The collection acts like an associative array, where you provide both a key and a value to the `setValue()`

method; you retrieve the value by passing the key to the getValue() method. The attributeNames() method returns a java.util.Enumeration, which allows you to iterate over the collection of keys stored in the associative array. A BeanInfo object could use this feature to provide special (possibly vendor-specific) information about itself that would help a particular tool do its job.

## The Bean Descriptor

The java.beans.BeanDescriptor is used to describe the classes that implement the Bean and the Bean customizer. This class has two constructors:

```
public BeanDescriptor(Class beanClass)
public BeanDescriptor(Class beanClass, Class customizerClass)
```

The first form of the constructor takes one parameter: the class that implements the Bean for which the BeanInfo is being prepared. The second form takes a second parameter for the class that implements the customizer for the Bean. We'll defer talking about the Bean customizer until Chapter 10, *Property Editors and Customizers*. If we wanted to create a java.beans.BeanDescriptor for the Thermostat object in the simulator, we could do it as follows:

```
BeanDesciptor bd = new
    BeanDescriptor(BeansBook.Simulator.Thermostat.class);
```

The user of the BeanDescriptor object would call the getBeanClass() or getCustomizerClass() methods to retrieve the classes that implement the Bean and its customizer, respectively. If a Bean does not have a customizer, the getCustomizerClass() method will return null. It is not valid to use the second form of the constructor to create a Bean descriptor for a Bean that does not have a customizer. If you pass null as the second argument, you will get a run-time exception thrown.

The getBeanDescriptor() method of the java.beans.BeanInfo interface is used to return an instance of a java.beans.BeanDescriptor class. Let's start creating a BeanInfo class for the BeansBook.Simulator.Thermostat class. The class is named BeansBook.Simulator.ThermostatBeanInfo, and its code is shown below:

```
package BeansBook.Simulator;

import java.beans.*;

public class ThermostatBeanInfo extends SimpleBeanInfo
{
    public BeanDescriptor getBeanDescriptor()
    {
        BeanDescriptor bd = new BeanDescriptor(Thermostat.class);
```

```
        bd.setDisplayName("Simulated Thermostat");
        return bd;
    }
}
```

The getBeanDescriptor() method creates an instance of BeansDescriptor, specifying Thermostat.class as the class that implements the Bean. Then the setDisplayName() method is used to specify that *Simulated Thermostat* is used for this Bean's display name.

## *Icons*

Every Bean can have an associated graphic icon that can be used by development tools for putting Beans into palettes or tool bars. The only supported format for icons is GIF, although other standard formats will probably be supported in the future. Currently, four kinds of icons are supported: 16×16 and 32×32 pixel icons in both color and monochrome representations. You are free to provide as few or as many of these as you like, and of course you are not forced to provide any.

I've created a simple 16×16 color GIF that can be used as an icon for the *Thermostat* Bean, and I've named the file *thermostat.gif*. This file is placed into the same directory as the *BeansBook.Simulator.Thermostat.class* file. This is not a requirement, but, as you'll see shortly, it is convenient.

In order to make this icon available via introspection, we implement the getIcon() method in the ThermostatBeanInfo class. The introspector calls this method with a single parameter: a constant specifying which of the four icon types the introspector is checking. Our implementation checks the iconKind parameter to see if it is BeanInfo.ICON_COLOR_16x16, which is the constant used to specify a 16×16 color icon, since this is the only kind of icon we're going to support. If this is not the requested format, we just return null indicating that we don't support that format. If the request is for a 16×16 color icon, we call the loadImage() method. Note that this method is provided by the SimpleBeanInfo class; don't confuse it with the getImage() methods provided by java.awt.Toolkit or java.applet.Applet. getImage() takes one string parameter that contains the name of the image file to load. The file is assumed to be in the same directory as the class that implements the Bean. That's why I put the *thermostat.gif* file in the same directory as *Thermostat.class*. The instance of java.awt.Image that is returned from loadImage() is then returned to the caller.

```
public java.awt.Image getIcon(int iconKind)
{
    if (iconKind == BeanInfo.ICON_COLOR_16x16)
    {
        java.awt.Image img = loadImage("thermostat.gif");
```

```
        return img;
    }

    return null;
}
```

Table 9-2 shows the BeanInfo constants that identify the different kinds of icons.

*Table 9-2. Icon Constants*

| Constant | Meaning |
|----------|---------|
| ICON_COLOR_16x16 | 16×16 color icon |
| ICON_COLOR_32x32 | 32×32 color icon |
| ICON_MONO_16x16 | 16×16 monochrome icon |
| ICON_MONO_32x32 | 32×32 monochrome icon |

Let's stop here and check that the `ThermostatBeanInfo` class is performing its function, using BeanBox to verify the information we've provided. We've added two new files that need to be added to the *Simulator.mf* manifest file from the previous chapter, as follows:

```
Name: BeansBook/Simulator/ThermostatBeanInfo.class
Java-Bean: False

Name: BeansBook/Simulator/thermostat.gif
Java-Bean: False
```

Now we create the new *Simulator.jar* file by issuing the following command:

```
jar cvfm Simulator.jar Simulator.mf BeansBook/Simulator/*.class
    BeansBook/Simulator/*.gif
```

Remember to put the *Simulator.jar* file into the *jars* directory of the BDK installation, and then start BeanBox. Figure 9-1 shows the BeanBox toolbox window. I've removed the sample Beans from the *jars* directory for clarity.

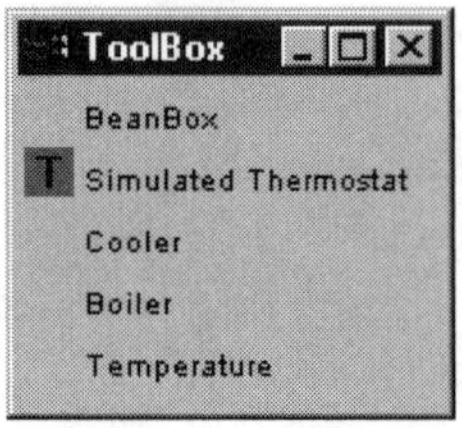

*Figure 9-1. Supplying an icon with BeanInfo*

Now the thermostat is shown in the toolbox with an icon next to it; its display name is *Simulated Thermostat*. So BeanBox is getting the information that we've explicitly specified using the `ThermostatBeanInfo` class. The rest of the information about properties, methods, and events for the thermostat is still coming from analysis performed by the Java reflection mechanism, since we didn't provide any explicit descriptors about them.

## Property Descriptors

Property descriptors are used to provide explicit information about the properties exposed by the associated Bean. The java.beans.PropertyDescriptor class gathers this information, which can be retrieved from the BeanInfo object by calling the getPropertyDescriptors() method. This method returns an array of PropertyDescriptor objects, one for each property exposed by the Bean. If properties should be determined by low-level reflection, the getPropertyDescriptors() method returns null.

There are three constructors for the java.beans.PropertyDescriptor class. The first form is used for a read/write property that supports the standard getPropertyName() and setPropertyName() design pattern:

```
public PropertyDescriptor(String propertyName, Class beanClass)
        throws IntrospectionException
```

The first parameter specifies the name of the property as a string, and the second specifies the class that implements the Bean. This constructor can throw a java.beans.IntrospectionException exception, which occurs if the specified class does not actually implement the standard get and set methods for the specified property name.

Let's start creating a BeanInfo class for the BeansBook.Simulator.Temperature class. We use the first form of the PropertyDescriptor constructor to expose the *Temperature* property explicitly, and we do so by implementing the getPropertyDescriptors() method. The code is as follows:

```
package BeansBook.Simulator;

import java.beans.*;
import java.lang.reflect.*;

public class TemperatureBeanInfo extends SimpleBeanInfo
{
    public BeanDescriptor getBeanDescriptor()
    {
        BeanDescriptor bd = new BeanDescriptor(Temperature.class);
        bd.setDisplayName("Temperature Source");
        return bd;
    }
```

```
    public PropertyDescriptor[] getPropertyDescriptors()
    {
       try
       {
          PropertyDescriptor pd = new PropertyDescriptor("Temperature",
                            Temperature.class);

          pd.setBound(true);
          pd.setConstrained(false);

          PropertyDescriptor[] pda = { pd };

          return pda;
       }
       catch (IntrospectionException e)
       {
          return null;
       }
    }


 }
```

After we create the property descriptor, pd, we call setBound(true) and setConstrained(false) to indicate that *Temperature* is a bound property, but that it is not constrained. This means that we should be firing propertyChange events for this property, but not firing vetoableChange events. The default value for both of these attributes is false, so we really didn't have to call the setConstrained() method. The last step is to create an array of PropertyDescriptor objects named pda. This object is created using the initializer {pd}, since we already know the objects that it should contain. pda is then returned to the caller.

The next form of the PropertyDescriptor constructor allows you to specify the method names for the get and set methods as strings. If the property is read-only or write-only, the appropriate method name can be replaced with null. The constructor looks as follows:

```
    public PropertyDescriptor(String propertyName, Class beanClass,
                          String getterName, String setterName)
         throws IntrospectionException
```

So we could implement the getPropertyDescriptors() method for the TemperatureBeanInfo class using this form of the constructor. This form also provides us with the freedom to name the property accessor methods anything we want, since we are not counting on the design pattern. Although I'm not going to show the change here, take it on my word that I've modified the BeansBook.Simulator.Temperature class to use the methods returnTemperature() and assignTemperature() for accessing the *Temperature* property. In this case we specify those names as parameters to the constructor, as shown here.

```
public PropertyDescriptor[] getPropertyDescriptors()
{
    try
    {
        PropertyDescriptor pd = new PropertyDescriptor("Temperature",
                                                Temperature.class,
                                                "returnTemperature",
                                                "assignTemperature");

        pd.setBound(true);
        pd.setConstrained(false);

        PropertyDescriptor[] pda = { pd };

        return pda;
    }
    catch (IntrospectionException e)
    {
        return null;
    }
}
```

The last form of the PropertyDescriptor constructor gets us involved in the reflection mechanism. Instead of passing method names as strings, we actually pass instances of java.lang.reflect.Method for the accessor parameters. This form of the constructor is:

```
public PropertyDescriptor(String propertyName, Method getter,
                          Method setter)
        throws IntrospectionException
```

Note that this constructor doesn't require a parameter for specifying the class that implements the Bean; the getter and setter parameters already carry that information as instances of java.lang.reflect.Method. The code for the getPropertyDescriptors() method using this form of the constructor is:

```
public PropertyDescriptor[] getPropertyDescriptors()
{
    try
    {
        Class c = Temperature.class;
        Class[] params = { java.lang.Double.TYPE };
        Method getter = c.getMethod("returnTemperature", null);
        Method setter = c.getMethod("assignTemperature", params);

        PropertyDescriptor pd = new PropertyDescriptor("Temperature",
                                                getter, setter);

        pd.setBound(true);
        pd.setConstrained(false);
```

```
        PropertyDescriptor[] pda = { pd };

        return pda;
    }
    catch (IntrospectionException e)
    {
        return null;
    }
}
```

In order to create the appropriate instances of java.lang.reflect.Method, we first need an instance of java.lang.Class. The variable c is assigned the value Temperature.class, the class that implements the Bean. Next we need an array of parameter objects that get passed to the assignTemperature() method. We create an array of Class objects called params, and we use the initializer { java.lang.Double.TYPE } to create its contents. The constant java.lang.Double.TYPE is used to identify the primitive data type double. Next the getMethod() method of the Class variable c is called to get the method instances getter and setter. Note that since the returnTemperature() method takes no parameters, null is passed to the getMethod() method where the parameters are normally specified.

Since we've changed the method names for the *Temperature* property to return-Temperature() and assignTemperature(), either of the last two implementations of the getPropertyDescriptor() method would work. You can check this out for yourself by adding the BeansBook.Simulator.TemperatureBeanInfo class to the *Simulator.jar* file and running BeanBox. Drop an instance of *Temperature Source* onto the BeanBox form, and then look at the property sheet. You should see an editor for changing the value of the *Temperature* property.

The java.beans.PropertyDescriptor class provides a number of methods for retrieving the get and set methods for the property, determining its data type, as well as determining if the property is bound or constrained. The property descriptor can also be used to specify a property editor class for the property. We'll talk about this in Chapter 10.

## *The Default Property*

It may also be desirable to specify that one of the properties supported by a Bean is the "default" property. In some development environments, the notion of a default property may have special meaning. For instance, a scripting language may allow you to assign a value to the object name directly without specifying the property name. For example, imagine that a Bean has a property named *Label,* and that this property is the default property. A scripting language may allow you to assign a value to this property in either of the following two ways:

```
Object.Label = "OK"
```

or

```
Object = "OK"
```

In the second case, the value would be applied to the *Label* property, just as in the first case. You can specify the default property by implementing the getDefault-PropertyIndex() method. The SimpleBeanInfo class implementation of this method returns −1, which indicates that there is no default property. You can override this method and return the 0-based index for the default property. This index corresponds to the PropertyDescriptor object that was in the specified position in the array returned by the getPropertyDescriptors() method.

In the following example, the associated Bean contains three properties named *Color, Font,* and *Size.* The default property index is 1, which refers to the *Font* property based on the ordering of the PropertyDescriptors array.

```
public PropertyDescriptor[] getPropertyDescriptors()
{
    try
    {
        PropertyDescriptor color = new PropertyDescriptor("Color",
                                                       Example.class);

        PropertyDescriptor font = new PropertyDescriptor("Font",
                                                       Example.class);

        PropertyDescriptor size = new PropertyDescriptor("Size",
                                                       Example.class);

        PropertyDescriptor[] pda = { color, font, size };

        return pda;
    }
    catch (IntrospectionException e)
    {
        return null;
    }
}

public int getDefaultPropertyIndex()
{
    // font is the default
    return 1;
}
```

## *Indexed Property Descriptors*

Indexed properties can be exposed explicitly by creating an instance of
java.beans.IndexedPropertyDescriptor (which is a subclass of the base class
java.beans.PropertyDescriptor), which accommodates the extra information
needed for indexed properties. Remember that indexed properties may support
basic methods for getting and setting the entire collection as an array, as well as
methods that allow you to specify an index for accessing a single entry in the
collection.

Just like the regular property descriptor class, this class has three constructors. The
first form assumes that the Bean implements both indexed and non-indexed
accessor methods according to the standard design pattern for indexed
properties:

```
public IndexedPropertyDescriptor(String propertyName,
                                 Class beanClass)
        throws IntrospectionException
```

In order to illustrate an indexed property descriptor, let's use the WatchList class
that we first introduced in Chapter 4, *Properties*. This Bean has an indexed property named *Stocks*, which is an ordered collection of java.lang.String objects.
Since we implemented all of the accessor methods according to the design
pattern, we can implement the getPropertyDescriptors() method of its associated BeanInfo class as follows:

```
public PropertyDescriptor[] getPropertyDescriptors()
{
    try
    {
        IndexedPropertyDescriptor ip =
            new IndexedPropertyDescriptor("Stocks", WatchList.class);
        PropertyDescriptor[] pda = { ip };
        return pda;
    }
    catch (IntrospectionException e)
    {
        return null;
    }
}
```

We create an instance of java.beans.IndexedPropertyDescriptor called ip,
specifying the name of the property as *Stocks* and the implementing class as
WatchList.class. We can put the ip variable into the java.beans.PropertyDe-
scriptor array because java.beans.IndexedPropertyDescriptor is a subclass of
java.beans.PropertyDescriptor.

There are two more forms of the java.beans.IndexedPropertyDescriptor, which are shown next. Each uses techniques similar to those already discussed for the java.beans.PropertyDescriptor constructors. Since the use of these constructors are similar in nature to those previously discussed, I'm not going to bother with any examples. The java.beans.IndexedPropertyDescriptor class adds methods to retrieve the indexed property data type, and to retrieve the indexed form of the property get and set methods. The base class provides the methods for accessing the information related to the methods and types for accessing the entire property array.

```
public IndexedPropertyDescriptor(String propertyName,
                                 Class beanClass,
                                 String getterName,
                                 String setterName,
                                 String indexedGetterName,
                                 String indexedSetterName)
        throws IntrospectionException

public IndexedPropertyDescriptor(String propertyName,
                                 Method getter,
                                 Method setter,
                                 Method indexedGetter,
                                 Method indexedSetter)
        throws IntrospectionException
```

## Method Descriptors

Normally, methods are exposed simply by making them public. The use of a method descriptor allows you to define explicitly which methods are available to be called on a Bean, and it also allows you to provide more descriptive information than can be provided via low-level reflection.

Methods are exposed by creating instances of java.beans.MethodDescriptor objects, and returning them as an array from the getMethodDescriptors() method of your BeanInfo class. The first form of the constructor for the method descriptor takes a single java.lang.reflect.Method object as its only parameter:

```
public MethodDescriptor(Method method)
```

The second form of the constructor allows you to provide descriptive information about the parameters of the method, beyond the basic type information that is contained directly within the java.lang.reflect.Method instance. The java.beans.ParameterDescriptor class is used to create descriptive information for the method parameters. This class is a subclass of java.beans.FeatureDescriptor, but it adds no new information to this class. The `java.beans.FeatureDescriptor` provides what we need for creating parameter descriptors. The form of the constructor that takes parameter descriptors is:

```
public MethodDescriptor(Method method,
                        ParameterDescriptor parameterDescriptors[])
```

The parameter descriptors are aggregated into an array. Remember that a parameter descriptor is used only for extra descriptive information about the parameters of the method. The actual parameter type information, as well as the return type, are part of the `Method` object itself. This array should contain an instance of `java.beans.ParameterDescriptor` for each parameter for the described method. To illustrate this, we add a couple of methods to the `WatchList` class. The first method, `clearStocks()`, removes all of the entries from the ordered collection of stock names. This method takes no parameters, and it has a void return type. The second method, `sortStocks()`, sorts the order of the stocks collection in either ascending or descending order, depending on the value of its single parameter of type int. The method returns a `boolean`, indicating whether or not any change to the ordering was actually required. The signatures of these two methods are as follows:

```
public synchronized void clearStocks()
public synchronized boolean sortStocks(int nOrder)
```

Now let's implement the `getMethodDescriptors()` method on the BeanInfo class for the `WatchList`. First we create a class variable named c and assign it the value `WatchList.class`. This is the class that implements the watch list, and we need it to get method instances. Next we create the method object named `clear` by calling the `getMethod()` method on variable c. The name of the method we're looking for is `clearStocks`, and the `null` indicates that the method takes no parameters. With this method variable, we create the instance of `java.beans.MethodDescriptor` named `clearDesc`. This is the variable that contains the method descriptor for the `clearStocks()` method of the `WatchList` class. Next we call the `setShortDescription()` method of the method descriptor, giving it a string that contains a short description of the method. That takes care of the method descriptor for the `clearStocks()` method.

Now we create a method descriptor for the `sortStocks()` method. This method takes a single parameter of type int. Since the `getMethod()` method requires an array of `java.lang.Class` objects for the parameters, we create the array variable `params` and use the initializer `{ java.lang.Integer.TYPE }` to indicate the parameter type. Now we can create an instance of `java.lang.reflect.Method` named sort by calling `getMethod()` on the Class variable c, passing it the string `sortStocks` and the `params` array. Since this method has parameters, we create an array of `java.beans.ParameterDescriptor` objects to describe them. There is only one parameter, so we create a single instance of the descriptor named pd, and call its setShortDescription() method to provide descriptive text about the parameter. Now we create an array of descriptors called s and initialize it with the pd variable. We use the second form of the java.beans.MethodDescriptor constructor to create the variable sortDesc, passing it both the method variable sort and the parameters descriptor array s. The setShortDescription() method is called to provide a description of the method, and then a java.beans.MethodDescriptor array named mda is created and returned to the caller.

```
public MethodDescriptor[] getMethodDescriptors()
{
    try
    {
        Class c = WatchList.class;

        Method clear = c.getMethod("clearStocks", null);
        MethodDescriptor clearDesc = new MethodDescriptor(clear);
        clearDesc.setShortDescription("Clears the list of stocks");

        Class[] params = { java.lang.Integer.TYPE };
        Method sort = c.getMethod("sortStocks", params);
        ParameterDescriptor pd = new ParameterDescriptor();
        pd.setShortDescription("Specifies the sort order");
        ParameterDescriptor[] s = { pd };
        MethodDescriptor sortDesc = new MethodDescriptor(sort, s);
        sortDesc.setShortDescription("Sorts the list of stocks");

        MethodDescriptor[] mda = { clearDesc, sortDesc };
        return mda;
    }
    catch (SecurityException e)
    {
        return null;
    }
    catch (NoSuchMethodException e)
    {
        return null;
    }
}
```

As you can see, this example created explicit information about the methods clearStocks() and sortStocks(). Because we only created method descriptors for these two methods, any other public methods on the WatchList class would not be exposed through introspection. Remember that if you choose to provide explicit introspection about a feature set, such as methods, you must provide information about all of the methods. This doesn't mean that the property accessor methods and event registration methods wouldn't be exposed, since these are handled separately. It also has nothing to do with your ability to write code by hand that uses the other public methods that might be available from the class. It only means that wherever the development tool relies on introspection to find methods, only those that are explicitly described by your method descriptors will be shown. It does mean that a development tool relying on introspection won't have access to methods of the Bean's base class, though you can get around this limitation by providing an additional BeanInfo class for the base class. We'll get to this subject a little later.

## Event Set Descriptors

Event set descriptors expose the events that can be fired by the Bean. Several events can be grouped together into a single event set by grouping their event methods in a single listener interface. So you can view an event set as implemented by an event-listener interface. To describe the interface, you create an event set descriptor, which is an instance of java.beans.EventSetDescriptor. To expose your event sets, your BeanInfo class must implement the method getEventSetDescriptors(), which returns an array of event set descriptors.

The constructor for the java.beans.EventSetDescriptor has many forms. The first one can be used when you've followed the design patterns for adding and removing an event listener, and when there is a single event whose method takes a single parameter that follows the design pattern. The signature of the constructor is as follows:

```
public EventSetDescriptor(Class sourceClass,
                          String eventSetName,
                          Class listenerType,
                          String listenerMethodName)
             throws IntrospectionException
```

For example, you could use this constructor if a SampleListener interface has a single method that takes a single parameter of type SampleEvent, and the class that implements the Bean implements the addSampleListener() and removeSampleListener() methods. This set of rules is relatively restrictive, but they are probably obeyed often enough to make this constructor worthwhile. All of the events that we created for the simulator Beans follow this model.

Let's look at the BeansBook.Simulator.TemperatureBeanInfo again. Since the Temperature object can fire a property change event, we implement the getEventSetDescriptors() method to explicitly expose the event set information. We create an instance of java.beans.EventSetDescriptor called ed. The first parameter to the constructor is Temperature.class, the class that implements the Bean. The next parameter is a string that describes the event. The documentation says that this should be the name of the event—in this case *prop-ertyChange*—but in cases where the event name isn't descriptive enough, something more would be useful. In fact, this parameter is just setting the display name of the event set descriptor to the string provided in this parameter. Thus it's nothing more than a shortcut for calling the setDisplayName() method after the descriptor is constructed. The next parameter is used to specify the interface class that implements the listener interface for this event set. In this case we pass PropertyChangeListener.class, the interface used to listen for property change events. The last parameter is a string that contains the name of the method on the listener interface used to fire the event, so we pass the string *propertyChange*. Now we just create an array of type java.beans.EventSetDescriptor, populate it with our event set descriptor, and return it to the caller.

```java
public EventSetDescriptor[] getEventSetDescriptors()
{
    try
    {
        EventSetDescriptor ed =
            new EventSetDescriptor(Temperature.class,
                                   "Property Change Event",
                                   PropertyChangeListener.class,
                                   "propertyChange");

        EventSetDescriptor[] eda = { ed } ;
        return eda;
    }
    catch (IntrospectionException e)
    {
        return null;
    }
}
```

The second form of the constructor allows for more flexibility in the names and number of methods in the listener interface. The first three parameters are the same: the class that implements the Bean, the name of the event set, and the class that implements the listener interface. The fourth parameter takes an array of strings where each entry represents the name of a method found in the event listener class. (It's not clear why this is needed, since we've already specified the event listener as an instance of java.lang.Class. This class could be analyzed to determine the methods, which would reduce the number of mistakes that are bound to occur due to programmer error. This is also true for the first constructor, where both the class and method name are required parameters.) The last two parameters take strings that specify the names of the methods implemented by the Bean class to add and remove a listener of the specified type.

```java
public EventSetDescriptor(Class sourceClass,
                          String eventSetName,
```

```
                        Class listenerType,
                        String listenerMethodNames[],
                        String addListenerMethodName,
                        String removeListenerMethodName)
        throws IntrospectionException
```

We can reimplement the getEventSetDescriptors() method using the second form of the constructor. The code for doing so is shown next. Note that an array of strings is created with the event method names (in this case just one string), and this array is passed to the constructor.

```
public EventSetDescriptor[] getEventSetDescriptors()
{
    try
    {

        String[] names = { "propertyChange" } ;
        EventSetDescriptor ed =
            new EventSetDescriptor(Temperature.class,
                                   "Property Change Event",
                                   PropertyChangeListener.class,
                                   names,
                                   "addPropertyChangeListener",
                                   "removePropertyChangeListener") ;

        EventSetDescriptor[] eda = { ed } ;
        return eda;
    }
    catch (IntrospectionException e)
    {
        return null;
    }
}
```

This form of the constructor provides you with the flexibility to name your event-listener registration methods anything you like, since you are specifying them explicitly here by name. It is still expected, however, that each of the event methods take a single parameter that follows the standard convention for the name of the event object.

Two additional forms of the constructor for the java.beans.EventSetDescriptor class use instances of java.lang.reflect.Method to specify the various methods that describe an event-listener interface, as well as the methods implemented by the Bean for adding and removing event listeners. The signatures for these constructors are:

```
public EventSetDescriptor(String eventSetName,
                          Class listenerType,
                          Method listenerMethods[],
```

```
                              Method addListenerMethod,
                              Method removeListenerMethod)
            throws IntrospectionException

   public EventSetDescriptor(String eventSetName,
                             Class listenerType,
                             MethodDescriptor listenerMethodDescriptors[],
                             Method addListenerMethod,
                             Method removeListenerMethod)
            throws IntrospectionException
```

The `java.beans.EventSetDescriptor` class provides methods that allow the caller to retrieve the listener methods as instances of `java.lang.reflect.Method` or `java.beans.MethodDescriptor`. In addition, the event set can be marked as being unicast, indicating that the associated Bean can only handle a single event listener of this type. The `setUnicast()` and `isUnicast()` methods are used to set and get this information, respectively.

### The Default Event Set

Just like a default property, it may also be desirable to specify that one of the event sets supported by a Bean is considered to be the default. You can specify the default event set by implementing the `getDefaultEventIndex()` method. The `SimpleBeanInfo` class implementation of this method returns –1, which indicates that there is no default event set. You can override this method and return the 0-based index for the default event set. This index corresponds to the `EventSet-Descriptor` object that was in the specified position in the array returned by the `getEventSetDescriptors()` method.

The use of a default event set is not as clear as that of a default property. Maybe a scripting environment will be able to do something useful if it knows what the default event set is. This might be nothing more than making an educated guess at the event the user wants to handle. This is more difficult with event sets because more than one event can be fired through a single event set, so even if an event set is specified as the default, it may be impossible to identify a single event as the actual default.

## Providing Additional BeanInfo Objects

I mentioned near the beginning of this chapter that when explicit information is provided for a given feature set of the Bean, the base classes are not examined for that feature set. This creates a problem when you create a Bean from a subclass that provides only some of the exposed properties, methods, and events, and the rest come from a base class. Let's say you have class AA that exposes a property named *propA*, and class BB that extends class AA and exposes its own property named *propB*. If you were to use low-level reflection to analyze class BB, you would find two properties named *propA* and *propB*. Now let's say you create a class called BBBeanInfo (the BeanInfo class for class BB). This class implements the getPropertyDescriptor() method by returning a property descriptor array that contains one element, an instance of java.beans.PropertyDescriptor for *propB*. The problem here is that the property named *propA* that comes from base class AA is no longer being exposed. It certainly isn't the responsibility of the BBBeanInfo class to create property descriptors for its base classes. First of all, if class AA changes then BBBeanInfo would have to be updated to reflect the change. That doesn't sound like a good idea. And if you had class CC that extends class BB, the BeanInfo class for CC would have to replicate the property descriptors for AA and BB. This is definitely not the right approach.

The java.beans.BeanInfo interface includes a method called getAdditional-BeanInfo(), which is used to provide other BeanInfo objects that are relevant to the Bean. This method returns an array of objects, each of which implements the java.beans.BeanInfo interface. When there is more than one BeanInfo object that collectively describes a single Bean, there is opportunity for conflicting information. When conflicts occur, the BeanInfo for the Bean being introspected takes precedence over any BeanInfo returned by the getAdditionalBeanInfo() method. Where conflicts exist among BeanInfo objects returned by the getAdditionalBeanInfo() method, the objects that come later in the array take precedence over those that come earlier. This is meant to model the precedence rules that are applied when low-level reflection is used. Basically, precedence is given to the BeanInfo at the bottom of the hierarchy first, and then to the BeanInfo for each successive superclass. If you are providing additional BeanInfo classes for multiple levels of inheritance, the BeanInfo for the class at the top of the hierarchy goes at position 0 of the array, and the rest are added to the array as you walk down the hierarchy. Figure 9-2 illustrates this for the classes AA, BB, and CC, discussed above. In this example, class CCBeanInfo provides an array of two additional BeanInfo objects to fully describe CC.

The getAdditionalBeanInfo() method of class CCBeanInfo returns an array (of size 2) that contains BeanInfos for class AA and class BB. These BeanInfo classes collectively describe a Bean based on class CC. It would have been nice if a method was provided to combine the BeanInfo objects according to the rules of precedence, because this is complicated enough to expect that some will get it wrong.

## The Introspector

The previous example raises another question; how does class BBBeanInfo know if there is a class AABeanInfo? It's unreasonable to expect one BeanInfo class to know about the existence of another. Therefore, we need another mechanism to

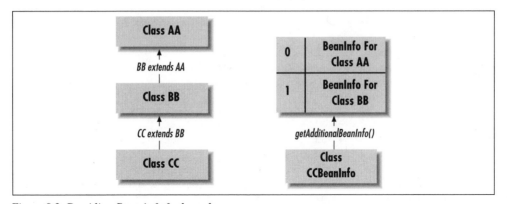

*Figure 9-2. Providing Bean info for base classes*

get a BeanInfo object for a specified class. The `java.beans.Introspector` class can be used to get a BeanInfo object for a specified class. If a specific BeanInfo class is not available, the introspector uses low-level reflection to build an appropriate BeanInfo object. The following code shows what the `getAdditionalBeanInfo()` method might look like for class `BBBeanInfo`:

```
public BeanInfo[] getAdditionalBeanInfo()
{
    try
    {
        BeanInfo[] bia = { Introspector.getBeanInfo(AA.class) };
        return bia;
    }
    catch (IntrospectionException e)
    {
        return null;
    }
}
```

Tool vendors can use the `java.beans.Introspector` to gather information about a Bean, and so can anyone else. You could write a reporting tool that analyzes a Bean through introspection and reports its findings. The BeanBox creators have already done this for you. The *Edit* menu has an entry called *Report* that analyzes the currently selected Bean and dumps a report of its findings to the console window. If you run the report on an instance of `BeansBook.Simulator.Temperature`, the following report will be created (you may want to redirect output to a file, as the report can scroll past rather quickly):

```
CLASS: BeansBook.Simulator.Temperature
    H => Hidden
    E => Expert
    [ => Indexed Property
```

```
Properties:
   Temperature double returnTemperature/assignTemperature
Event sets:
   Property Change Event
      addPropertyChangeListener/removePropertyChangeListener
      propertyChange
Methods:
   public void BeansBook.Simulator.Temperature.assignTemperature(double)
   public final void java.lang.Object.wait(long,int)
   public void BeansBook.Simulator.Temperature.removePropertyChangeListener
         (java.beans.PropertyChangeListener)
   public final native void java.lang.Object.notifyAll()
   public double BeansBook.Simulator.Temperature.returnTemperature()
   public final void java.lang.Object.wait()
   public java.lang.String java.lang.Object.toString()
   public final native void java.lang.Object.notify()
   public void BeansBook.Simulator.Temperature.addPropertyChangeListener
         (java.beans.PropertyChangeListener)
   public native int java.lang.Object.hashCode()
   public final native java.lang.Class java.lang.Object.getClass()
   public void BeansBook.Simulator.Temperature.temperaturePulse
         (BeansBook.Simulator.TemperaturePulseEvent)
   public final native void java.lang.Object.wait(long)
   public boolean java.lang.Object.equals(java.lang.Object)
```

This report shows the properties, event sets, and methods for the class Beans-
Book.Simulator.Temperature. You should notice that there is one property
named *Temperature* of type double, and the methods returnTemperature() and
assignTemperature() are used to get and set its value. There is a single event set
named Property Change Event. Listeners are added and removed by calling the
addPropertyChangeListener() and removePropertyChangeListener() methods, and the event method is called propertyChange(). The methods that are
exposed include those that are defined by the base classes and interfaces of
BeansBook.Simulator.Temperature: java.lang.Object, BeansBook.Simula-
tor.TemperaturePulseListener, and java.io.Serializable.

## *Introspecting the Environment*

The Java introspection mechanism is designed to allow you to explicitly expose
various features of your Beans. This is essentially the environment asking for information about a Bean. However, there is some information that a Bean might want
to know about its environment. Your Bean may want to know whether it is
running in an environment that supports a graphical user interface (GUI), and it
may also want to know if it is running in a development environment that is
considered to be operating in design mode. Although these issues are not covered

by the introspection mechanism, they seem to follow the same model; one object asks for information about another.

## Design-time vs. Run-time

It is certainly possible that you would want to design a Bean that behaved differently at design-time than it does at run-time. Maybe the Bean does an enormous amount of processing, or it has some other feature that just doesn't lend itself well to a design-time environment. A development tool can call the setDesignTime() method on the java.beans.Beans class to indicate whether or not the system is running in design mode. In turn, your Bean can call the isDesignTime() method on the same class to find out if it is running in design mode. This call could be made at the time the Bean is instantiated and stored in a variable. This way the Bean can always check the state of this variable before performing a function that is dependent upon whether it is running in design mode.

The problem is that some development tools may be able to switch between design-time mode and run-time mode on the fly, without having to create different instances of the Bean. The current JavaBeans architecture does not provide a way for Beans to listen for changes in the design mode. Therefore, even though you can get this information at any time by calling isDesignTime(), you have no way of knowing if and when you should be calling it. Depending on the development tool you are using, this could be a real problem. Hopefully, future versions of the JDK will allow Beans to become event listeners for changes to the design mode status.

## Running Without a Graphical User Interface

Beans may not always be running on a system that has a GUI. Although we usually think of Beans running on a desktop that supports a windowing system, Beans may also prove useful in a server environment. The java.beans.Beans class contains the method setGuiAvailable(), which can be used by the environment to specify whether a GUI is available. Your Beans can call isGuiAvailable() to get this information. This is important so that Beans don't attempt to interact with the user through dialog boxes or other windows that cannot be created. Some Beans may not be able to do anything useful at all without the support of a GUI.

This mechanism suffers from the same problem as the mechanism for determining if the Bean is running in design mode. If there is a chance that the availability of a GUI can change during the lifetime of the Bean, it would be useful to have a notification mechanism.

## The Visibility Interface

The `java.beans.Visibility` interface can be implemented by a Bean that wishes to behave well in an environment that may not be supporting a GUI. The method `dontUseGui()` can be called on a Bean that implements this interface to instruct it not to attempt to use the GUI. This way the Bean can be notified that the GUI is not available. The method `avoidingGui()` is called to determine if the Bean is avoiding the use of the GUI, presumably because it has already had the `dontUseGui()` method invoked. These two methods allow the environment to inform the Bean that the GUI is not available, and to determine if the Bean is properly avoiding its use. If the GUI becomes available, the environment can call the `okToUseGui()` method on the Bean, indicating that it is now okay for the Bean to make use of the GUI. The interface also defines the method `needsGui()`, which can be called to determine if a Bean absolutely must have a GUI in order for it to operate properly. In this case, the environment can decide not to use the Bean.

# The BeansBook.Simulator BeanInfo Classes

This section contains the code for the BeanInfo classes for the `BeansBook.Simulator` package. All of the concepts and techniques used by these classes have been discussed in this chapter. Instead of boring you by describing the code, I'm just including it here for you to look at if you wish.

## The BeansBook.Simulator.TemperatureBeanInfo Class

```
package BeansBook.Simulator;

import java.beans.*;
import java.lang.reflect.*;

public class TemperatureBeanInfo extends SimpleBeanInfo
{
    // return a bean descriptor for the Temperature object
    public BeanDescriptor getBeanDescriptor()
    {
        // create an instance of BeanDescriptor
        BeanDescriptor bd = new BeanDescriptor(Temperature.class);

        // set the display name
        bd.setDisplayName("Temperature Source");
```

```java
      // return the descriptor
      return bd;
}


// return the property descriptors
public PropertyDescriptor[] getPropertyDescriptors()
{
   try
   {
      // get the Temperature class
      Class c = Temperature.class;

      // get the get method for the Temperature property
      Method getter = c.getMethod("returnTemperature", null);

      // create the parameters array for the set method of the
      // Temperature property
      Class[] params = { java.lang.Double.TYPE };

      // get the set method
      Method setter = c.getMethod("assignTemperature", params);

      // create a property descriptor for the Temperature property
      PropertyDescriptor pd = new PropertyDescriptor("Temperature",
                                                getter, setter);

      // the Temperature property is bound
      pd.setBound(true);

      // the Temperature property is not constrained
      pd.setConstrained(false);

      // create the property descriptor array and return it
      PropertyDescriptor[] pda = { pd };
      return pda;
   }
   catch (NoSuchMethodException e)
   {
      return null;
   }
   catch (SecurityException e)
   {
      return null;
   }
}


// return the event set descriptors
public EventSetDescriptor[] getEventSetDescriptors()
{
   try
```

```
      {
         // the method names for the listener interface
         String[] names = { "propertyChange" } ;

         // create the event set descriptor
         EventSetDescriptor ed =
            new EventSetDescriptor(Temperature.class,
                                   "Property Change Event",
                                   PropertyChangeListener.class,
                                   names,
                                   "addPropertyChangeListener",
                                   "removePropertyChangeListener");

         // create the descriptor array and return it
         EventSetDescriptor[] eda = { ed } ;
         return eda;
      }
      catch (IntrospectionException e)
      {
         return null;
      }
   }
}
```

## The BeansBook.Simulator.ThermostatBeanInfo Class

```
   package BeansBook.Simulator;

   import java.beans.*;

   public class ThermostatBeanInfo extends SimpleBeanInfo
   {
      // return the bean descriptor
      public BeanDescriptor getBeanDescriptor()
      {
         // create the bean descriptor
         BeanDescriptor bd = new BeanDescriptor(Thermostat.class);

         // set the display name
         bd.setDisplayName("Simulated Thermostat");

         // return the object
         return bd;
      }

      // get an icon
      public java.awt.Image getIcon(int iconKind)
      {
         // we're only supporting 16x16 color icon
         if (iconKind == BeanInfo.ICON_COLOR_16x16)
```

```
       {
           // load the thermostat.gif file
           java.awt.Image img = loadImage("thermostat.gif");

           // return the image
           return img;
       }

       // return null for all other icon formats
       return null;
   }
}
```

# The BeansBook.Simulator.BoilerBeanInfo Class

```
package BeansBook.Simulator;

import java.beans.*;
import java.lang.reflect.*;

public class BoilerBeanInfo extends SimpleBeanInfo
{
    // return the bean descriptor
    public BeanDescriptor getBeanDescriptor()
    {
        // create the bean descriptor object
        BeanDescriptor bd = new BeanDescriptor(Boiler.class);

        // set the display name
        bd.setDisplayName("Simulated Boiler");

        // return the descriptor object
        return bd;
    }

    // return the property descriptors
    public PropertyDescriptor[] getPropertyDescriptors()
    {
        // for now this class defines none of its own properties,
        // but this is implemented as a place holder
        try
        {
            // create an empty array of descriptors
            PropertyDescriptor[] pda = { };

            // return the array
            return pda;
        }
```

```
        catch (Exception e)
        {
            return null;
        }
    }


    // return the additional bean info objects for the bean
    public BeanInfo[] getAdditionalBeanInfo()
    {
        try
        {
            // Create a bean info array that contains one object, which is
            // the bean info for the base TemperatureModifier class.  This
            // bean info is retrieved via the Introspector.
            BeanInfo[] bia =
                { Introspector.getBeanInfo(TemperatureModifier.class) };

            // return the bean info array
            return bia;
        }
        catch (Exception e)
        {
            return null;
        }
    }
}
```

## The BeansBook.Simulator.CoolerBeanInfo Class

```
    package BeansBook.Simulator;

import java.beans.*;
import java.lang.reflect.*;

public class CoolerBeanInfo extends SimpleBeanInfo
{
    // return the bean descriptor
    public BeanDescriptor getBeanDescriptor()
    {
        // create the bean descriptor object
        BeanDescriptor bd = new BeanDescriptor(Cooler.class);

        // set the display name
        bd.setDisplayName("Simulated Cooler");

        // return the descriptor object
        return bd;
    }
```

```java
    // return the property descriptors
    public PropertyDescriptor[] getPropertyDescriptors()
    {
        // for now this class defines none of its own properties,
        // this is implemented as a place holder
        try
        {
            // create an empty array of descriptors
            PropertyDescriptor[] pda = { };

            // return the array
            return pda;
        }
        catch (Exception e)
        {
            return null;
        }
    }

    // return the additional bean info objects for the bean
    public BeanInfo[] getAdditionalBeanInfo()
    {
        try
        {
            // Create a bean info array that contains one object, which is
            // the bean info for the base TemperatureModifier class.  This
            // bean info is retrieved via the Introspector
            BeanInfo[] bia =
                { Introspector.getBeanInfo(TemperatureModifier.class) };

            // return the bean info array
            return bia;
        }
        catch (IntrospectionException e)
        {
            return null;
        }
    }
}
```

# 10

# Property Editors
# and Customizers

One of the most important aspects of a visual programming tool is that it allows you to modify the properties and behaviors of components. Instead of having to write code, you are provided with some kind of user interface that presents the options that can be specified for a given instance of an object. The most common form of this interface is a property sheet, which is used to set the values of the component's properties. Each property is listed along with a user interface element for viewing and altering its value. These user interface elements are called *property editors*.

For most simple Beans, the property sheet is sufficient. For more complex Beans, however, the property sheet may not be enough. Perhaps it's just a matter of presenting the information to the user in a different way; in other cases there may be configuration options that are not exposed as properties, and these options may have a degree of complexity that requires a more sophisticated user interface in order to be configured correctly. Whatever the reason, Beans may have their own custom user interfaces that exist just for this purpose. These user interfaces are known as customizers.

## Property Editors

It's pretty safe to say that almost every visual development tool that deals with components will have a property sheet, or something like it. Even the BeanBox test tool has a property sheet. When you select a Bean on the form, the property sheet updates its contents to reflect the exposed read/write properties of the Bean. Figure 10-1 shows the BeanBox property page when an instance of `Beans-Book.Simulator.Boiler` is the currently selected Bean. An edit box is used to change the value of the *Rate* property, which is an `int`. The *Running* property, on the other hand, uses a choice (dropdown) list component for changing its boolean value. But how does BeanBox know how to present an appropriate user interface for the property types? Actually, it doesn't use any of its own classes for the user interface elements used for editing property values. Instead, it uses Java classes that exist just for editing the value of properties of the given type.

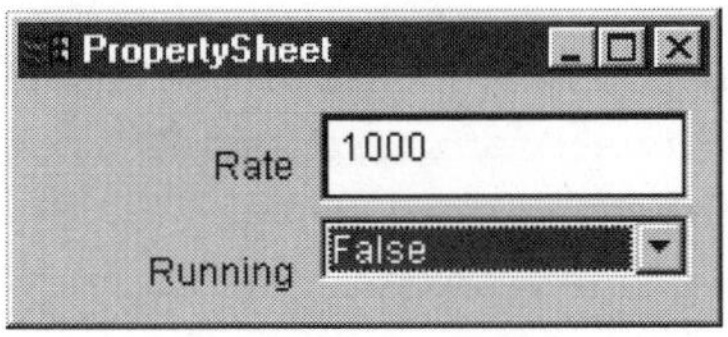

*Figure 10-1. Property sheet for the boiler*

## *Implementing the PropertyEditor Interface*

A property editor is a class that exists solely for editing a property of a specific type. The type can be one of the primitive Java data types, a class provided by one of the standard JDK packages, or a custom class that you or someone else has written. All property editors must implement the `java.beans.PropertyEditor` interface; this ensures that they will behave in a manner that is consistent across all instances of property editors, regardless of the property type.

There are different models of support that a property editor can implement. As we'll see, the level of support that a particular property editor implements will be based largely on the data type of the property. Simple editors may not need anything more than the ability to get and set the property value as text, while others may require custom user interfaces in order to properly manipulate their value.

In order to illustrate the various styles of property editors, we need a way of associating a property editor with a given property. Later in this chapter we'll cover the various techniques which can be used to locate an appropriate property editor for a given property. For now, we'll be explicitly declaring a property editor as part of a BeanInfo class for a Bean. The `java.beans.PropertyDescriptor` class, which provides explicit information about a property, also provides a `setPropertyEditorClass()` method that is used to identify a specific property editor class to be used for the property being described. This method takes a single parameter: the class that implements the property editor to use for the associated property.

Throughout this chapter we'll use the `BeansBook.Simulator.Boiler` class to illustrate the various techniques. For now let's concentrate on the *Running* property, which is provided by the `BeansBook.Simulator.TemperatureModifier` class. Remember that this is the base class for `BeansBook.Simulator.Boiler`. This raises an interesting question: which BeanInfo should be used to specify the property editor, `BeansBook.Simulator.BoilerBeanInfo` or `BeansBook.Simulator.TemperatureModifierBeanInfo`? Let's implement the property descriptor in a BeansBook.Simulator.TemperatureModifierBeanInfo class so that it will be available to all of its subclasses. The appropriate place to specify the property editor is where we implement the associated BeanInfo for the property—in this case, in the superclass's BeanInfo property descriptor. We'll implement this class a little later. Right now, let's concentrate on the property editor itself.

The property editor that we are going to create will be named BeansBook.Simulator.RunningEditor. This class implements the java.beans.PropertyEditor interface. But this interface contains many methods that are not necessary for the simple editor that we're going to create now. A class called java.beans.PropertyEditorSupport makes things a little easier by saving us the trouble of writing methods we don't need. By now we've seen this approach many times over. This class provides basic implementations of the methods in the java.beans.PropertyEditor interface. These default implementations are meant to be overridden by subclasses that provide the specific functionality for the methods. So the BeansBook.Simulator.RunningEditor class extends the java.beans.PropertyEditorSupport class. Let's take a look at the code:

```
package BeansBook.Simulator;

import java.beans.*;

public class RunningEditor extends PropertyEditorSupport
{
    // the current state of the property
    protected boolean bRunning;

    // set the object being edited
    public void setValue(Object o)
    {
        // get the primitive data value from the object version
        bRunning = ((Boolean)o).booleanValue();
    }

    // get the current value of the property
    public Object getValue()
    {
        // return the object version of the primitive type
        return new Boolean(bRunning);
    }

    // get the value of the property as text
    public String getAsText()
    {
        if (bRunning)
        {
            // return the text that indicates running
            return "YES";
        }
```

```
        else
        {
            // return the text that indicates not running
            return "NO";
        }
    }

    // set the value of the property as text
    public void setAsText(String s)
    {
        if (s.equals("YES"))
        {
            // the state is running
            bRunning = true;
        }
        else
        {
            // the state is not running
            bRunning = false;
        }

        // let any interested listeners know about the change
        firePropertyChange();
    }
}
```

Every property editor implements setValue(), which is used to give the property editor an object that represents the current value of the property being edited. The parameter is an instance of java.lang.Object; properties that are primitive data types are passed using their corresponding object representations. For our editor, we first cast the parameter to Boolean, and then call its booleanValue() method. This way we can store the current property value internally as a primitive boolean called bRunning. The getValue() method is implemented to return the current value of the property. This method returns an instance of java.lang.Object, so we return an instance of java.lang.Boolean based upon the variable bRunning. Normally, I think that it would be wise for the local instance of the property to have the same data type as the property itself—I could have changed the data type of bRunning to BeansBook.Simulator.Running. In this case, however, I found it a convenient shortcut to leave bRunning as a boolean variable, since this way I didn't have to change any other code. In practice I would probably have gone through the effort of converting its type, as well as the code that was affected by that change.

The BeansBook.Simulator.RunningEditor class provides the simplest form of property editor functionality; it only supports the ability to get and set the property value as a text string. To do this, we implement getAsText() and setAsText(). Our editor uses the strings *YES* and *NO* to indicate that the *Running* property is in the running or not running state, respectively. So when the getAs-Text() method is called, we return either *YES* or *NO* based upon the value of bRunning. When the setAsText() method is called to set the value of the property we compare the value of the string parameter to *YES*. If the parameter is equal to *YES*, we set bRunning to true; if not, then bRunning is set to false. You might be wondering why the string parameter isn't compared to *NO*, so that the value of bRunning will only be changed to false if that condition is met. The problem is that if neither of these two conditions were met, we would have a text representation of the property value that may not coincide with its actual value. This would be very confusing to the user. For this editor, we're really saying that the string *YES* indicates that the *Running* property is in the running state, and any other string value indicates that it is not in the running state.

When it has set the property value, setAsText() calls firePropertyChange(). This fires a property change event to any objects that registered an interest. It turns out that the property sheet itself is interested in these events, so that BeanBox knows when to update the instance of the Bean. The firePropertyChange() method uses the instance of the property editor as the source of the event. The BeansBook.Simulator.RunningEditor inherits the addPropertyChangeListener() and removePropertyChangeListener() methods from the java.beans.PropertyEditorSupport class. In turn, the java.beans.PropertyEditorSupport class uses an instance of java.beans.PropertyChangeSupport to handle property change listeners.

Before we rebuild the *Simulator.jar* file to include the property editor, we need to create the BeansBook.Simulator.TemperatureModifierBeanInfo class. The getPropertyDescriptors() method creates two instances of java.beans.PropertyDescriptor named, pd1 and pd2, for the *Rate* and *Running* properties. The call to setPropertyEditorClass() on the property descriptor for the *Running* property (pd2) identifies RunningEditor.class as the property editor for the *Running* property. The code for the BeansBook.Simulator.TemperatureModifierBeanInfo class looks like this:

```
package BeansBook.Simulator;

import java.beans.*;
import java.lang.reflect.*;

public class TemperatureModifierBeanInfo extends SimpleBeanInfo
{
    // return the property descriptors
    public PropertyDescriptor[] getPropertyDescriptors()
    {
        try
        {
```

```
            // create a descriptor for the Rate property
            PropertyDescriptor pd1 = new PropertyDescriptor("Rate",
                                             TemperatureModifier.class);

            // create a descriptor for the Running property
            PropertyDescriptor pd2 = new PropertyDescriptor("Running",
                                             TemperatureModifier.class);

            // specify the property editor for Running
            pd2.setPropertyEditorClass(RunningEditor.class);

            // create an array of descriptors and return it to the caller
            PropertyDescriptor[] pda = { pd1, pd2 };

            return pda;
        }
        catch (Exception e)
        {
            return null;
        }
    }
}
```

Now rebuild the *Simulator.jar* file, and put it into the *jars* directory of the BDK installation. Remember to modify the *Simulator.mf* file to include an entry for the `BeansBook.Simulator.RunningEditor` and `BeansBook.Simulator.TemperatureModifierBeanInfo` classes. The entries look like this:

```
Name: BeansBook/Simulator/RunningEditor.class
Java-Bean: False

Name: BeansBook/Simulator/TemperatureModifierBeanInfo.class
Java-Bean: False
```

Let's start BeanBox to test the behavior of the property sheet with the new property editor. Add an instance of the boiler to the BeanBox form. Figure 10-2 shows what the property sheet looks like. The *Rate* property still uses the same text editor, but the *Running* property now uses a text editor that shows the text *NO*.

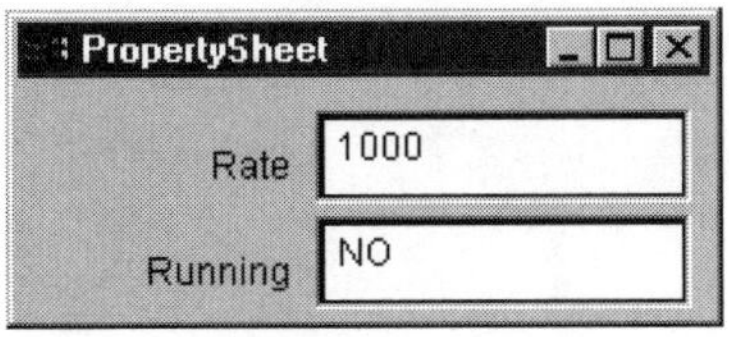

*Figure 10-2. Supplying our own property editor for Running*

By implementing the basic `setAsText()` and `getAsText()` methods, we've indicated to the property sheet that a simple text editing field is sufficient. The property defaults to *NO* because the default state of the *Running* property is not running. If you change the text in the edit field for the *Running* property to *YES*, the instance of the boiler Bean will turn red and change its text to *BOILER ON*, indicating that its *Running* property has changed. Remember that this implementation assumes that any text other than *YES* means that the value of the *Running* property is not running. Try this by changing the text to anything other than *YES*; the boiler Bean in turn is changed back to yellow with the text *BOILER OFF*.

This implementation fails to deal properly with the fact that there are really only two text strings that have any meaning to the *Running* property. It would be nice if we could somehow limit the choices to the strings *YES* and *NO*. The `java.beans.PropertyEditor` interface includes a method called `getTags()`, which returns an array of `java.lang.String` objects, each representing a valid string value for the property. If this method returns an array, instead of `null`, the caller can provide a smarter user interface for choosing these string values. This seems to suit our needs better than allowing arbitrary text, so let's add the `getTags()` method to the `BeansBook.Simulator.RunningEditor`, as follows:

```
// get the string tags
public String[] getTags()
{
    // the only two valid strings are YES and NO
    String[] s = { "YES", "NO" };
    return s;
}
```

Rebuild the *Simulator.jar* file and start BeanBox, again adding an instance of the boiler Bean. Figure 10-3 shows what the property sheet presents to the user. Instead of a text edit field, a choice (dropdown) list is presented to the user which contains two entries with the text *YES* and *NO*. This way the user can't provide arbitrary strings for the value of the *Running* property; only the desired values of *YES* and *NO* will be used, since these are the only choices available in the list. Whenever the selected string in the list changes, the boiler Bean is updated to reflect the change. This is no different than the first example, and in fact the same mechanism is used. The `setAsText()` method is still called to set the value of the property.

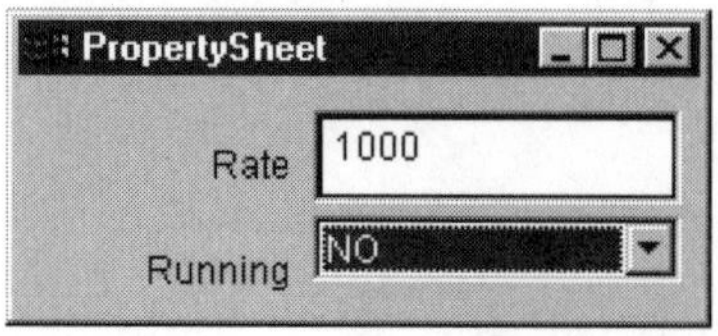

*Figure 10-3. A property editor using a choice*

This mechanism seems very appropriate for setting the value of the *Running* property. Other properties, however, may not fit so well into either the simple text scheme or the one that uses a set of predefined text tags. For these properties, the property editor has to be more elaborate. You can return null from the getAs-Text() method of the property editor, indicating that the value of the property can't be represented as text.

Instead of relying on the property sheet to provide a user interface element for manipulating the property value, a property editor can choose to paint a suitable representation of the property value into a defined area of the screen. If this technique is used, the property editor can also provide a custom user interface for setting the property value. The BeanBox property sheet uses these two techniques in conjunction with each other; a single click in the painted area for a property launches the custom property editor. Now let's implement a custom property editor for the *Running* property.

We no longer want to deal with text strings for the property value, so we remove the getAsText() and setAsText() methods from the BeansBook.Simulator.RunningEditor class. The implementation of getAsText() provided by the base class java.beans.PropertyEditorSupport returns null, indicating that this property editor does not support getting and setting the *Running* property as a text string.

We have to implement two methods to paint the property value. The first method is called isPaintable(): this method is called to determine whether the property editor is able to paint its property value. The default implementation provided by our base class returns false, so we override it and return true. We also need to override the paintValue() method, which is called when the property editor should paint its value. The java.awt.Graphics object to paint on is passed as the first parameter, and the second parameter is an instance of java.awt.Rectangle indicating the area of the screen on which to paint the property value. Let's take a look at the implementation of these two methods in the BeansBook.Simulator.RunningEditor class:

```
// indicate that we support paintValue
public boolean isPaintable()
{
    return true;
}

// implement the paintValue() method
public void paintValue(Graphics gfx, Rectangle box)
{
    // the string variable that holds the string to draw
    String s;
```

```
        if (bRunning)
        {
           // if running we paint YES
           s = "YES";
        }
        else
        {
           // if not running we paint NO
           s = "NO";
        }

        // set the background color to white
        gfx.setColor(Color.white);

        // fill the rectangle with the background color
        gfx.fillRect(box.x, box.y, box.width, box.height);

        // set the color to black for drawing text
        gfx.setColor(Color.black);

        // find a reasonable place to draw the string based on the font
        FontMetrics fm = gfx.getFontMetrics();
        int w = fm.stringWidth(s);
        int x = box.x + (box.width - w) / 2;
        int y = box.y + box.height / 2;

        // draw the string that represents the value of the property
        gfx.drawString(s, x, y);
    }
```

Our implementation of the paintValue() method is relatively simple. We are just
going to paint the string *YES* or *NO* in black text on a white background, based on
the current value of the *Running* property. The java.lang.String variable s is
used to hold the value of the string that we paint on the graphics object. The
value of the bRunning variable is checked, and the appropriate string is assigned
to s accordingly. Next the setColor() method is called on the gfx parameter,
passing the constant Color.white as its parameter. We can use the fields of box as
parameters when we call the fillRect() method on gfx, resulting in the entire
area provided for painting the property value being filled with white. Now we call
the setColor() method on gfx again, this time passing it the constant
Color.black. This is done because we want our strings drawn in black. The font
metrics are used to determine an appropriate place to draw the string, essentially
in the center of the rectangle. Finally we just draw the string by calling the draw-
String() method on gfx.

In order to support a custom user interface for editing the *Running* property, we
need to implement two more methods. The supportsCustomEditor() method is

called to determine if a property editor supports a custom editor. The default implementation of this method provided by the `java.beans.PropertyEditor-Support` class returns `false`, so we override it and return `true`. The `getCustomEditor()` method is called on a property editor to get an instance of its custom editor. This method returns `java.awt.Component`, which indicates that the custom editor must be a subclass of `java.awt.Component`. We create our own custom editor class called `BeansBook.Simulator.RunningPanel`. The `getCustom-Editor()` method creates an instance of the custom editor and returns it to the caller.

```
// we support a custom editor
public boolean supportsCustomEditor()
{
    return true;
}


// return the custom editor
public Component getCustomEditor()
{
    // create an instance of the custom editor
    return new RunningPanel(this);
}
```

Since the custom editor is only going to be used by the property editor, we can just define it right in the same code module as `BeansBook.Simulator.Running-Editor`. The only restriction here is that we can't make the custom editor `public`, but we don't need to anyway. Our custom editor provides two buttons; one to set the value of the *Running* property to *YES*, and one to set it to *NO*. So we extend the `java.awt.Panel` class, and we implement `java.awt.event.ActionListener` to handle button pushes from the *YES* and *NO* buttons. Let's take a look at the code for the `BeansBook.Simulator.RunningPanel` class:

```
class RunningPanel extends Panel implements ActionListener
{
    // create the YES button
    protected Button yes = new Button("YES");

    // create the NO button
    protected Button no = new Button("NO");

    // the instance of the editor that we're working for
    protected RunningEditor editor;

    // the constructor
    public RunningPanel(RunningEditor ed)
    {
        // save a reference to the editor we're working for
        editor = ed;
```

```
        // set the size of the buttons to 50x50
        yes.setSize(50,50);
        no.setSize(50,50);

        // add the buttons to the panel
        add(yes);
        add(no);

        // become an action listener for the yes and no buttons
        yes.addActionListener(this);
        no.addActionListener(this);
    }

    // handle the action performed event
    public void actionPerformed(ActionEvent evt)
    {
        if (evt.getSource() == yes)
        {
            // tell the editor about the new value
            editor.setValue(new Boolean(true));
        }
        else
        {
            // tell the editor about the new value
            editor.setValue(new Boolean(false));
        }

        // tell the editor to fire a property change event to
        // its listeners
        editor.firePropertyChange();
    }
}
```

Two instances of java.awt.Button are created, named yes and no. These buttons are used to set the value of the *Running* property, and are labeled *YES* and *NO* respectively. The constructor takes an instance of BeansBook.Simulator.RunningEditor, because it needs to call the editor as the user presses the buttons. The editor variable stores the reference to the property editor. Next, the sizes of the buttons are both set to 50×50 by calling the setSize() method, and they are added to the panel by passing them as parameters to the add() method. The next step is to pass this to the addActionListener() method on both buttons so that we can handle the action event that is generated when the user presses a button.

The only other method we need in our custom editor is actionPerformed(), which handles action events from the yes and no buttons. We figure out which button was pressed by calling the getSource() method on the evt parameter, and comparing the result to the yes variable. In order to tell the property editor about the new value of the property, we call the `setValue()` method on the `editor` variable. (Remember that this method is used to tell the editor about the current value of the property. Since the property type is boolean, we need to pass an instance of `java.lang.Boolean` that represents its value. Again, this is because the `setValue()` method of a property editor takes an instance of `java.lang.Object` as a parameter.) The last step is to call the `fireProperty-Change()` method on the `editor` variable so that the `editor` in turn will notify its listeners of the property change. Add the `BeansBook.Simulator.RunningPanel` class to the *Simulator.mf* manifest file using the following entry:

```
Name: BeansBook/Simulator/RunningPanel.class
Java-Bean: False
```

Rebuild the *Simulator.jar* file and put it into the *jars* directory of the BDK installation. Now start BeanBox, and put an instance of the boiler Bean onto the form. Now the BeanBox property sheet will look like Figure 10-4.

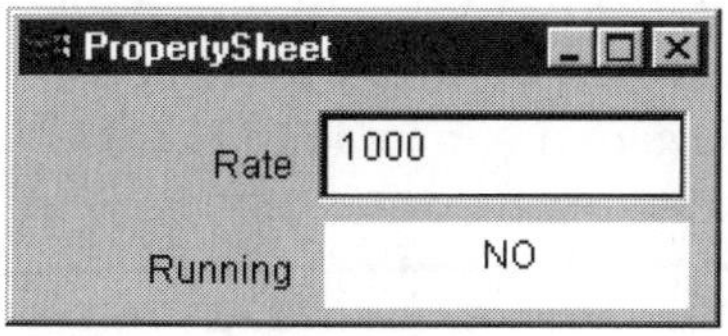

*Figure 10-4. Painting the value of a property*

Since the `BeansBook.Simulator.Boiler` class is not running by default, the string *NO* is painted into the display area next to the label for the *Running* property. In order to modify the value of the property we need to invoke its custom editor. In the BeanBox property sheet, this is accomplished by clicking once in the painted area for the property. When you do so, the custom editor for the *Running* property will be displayed as shown in Figure 10-5.

*Figure 10-5. A custom property editor for Running*

The custom property editor that we created is housed in a modal dialog box created by BeanBox. The buttons labeled *YES* and *NO* are provided by the `Beans-Book.Simulator.RunningPanel` class. Press the *YES* button and two things will happen: the painted area for the *Running* property will be repainted with the string *YES*, handled by the `paintValue()` method of the `BeansBook.Simu-lator.RunningEditor` class; and the instance of the boiler Bean on the BeanBox form is updated to reflect the change in its *Running* property value. The boiler reflects this change by setting its background color to red and changing its text to *BOILER ON*.

The button labeled *Done* is provided as part of the property editor dialog. This button is only used to dismiss the dialog; the *Running* property was updated on the fly when the *YES* and *NO* buttons were pressed.

## Locating Property Editors

As we've already seen, you can use a property descriptor in a Bean's BeanInfo object to specify explicitly which property editor to use for a specific property. However, this isn't always the best approach. Every Bean may not supply a Bean-Info class; it would certainly be inconvenient if we had to write a BeanInfo class just to specify a property editor. So it might be better to rely on another method for locating an appropriate property editor. Actually, we're already doing this: whenever we don't supply a property editor, the development tool (in this case, BeanBox) automatically selects an appropriate default editor. Since the *Running* property is of type `boolean`, we automatically get the default editor for `boolean` values. To illustrate how the location process works, let's make some changes to our simulator. Then we'll create an editor for the *Running* property that can be located using this process.

How would a development tool find a property editor if the *Running* property were based on a custom type that we created? Let's define a new class called `BeansBook.Simulator.Running`, which is used for properties that represent the running state of an object. Its constructor takes a `boolean` argument, and its value can be retrieved by calling its `value()` method. The code for the class is shown here:

```
package BeansBook.Simulator;

public class Running
{
    // the value of the running object
    protected boolean bRunning;

    // constructor
    public Running(boolean b)
    {
        // save the state
        bRunning = b;
    }
```

```
        // return the value of the object
        public boolean value()
        {
            return bRunning;
        }
    }
```

There are a number of changes that have to be made in the BeansBook.Simulator package to accommodate the use of the BeansBook.Simulator.Running class. First, let's update the BeansBook.Simulator.TemperatureModifier class. We have to change the setRunning() method to take an instance of Beans-Book.Simulator.Running instead of a boolean. We can continue to store the state of the *Running* property internally using the boolean variable running, but we have to make some changes where the passed parameter b is referenced; instead of using b directly we use b.value(). Here's the code for the updated setRunning() method:

```
    public void setRunning(Running b)
    {
        // don't bother if there is no change
        if (running == b.value())
        {
            return;
        }

        // save the new value
        running = b.value();

        // set the appropriate label text and background color
        if (running)
        {
            setText(onText);
            setBackground(onColor);
        }
        else
        {
            setText(offText);
            setBackground(offColor);
        }
    }
```

We also have to change the isRunning() method. The first step is to change its name to getRunning(), because the property type is no longer boolean and we should therefore not be using the design pattern for boolean properties. The getRunning() method returns an instance of BeansBook.Simulator.Running, which it creates based on the value of the running variable. Here's the code:

```
    // get the value of the Running property
    public Running getRunning()
```

```
{
    return new Running(running);
}
```

The `BeansBook.Simulator.Boiler` and `BeansBook.Simulator.Cooler` class both make calls to the `setRunning()` method provided by their base class, which is `BeansBook.Simulator.TemperatureModifier`. This is done when they get a service request event fired on them. These events are handled by the `coolingRequest()` and `heatingRequest()` methods of the `BeansBook.Simulator.Cooler` and `BeansBook.Simulator.Boiler` classes respectively. Note that the `isStart()` method of the `BeansBook.Simulator.ServiceRequestEvent` is returning a boolean. This value is used to construct an instance of `BeansBook.Simulator.Running` that can be passed to the updated `setRunning()` method. The modified code for these two classes is:

```
// handle a cooling request event
public void coolingRequest(ServiceRequestEvent evt)
{
    // set the Running property based on the value returned
    // by the isStart() method from the event
    setRunning(new Running(evt.isStart()));
}

// handle a heating request event
public void heatingRequest(ServiceRequestEvent evt)
{
    // set the Running property based on the value returned
    // by the isStart() method from the event
    setRunning(new Running(evt.isStart()));
}
```

We also need to change the `BeansBook.Simulator.RunningEditor` class, because it assumes a boolean property type. The `setValue()` and `getValue()` methods have to be changed to use an instance of `BeansBook.Simulator.Running`. We'll continue to use the boolean variable `bRunning` to represent the state of the *Running* property inside of the property editor. The `setValue()` method casts the parameter to an instance of `BeansBook.Simulator.Running`, and then calls its `value()` method to set the value of the `bRunning` variable. The `getValue()` method uses the `bRunning` variable to construct an instance of `BeansBook.Simulator.Running` to return to the caller. The new code is as follows:

```
// set the value of the property
public void setValue(Object o)
{
    // save the current value
    bRunning = ((Running)o).value();
}
```

```
// get the value of the property
public Object getValue()
{
    // return the property value
    return new Running(bRunning);
}
```

Finally, the custom property editor class `BeansBook.Simulator.RunningPanel` has to be updated to accommodate the new type for the *Running* property. The `actionPerformed()` method calls the `setValue()` method of the property editor, which we just modified. We need to change the parameter that is constructed for the `setValue()` calls to be of the appropriate type, as the following code shows:

```
// handle the action performed event
public void actionPerformed(ActionEvent evt)
{
    if (evt.getSource() == yes)
    {
        // tell the editor about the new value
        editor.setValue(new Running(true));
    }
    else
    {
        // tell the editor about the new value
        editor.setValue(new Running(false));
    }

    // tell the editor to fire a property change event to
    // its listeners
    editor.firePropertyChange();
}
```

If you rebuild these classes and create a new *Simulator.jar* file, you'll find that everything works as before—but let's not stop there. The point of these changes is to show alternative methods of locating a suitable property editor. So let's go back into the `BeansBook.Simulator.TemperatureModifierBeanInfo` class and make a subtle change. Remember that we specified the property editor class for the *Running* property by calling the `setPropertyEditorClass()` method on its property descriptor variable pd2. Let's remove that call and force a different method of locating the property editor to be used.

### Registering a property editor

The class `java.beans.PropertyEditorManager` is used to locate a property editor for a specified class when one is not declared explicitly in a property descriptor. The `findEditor()` method can be called on the class to find a property editor for a specified class. This method will try all of its techniques for locating a property editor. The first of these techniques is based on editor registration. The method called `registerEditor()` is used to register or unregister a property editor for a specified class. The `registerEditor()` method takes two parameters: the property type class and the property editor class. If you pass `null` in place of the property editor class, any registered property editor for the specified property type will be unregistered. Although this is perfectly usable, it seems to violate the patterns of methods we've seen throughout most of the packages provided by the JDK.*

In order to make use of this technique we need to find an appropriate place to register our property editor. Registration is a run-time attribute of the system; it does not get saved anywhere. Since the property editor relates to the `BeansBook.Simulator.Running` class, let's find a suitable way to put it right there. We can use a static block of code within the class to register the property editor. A static block is only executed one time on behalf of all instances of `BeansBook.Simulator.Running`, so this seems like a good place to perform the registration. We call the `registerEditor()` method, specifying that the `BeansBook.Simulator.RunningEditor` class is used to edit properties of type `BeansBook.Simulator.Running`. The updated code for the class follows:

```
package BeansBook.Simulator;

public class Running
{
    static
    {
        // register a property editor for the Running object
        java.beans.PropertyEditorManager.registerEditor(Running.class,
                                                RunningEditor.class);
    }

    // the value of the running object
    protected boolean bRunning;

    // constructor
    public Running(boolean b)
    {
        // save the state
        bRunning = b;
    }

    // return the value of the object
    public boolean value()
```

---

* I think it would have been more consistent to provide an `unregisterEditor()` method, instead of allowing the use of a `null` parameter to imply that a property editor should be unregistered.

```
     {
         return bRunning;
     }
 }
```

### Following a standard naming convention

When an editor hasn't been explicitly registered, the `java.beans.PropertyEditorManager` looks for a suitable property editor for the specified class using a standard naming convention. The fully qualified name of the class for which an editor is needed is concatenated with the string *Editor*, and an attempt is made to load the resulting class name. If you were requesting an editor for type `Package.Type`, the property editor manager would look for the class `Package.TypeEditor`.

It turns out that our property editor already follows this naming convention; we use `BeansBook.Simulator.RunningEditor` to edit properties of type `BeansBook.Simulator.Running`. So we could remove the static block of code which calls the `registerEditor()` method to explicitly register the property editor with the property editor manager.

### Looking in the default path

Finally, if this class isn't found, the editor manager searches for the property editor in a default path. The string *Editor* is appended to the class name for the property type, without using the full package path. Then the editor is searched for in the package paths that are considered to be the default for locating property editors. The default search path is the package `sun.beans.editors`. This package contains the default property editors for the primitive data types, as well as an editor for properties of types `java.awt.Color`, `java.awt.Font`, and `java.lang.String`. This is why we were able to modify our properties using the BeanBox property sheet without ever creating a custom property editor. The default search path for property editors can be accessed and changed by calling the `getEditorSearchPath()` and `setEditorSearchPath()` methods of the `java.beans.PropertyEditorManager` class, respectively. Calling the `setEditorSearchPath()` method allows you to define one or more default package paths for locating property editors. Third-party development tools will probably use this technique to provide vendor-specific property editors for use within their own property pages.

## Choosing an Appropriate Locator Technique

Which technique you use is really dependent on the design of your Bean and the environment in which it is running. I wouldn't put any new property editors into the default package sun.beans.editors. This is where the default editors for the primitive data types are, but there is no guarantee that they will be there in the future. Even if they remain there forever, this is a package created by Sun and should really contain only classes produced by that organization. Of course, if your Bean's properties are based on primitive types, it is perfectly acceptable to take advantage of the default property editors. If your Bean has a property type based on a class from a package you are creating, it's more reasonable to create an editor class for that type by putting it into the same package and appending *Editor* to the fully qualified class name of the type. This way all properties of that type will use the same editor by default. If the choice of property editor can change over time, it may be beneficial to register these editors at run-time by calling the registerEditor() method.

## *Supporting Automatic Source Code Generation*

Property editors can also play a part in supporting source code generation. Some development tools may choose to generate Java source code based on the property values that are specified for a Bean at design-time. The java.beans.PropertyEditor interface defines a method called getJavaInitializationString() which is used for this purpose. The default implementation provided by the java.beans.PropertyEditorSupport class returns the string ???. This is not exactly a friendly response; it is designed to be flagged by the compiler so that the user is aware that something useful could not be specified. The idea is to override the method and supply a string that is actual Java code, to be used as the right side of an assignment statement.

Consider the BeansBook.Simulator.RunningEditor class, used to edit property values of type BeansBook.Simulator.Running. The editor is maintaining the current value of the *Running* property in a boolean variable named bRunning. We could implement the getJavaInitializationString() method as follows:

```
public String getJavaInitializationString()
{
   // a string variable to hold the code fragment
   String theCode;

   if (bRunning)
   {
      // the property is in the running state
      theCode = "new BeansBook.Simulator.Running(true)";
   }
   else
   {
      // the property is not in the running state
      theCode = "new BeansBook.Simulator.Running(false)";
   }
```

```
    return theCode;
}
```

A source code generator might call the `getJavaInitializationString()` method on an instance of `BeansBook.Simulator.RunningEditor` that is being used to edit the value of the *Running* property for a `BeansBook.Simulator.Boiler` object. If the boiler wasn't running, the source code generator might create the following code snippet:

```
// set the value of the Running property
theBoiler.setRunning(new BeansBook.Simulator.Running(false));
```

# *Customizers*

A customizer is a user interface for customizing an entire Bean, as opposed to a single property. The characteristics and behaviors of the Bean that can be modified by a customizer are not limited to its exposed properties. There can be any number of other settings that are needed to configure a Bean that are not considered properties.

The complexity of the configuration options for a Bean is another possible reason to provide a customizer. This gives you an opportunity to present these choices in a way that makes more sense to a user, and might even provide a mechanism which can guide the user through the process.

If you provide a customizer, you must also provide a BeanInfo class for your Bean in order to identify its associated customizer class. There is no standard naming convention that can be followed, nor is there any kind of customizer manager class provided by the JDK. This is another area that seems inconsistent. I don't see any reason why a run-time registration mechanism, like that provided by the `java.beans.PropertyEditorManager`, could not have been provided for registering Bean customizers at run-time. Likewise, I think a naming convention that appends the string `Customizer` to the Bean class name would have been useful, allowing for the creation of customizers without the need for creating a BeanInfo class. However, it is almost trivial to create a BeanInfo class solely for the purpose of specifying an associated customizer class.

Although customizers are generally thought of as design-time elements, it is certainly possible to launch a Bean customizer at run-time. One could easily imagine providing an interface on a Bean that, when invoked, launches that Bean's customizer. Such a customizer would not want to expose customization options that are not appropriate at run-time; however, this is purely a design issue. There is nothing to stop you from launching the customizer at run-time if you so choose.

Let's take another look at the constructors for the `java.beans.BeanDescriptor` class. One form of this constructor takes both the class that implements the Bean and the class that implements the Bean customizer. So you could create a very simple BeanInfo that does nothing more than implement the `getBeanDescriptor()` method and returns an instance of `java.beans.BeanDescriptor` that identifies the customizer class.

Once again we'll work with the `BeansBook.Simulator.Boiler` class to illustrate these concepts. We are going to create a customizer for this class named `BeansBook.Simulator.BoilerCustomizer`. Before we do so, let's consider the changes we need to make to the `BeansBook.Simulator.BoilerBeanInfo` class. The only thing we have to modify is the construction of the Bean descriptor inside of the `getBeanDescriptor()` method. This time we use the second form of the constructor, passing the customizer class as the second parameter. Here's what the code looks like now:

```
// return the bean descriptor
public BeanDescriptor getBeanDescriptor()
{
    // create the bean descriptor object
    BeanDescriptor bd = new BeanDescriptor(Boiler.class,
                                    BoilerCustomizer.class);

    // set the display name
    bd.setDisplayName("Simulated Boiler");

    // return the descriptor object
    return bd;
}
```

Let's create the `BeansBook.Simulator.BoilerCustomizer` class. All Bean customizers must implement the `java.beans.Customizer` interface. It may surprise you to find that this interface is very simple; it only defines three methods. There are the familiar `addPropertyChangeListener()` and `removePropertyChangeListener()` methods, which are needed so that other objects can listen for property changes that are performed by the customizer. The third method is called `setObject()`, which takes a single instance of `java.lang.Object` as its only parameter; this parameter represents the Bean that is being customized. Besides these methods, there are two more requirements imposed on customizers: they must subclass `java.awt.Component`, and they must provide a default constructor. The first requirement exists so that the customizer can be added to a `java.awt`-based panel or dialog box. A default constructor is needed because the customizer class itself will be instantiated by a call to the `newInstance()` method on a `java.lang.Class` object that represents it. The `newInstance()` method requires that the class it is instantiating have a default constructor.

Before we start creating the customizer, let's define exactly what the customizer will allow the user to do. Certainly it makes sense to manipulate the *Rate* and *Running* property values for the Bean, but let's go beyond that. Let's provide access to some functionality that is not currently exposed by a property. The BeansBook.Simulator.Boiler constructor calls the superclass constructor with a number of parameters, the first of which defines the operating temperature of the device. The boiler class passes the value 100.0 as the first parameter, specifying that the boiler Bean will operate at that temperature. That value is not exposed as a property, but it might be useful to be able to modify it. Let's add some methods to the BeansBook.Simulator.TemperatureModifier class to read and write the operating temperature. We don't want these methods to be confused with property accessor methods, so we make sure to name them accordingly. Actually, since we provide a BeanInfo class for the temperature modifier, we could really name these methods anything we like. As long as we don't create a property descriptor for the operating temperature, everything will be fine. Let's play it safe and name the method that sets the operating temperature assignOperatingTemperature(), which takes a parameter of type double. The method to get the operating temperature value is named retrieveOperatingTemperature(), which returns a double. The BeansBook.Simulator.TemperatureModifier class already keeps track of the operating temperature in a double variable called temp, so all we need to do is implement the two new methods as follows:

```
// set the operating temperature
public void assignOperatingTemperature(double t)
{
    temp = t;
}

// get the operating temperature
public double retrieveOperatingTemperature()
{
    return temp;
}
```

The TemperatureModifier constructor also takes a Color parameter to define the color of the component when it is on (running). This also hasn't been exposed as a property, but we can make it available through the Bean customizer. Again, we name the methods in a way that won't be confused with properties. The methods will be called assignOnColor() and retrieveOnColor() as shown:

```
// set the "on" color
public void assignOnColor(Color c)
{
    onColor = c;
    if (running)
```

```
        {
            setBackground(onColor);
        }
    }

    // get the "on" color
    public Color retrieveOnColor()
    {
        return onColor;
    }
```

Let's take this opportunity to think about any problems we may run into by allowing the operating temperature to be modified. The one problem that occurs to me is that the boiler can be used to veto a change to the comfort temperature of the thermostat. We did this so that the user could never specify a desired temperature higher than the operating temperature of the boiler. However, the following scenario could now take place. The user could change the operating temperature of the boiler to 125 degrees Celsius, and then specify a comfort temperature of 115 degrees. After the temperature of the system reaches 115 degrees, the user changes the operating temperature back to 100 degrees. Now when the user tries to reduce the comfort temperature on the thermostat, a vetoable change event is sent to the boiler specifying a desired temperature of 114 degrees. Since this value is greater than the operating temperature of 100 degrees, the change is vetoed. This is no good!

To solve this problem, we need to modify the vetoableChange() method on the BeansBook.Simulator.Boiler class. What we really want to veto is a desired comfort temperature that is greater than the operating temperature of the boiler, and is larger than the current comfort temperature. In other words, we don't want the user to increase the value of the comfort temperature if it is already greater than the operating temperature, but we do want to allow a decrease in this value. We now get both the new and old values from the PropertyChangeEvent object and determine if the proposed new value is an increase over the old value. We veto the change if the value is increasing and the new value is greater than the current operating temperature. Otherwise we let the change stand.

```
    // handle a vetoable change event
    public void vetoableChange(PropertyChangeEvent evt)
            throws PropertyVetoException
    {
        // only interested in ComfortTemperature
        if (evt.getPropertyName().equals("ComfortTemperature"))
        {
            // get the proposed temperature
            Double d = (Double)evt.getNewValue();
```

```
        // get the old value
        Double old = (Double)evt.getOldValue();

        // determine if the temperature is increasing
        boolean bIncreasing = (d.doubleValue() > old.doubleValue());

        // veto a rising temperature over the operating temperature
        if (bIncreasing && d.doubleValue() >
              retrieveOperatingTemperature())
        {
        throw new PropertyVetoException("Invalid Comfort Temperature",
                                    evt);
        }
    }
}
```

Now we're ready to build the customizer. The java.beans package does not provide any support class implementation for a customizer, so we have to start from scratch. The user interface for this customizer is pretty simple. We use a java.awt.Choice list for the *Running* property, and instances of java.awt.Text-Field for the *Rate* property and the operating temperature. We will also need some way to alter the color to use when the boiler is running. The Color property editor implements a custom editor that is perfect for this. Even though we haven't made the running color a property, we can still take advantage of the Color property editor. You'll see how to do this shortly when we get into the code. All of the fields on the customizer user interface will be preceded by descriptive labels. Since this class is rather long, I'm going to intersperse my description with the code.

The class extends java.awt.Panel and implements java.beans.Customizer, which imposes the requirements mentioned earlier. The customizer implements the java.awt.ItemListener interface so that it gets events from the java.awt.Choice list. It also implements java.awt.ActionListener for action events that come from the text fields. The actionPerformed event is fired by a text field when the *Enter* key is pressed. This will be the user action that causes the *Rate* and operating temperature values to be updated. This way we don't react prematurely to every keystroke in the text fields. The PropertyChangeListener interface is used for handling property change events that are fired by the Color property editor.

```
    package BeansBook.Simulator;

import java.awt.*;
import java.awt.event.*;
import java.beans.*;
```

```
public class BoilerCustomizer extends Panel
                implements Customizer, // to be a bean customizer
                ItemListener,          // to handle Choice list events
                ActionListener,        // to handle action events
                PropertyChangeListener // color property changes
```

The variable named theBoiler keeps track of the boiler Bean that is being customized. This value is passed to the customizer at run-time. To simplify the handling of property change listeners, we use an instance of java.beans.PropertyChangeSupport named support. The last three variables are the user interface elements used to customize the Bean. The variable runningChoice is a java.awt.Choice list that represents the value of the *Running* property. It will contain the strings *YES* and *NO*, indicating whether the boiler is running. The rateField and tempField variables are both instances of java.awt.TextField, and will be used for editing the value of the *Rate* property and the operating temperature, respectively. We define the colorEditor as an instance of the interface PropertyEditor, because we will be finding the Color property editor at run-time.

```
{
    // the boiler that we are customizing
    protected Boiler theBoiler;

    // an instance of property change support
    protected PropertyChangeSupport support;

    // the Choice list for the Running property
    protected Choice runningChoice = new Choice();

    // a text field for the Rate property
    protected TextField rateField = new TextField("*******");

    // a text field for the operating temperature
    protected TextField tempField = new TextField("*******");

    // the property editor for the running color
    protected PropertyEditor colorEditor;
```

The constructor sets up all of the objects used by the customizer. First, it creates the property change support object. Next, a label for the *Running* property is created and added to the panel, followed by the runningChoice list. Now a label is added for the *Rate* property, along with the text field variable rateField. The same thing is done for the operating temperature; a label and the tempField objects are added to the panel. Next, we add a label for the running color. We call the findEditor() method of the PropertyEditorManager to find an editor for class java.awt.Color. Then we get its custom editor and add it as a component to the customizer panel. The next step is to add the *NO* and *YES* strings to the runningChoice object, representing the available choices for the state of the *Running* property. Finally, we register the customizer as an event listener for the user interface elements.

```
// the empty constructor
public BoilerCustomizer()
{
    // create the instance of the support object
    support = new PropertyChangeSupport(this);

    // add a label for the Running property
    add(new Label("Running State: "));

    // add the Running property choice list
    add(runningChoice);

    // add a label for the Rate property
    add(new Label("Pulse Rate: "));

    // add the Rate property field
    add(rateField);

    // add a label for the operating temperature
    add(new Label("Operating Temp: "));

    // add the operating temperature field
    add(tempField);

    // add a label for the color editor
    add(new Label("Running Color: "));

    // find the editor and add its custom editor to the panel
    colorEditor =
        PropertyEditorManager.findEditor(java.awt.Color.class);
    add(colorEditor.getCustomEditor());

    // add the choice strings to the Running choice
    runningChoice.add("NO");
    runningChoice.add("YES");

    // become an item listener for the Choice list
    runningChoice.addItemListener(this);

    // become an action listener for the edit fields
    rateField.addActionListener(this);
    tempField.addActionListener(this);
}
```

The object passed to the setObject() method is the instance of BeansBook.Simulator.Boiler that we are customizing, so we cast it and save it in the variable theBoiler. Then we call the getRunning() method on the boiler, in turn calling the value() method on the returned object. This tells us the current value of the *Running* property, and we select the appropriate item in the choice list. The next step is to get the value of the *Rate* property by calling the getRate() method on theBoiler. We then get a string representation of the rate and pass it to rate-Field via its setText() method. We use the same approach to set up the operating temperature field. Next we need to set the initial value of colorEditor. We get the value by calling retrieveOnColor() on theBoiler and pass the result to the setValue() method of the editor. To receive the property change events fired by the color editor, we register our customizer as a listener by calling addPropertyChangeListener().

```
public void setObject(Object o)
{
    // save a reference to the bean we're customizing
    theBoiler = (Boiler)o;

    // get the state of the Running property and select it
    // in the Choice list
    if (theBoiler.getRunning().value())
    {
        runningChoice.select("YES");
    }
    else
    {
        runningChoice.select("NO");
    }

    // put the current value of the Rate property into the field
    int rate = theBoiler.getRate();
    rateField.setText(String.valueOf(rate));

    // put the current value of the operating temp into the field
    double temp = theBoiler.retrieveOperatingTemperature();
    tempField.setText(String.valueOf(temp));

    // hook up the color editor
    colorEditor.setValue(theBoiler.retrieveOnColor());
    colorEditor.addPropertyChangeListener(this);
}

public void addPropertyChangeListener(PropertyChangeListener l)
{
    // defer to the support object
    support.addPropertyChangeListener(l);
}

public void removePropertyChangeListener(PropertyChangeListener l)
{
```

```
        // defer to the support object
        support.removePropertyChangeListener(1);
    }
```

The addPropertyChangeListener() and removePropertyChangeListener() methods simply defer to their corresponding methods on the support variable.

You may be wondering why I've implemented both preferredSize() and getPreferredSize(). You may already be aware that preferredSize() is a deprecated method that was replaced by getPreferredSize(). The problem is that there are still products that call preferredSize(), and BeanBox is one of them (as of the February 1997 release of the BDK). The best thing to do in a case like this is to implement the deprecated method in terms of the new one.* In any event, the purpose of these two methods is to provide the caller with the desired size of the customizer panel, in this case, 480×80.

```
    public Dimension preferredSize()
    {
        // defer to the getPreferredSize() method
        return getPreferredSize();
    }

    public Dimension getPreferredSize()
    {
        // we prefer a dimension of 480x80
        return new Dimension(480, 80);
    }

    // handle an item state changed event
    public void itemStateChanged(ItemEvent evt)
    {
        // if a new selection is made in the Running choice list...
        if (evt.getSource() == runningChoice &&
            evt.getStateChange() == ItemEvent.SELECTED)
        {
```

When a new selection is made in the runningChoice list, we know we're going to modify the value of the *Running* property. First, we get the instance of the java.awt.Choice by calling getSource() on the event object, and then the string value of the selected item is retrieved. Next we determine the new boolean state of the property by comparing the string value of the selected item to the string *YES*. This boolean variable is used to create a new instance of Beans-Book.Simulator.Running, which is passed to the setRunning() method on

---

* Someday you'll be able to remove the deprecated method; a subsequent release of BeanBox promises to solve this problem. This technique is still good practice for a while, because other applications may still be calling deprecated methods.

theBoiler. The last step is to ask the support object to fire an appropriate property change event to any listeners.

```
// get the instance of the choice list
Choice pp = (Choice)evt.getSource();

// determine the newly selected item string
String sel = pp.getSelectedItem();

// the desired boolean state of the Running property
boolean state;
if (sel.equals("YES"))
{
   state = true;
}
else
{
   state = false;
}

// create a new instance of Running
Running newState = new Running(state);

// set the Running property of the boiler bean
theBoiler.setRunning(newState);

// fire a Running property change event
support.firePropertyChange("Running", null, newState);
   }
}
```

When the actionPerformed() method is called, it means that the user has pressed the *Enter* key in either the *Rate* property field or the operating temperature field. If it was the *Rate* field, the text is retrieved from the field and converted into an int variable. This variable is then passed to the setRate() method on theBoiler, and then we ask the support object to fire a property change event to the listeners. In this case, we don't specify the name of the property or its old and new values; we leave it up to the listener to figure it out. If the event came from the operating temperature field, the text is retrieved and converted into a double variable. This variable is then passed to the assignOperatingTemperature() method of theBoiler.

```
// handle an actionPerformed event
public void actionPerformed(ActionEvent evt)
{
   if (evt.getSource() == rateField)
   {
      // the event came from the rate field
```

```
        // get the text from the field
        String s = rateField.getText();

        // get an integer representation of the new value
        int r = Integer.valueOf(s).intValue();

        // set the Rate property
        theBoiler.setRate(r);

        // fire an unspecified property change event
        support.firePropertyChange("", null, null);
    }
    else
    {
        // the event came from the operating temp field

        // get the text from the field
        String s = tempField.getText();

        // get a double representation of the new value
        double r = Double.valueOf(s).doubleValue();

        // set the new operating temperature
        theBoiler.assignOperatingTemperature(r);
    }
}
```

The last thing we need to do is implement the propertyChange() method, which will be called whenever the user changes the color in the color editor. We retrieve the color by calling the getValue() method on the event object and cast it to Color, and then we pass the new color to theBoiler through its assignOn-Color() method. It turned out to be very little work to make use of the custom color editor, saving us the task of writing our own color picker.

```
    public void propertyChange(PropertyChangeEvent evt)
    {
        Color c = (Color)colorEditor.getValue();
        theBoiler.assignOnColor(c);
    }
}
```

Like we've done so many times before, we add an entry to the *Simulator.mf* manifest file for the BeansBook.Simulator.BoilerCustomizer class:

```
Name: BeansBook/Simulator/BoilerCustomizer.class
Java-Bean: False
```

All that's left is to rebuild the *Simulator.jar* file and run BeanBox. Once again, add an instance of the boiler Bean to the BeanBox form. With the boiler Bean selected, go to the BeanBox *Edit* menu and select *Customize*. The customizer dialog box will be launched as shown in Figure 10-6.

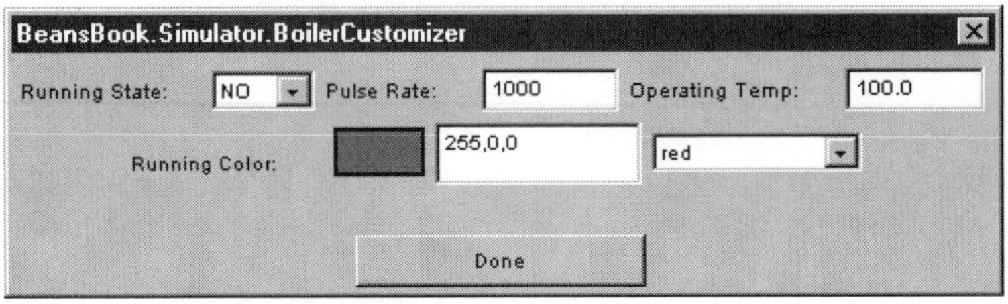

*Figure 10-6. A customizer for the boiler*

The customizer that we created in `BeansBook.Simulator.BoilerCustomizer` is presented in the dialog box along with a button labeled *Done* for dismissing the dialog. Change the value of the *Running* property by selecting *YES* or *NO* in the choice list. The result is that the paintable area for the *Running* property is updated in the BeanBox property sheet, and the boiler Bean itself is repainted to reflect the change.

You can change the *Rate* property by entering a new integer value in the field labeled *Pulse Rate*. After you've entered the desired value, press the *Enter* key. Although there is no visible change to the Bean itself, the new value is now shown for the *Rate* property in the BeanBox property sheet.

You can change the operating temperature of the boiler by changing the value in the field labeled *Operating Temp*, and then pressing the *Enter* key. The only way you'll be able to prove that this works is to wire a `vetoableChange` event from a thermostat Bean to the boiler, and then try changing the comfort temperature. The boiler will veto an increase in comfort temperature that is greater than the operating temperature you specified.

The running color of the boiler can be changed by entering a comma-separated RGB value, or by using the dropdown list and choosing a color by name. The interface for changing the color is provided by the custom editor that we got from the `Color` property editor.

Keep in mind that customizers are meant, for the most part, to be used to configure the characteristics or behavior of a Bean at design-time. As with property editors, the expectation is that the changes you make with the customizer will be part of the persistent state of the Bean. Your customizer should not modify any value internal to the Bean that is not saved and restored as part of its persistent state. This may seem obvious; after all, it is up to you, as the programmer, to make sure that property values are saved. But it is easy to overlook this issue for internal state that is not exposed as a property, so be aware of it.

# 11

# *ActiveX*

JavaBeans is a powerful and flexible component architecture, but it's not the only game in town. Microsoft's ActiveX technology is widely used; in fact, it's used on virtually every computer running Windows 95 or Windows NT. There's really no point in engaging in a long-winded debate about whether one technology is better than the other. The reality of the situation is that ActiveX is here, it works, and it's not going away. The best way to deal with this fact is to find a way to play in both worlds.

That's where the ActiveX Bridge comes in. This technology is designed to bridge the gap between the two component architectures, essentially allowing Beans to act like ActiveX components. I'll be talking much more about the ActiveX Bridge shortly. (Other bridges are planned to integrate Java Beans into other component architectures.)

ActiveX is really a term used to describe a wide range of technologies. We'll look primarily at visible ActiveX controls, whose counterparts are visible Java Beans (those that are subclasses of `java.awt.Component`). There is certainly a relationship between nonvisible Beans and nonvisible ActiveX components, but we won't be covering that aspect of the two technologies here.

Both of these technologies are based on the principles of component architectures that were described in the first chapter. Basically, Beans and ActiveX controls expose properties, methods, and events. The main difference is in the way these attributes are exposed. As we've seen, Beans use the introspection mechanism to expose the details of a component; ActiveX components use type libraries, which are binary files that contain the same kind of information provided by a BeanInfo class.

I'm not going to attempt to cover the details of ActiveX; that subject has been covered very well in a variety of other books.* This chapter is not meant to cover ActiveX, nor is it intended to be a guide for using ActiveX, with or without Java-Beans. If you don't have any knowledge of ActiveX, you may find some useful information in this chapter that will inspire you to investigate the topic further. If you already have some familiarity with ActiveX, you'll probably understand the references that I'll make to portions of that technology.

It is important that Beans are usable in an ActiveX environment without having to write any extra code. As Java developers, we should be concentrating on Java, without being distracted by the technical details of making our Beans available to other component architectures. That's the perfect-world scenario. In the real world, there are going to be technical obstacles that will have impact on our designs. I'll point some of these out along the way.

As of this writing, the Bridge is in its second beta release, but most of what I'm going to talk about will be relevant when it gets to final release as well. The Bridge is available from JavaSoft's web site at *http://java.sun.com/*. After you install the Bridge, you should go back and check your CLASSPATH environment variable. The beta releases tend to mess this up; your CLASSPATH should point to wherever it pointed before you installed the Bridge, with the *bridge/classes* directory appended. For example, my CLASSPATH variable points to the *classes.zip* file from the JDK, the root directory of the packages I am developing, and the Bridge classes, as shown below:

```
c:\jdk1.1\lib\classes.zip;c:\java\projects;c:\bdk\bridge\classes
```

# The JavaBeans ActiveX Bridge

The ActiveX Bridge is a technology developed by Sun to bridge JavaBeans components to the world of ActiveX. The Bridge sits between the Bean and the ActiveX container, acting like a proxy for the events, methods, and properties, as illustrated in Figure 11-1. Its job is to expose the Bean to the ActiveX container as if it were an ActiveX component. The container and the Bean never communicate directly with each other; everything happens through the Bridge.

## The Obstacles

We're going to make the Beans from the BeansBook.Simulator package available as ActiveX components. Before we do that, we have a few technical difficulties to overcome. The first of these has to do with invisible Beans. The Beta 2 version of

---

* For more information, check out *Understanding ActiveX and OLE,* by David Chappell (Microsoft Press).

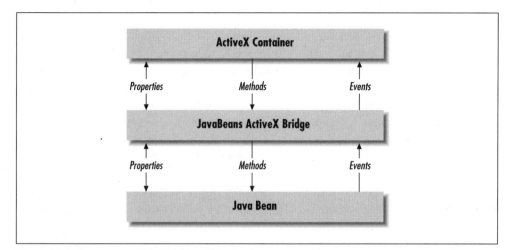

*Figure 11-1. Communications between a Bean and an ActiveX container*

the Bridge does not support invisible Beans.* At present, we have to do something now to deal with this limitation, because the BeansBook.Simulator.Temperature class is not visible; it doesn't subclass java.awt.Component. Let's create a new Bean class called BeansBook.Simulator.VisualTemperature which has all of the functionality of its nonvisible counterpart, and extends java.awt.Panel. (Here's a situation where I'd love to be able to use multiple inheritance, so that I could derive my new class from both BeansBook.Simulator.Temperature and java.awt.Panel.†) The code for the temperature object is small, so I'm just going to copy it to create the visual version of the class.

There's a subtle problem related to property change and vetoable change events that you'll have to deal with. These events are not exposed directly by the ActiveX wrapper for your Bean. In ActiveX, property changes are handled through the IPropertyNotifySink interface. This is a well-known interface in ActiveX; the Bridge uses it to fire property events to the component's container. In Visual Basic, the form itself implements IPropertyNotifySink on your behalf. This means that you won't be able to get these events in the same way that you handle custom events. Obviously, if you are writing your own ActiveX container to house the Beans, you can implement the IPropertyNotifySink interface and receive property change events from the Bridge. But the real point of the Bridge is to be able to run the Beans in any ActiveX container, so you may want to consider

---

* The Beta 3 version, now available from JavaSoft, includes support for invisible Beans.

† The issue of multiple inheritance is being addressed by JavaSoft, in a specification proposal entitled, *A Draft Proposal for an Object Aggregation/Delegation Model for Java and JavaBeans* (currently version 0.5).

designing custom events that get fired from your Bean either in place of, or at least as well as, the property change events.

The final obstacle has to do with the way the Bridge passes events to its container. The Bridge registers itself as a listener for all of the events that are fired by the underlying Bean, and it fires events to its container using the ActiveX event firing mechanism. This creates a problem for a Bean that is a listener for an event from a unicast event source. If the Bridge has already taken the only available listener slot, then no other Bean will be able to register. I'd like to be able to write some code in a language like Visual Basic that wires the Beans together the way I did in Java in Chapter 8, *Putting It All Together*. In that example, I registered the temperature object as a temperature pulse listener on the boiler and cooler objects. Now that the Bridge has registered for those events I'll need to find another way to get the information to the temperature object.

I'll handle the temperature pulse events at the container level and pass the information back to the temperature object by a method call. To accommodate this, we add a method called `directTemperaturePulse()`, which takes a parameter of type `double` as the temperature of the pulse. This feels like a kludge! In spite of its amateur feel, there is simply no way to register both the temperature object and the Bridge for the unicast temperature pulse events. You should keep this in mind when you're designing a Bean as a unicast event source. With these two changes in place, let's look at the code for the `BeansBook.Simulator.VisualTempera-ture` class:

```
package BeansBook.Simulator;

import java.beans.*;
import java.awt.*;

// the temperature bean class definition
public class VisualTemperature extends Panel
    implements TemperaturePulseListener,  // listens for temp pulses
            java.io.Serializable        // declare Serializable
{
    // support object for bound property listeners
    protected PropertyChangeSupport boundSupport;

    // the current temperature
    protected double theTemperature = 22.0;

    // constructor
    public VisualTemperature()
    {
        // construct the support object
        boundSupport = new PropertyChangeSupport(this);
    }
```

```java
// add a property change listener
public void addPropertyChangeListener(PropertyChangeListener l)
{
   // defer to the support object
   boundSupport.addPropertyChangeListener(l);
}

// remove a property change listener
public void removePropertyChangeListener(PropertyChangeListener l)
{
   // defer to the support object
   boundSupport.removePropertyChangeListener(l);
}

// get the value of the Temperature property
public double getTemperature()
{
   return theTemperature;
}

// set the value of the Temperature property
public void setTemperature(double t)
{
   // don't bother if the value didn't change
   if (t == theTemperature)
   {
      return;
   }

   // save the old value
   Double old = new Double(theTemperature);

   // save the new value
   theTemperature = t;

   // fire the property change event
   boundSupport.firePropertyChange("Temperature", old,
                                 new Double(t));
}

// handle a temperature pulse event
public void temperaturePulse(TemperaturePulseEvent evt)
{
   // get the pulse temperature
   double p = evt.getPulseTemperature();

   // get the current temp
   double c = getTemperature();
```

```
    // if the pulse temp is greater than the current temp
    if (p > c)
    {
        // only change if the difference is more than 1
        if ((p - c) >= 1.0)
        {
            // add 1 to the current temperature
            setTemperature(c + 1.0);
        }
    }
    else if (p < c) // pulse less than the current temperature
    {
        // only change if the difference is more than 1
        if ((c - p) >= 1.0)
        {
            // subtract 1 from the current temperature
            setTemperature(c - 1.0);
        }
    }
}

// take a temperature pulse by a direct method call
public void directTemperaturePulse(double pulse)
{
    // emulate a regular temperature pulse
    temperaturePulse(new TemperaturePulseEvent(this, pulse));
}
}
```

For the most part, the code is the same as that for the `BeansBook.Simu-`
`lator.Temperature` class. The new class now extends `java.awt.Panel` so that it
can be used by Beta 2 of the Bridge. The only other change is the addition of the
`directTemperaturePulse()` method. This is the method that we'll call when a
pulse is received by the ActiveX container. It is implemented in terms of the
`temperaturePulse()` method. The `pulse` parameter is used to create an instance
of `BeansBook.Simulator.TemperaturePulseEvent`, which is passed along as if it
came directly from the original source of the pulse. The `BeansBook.Simu-`
`lator.VisualTemperature` class must be added to the *Simulator.jar* file using the
same techniques we've been using throughout.

## Packaging a Bean

The process of preparing a Bean to be used as an ActiveX component is called
packaging. In order for a Bean to be packaged, it must be in a JAR file. The result
of packaging a Bean is the creation of a type library file, a registry file, and Java

stub files. The type library is the binary file that contains information about the component's properties, methods, and events. The registry file contains information for editing the Windows system registry to include the details of the new component, such as its location, the JAR file that contains the Bean, and the ActiveX component that implements the Bridge. This is an interesting aspect of the Bridge. One ActiveX component, named *beans.ocx*, implements the features of any and all Beans that are packaged for use with ActiveX. This is convenient because we don't have to create a new ActiveX component for every Bean we package.

Let's go through the steps of packaging the *BeansBook.Simulator.Thermostat* Bean. I've created a directory called *c:\java\projects\BeansBook\ActiveX* that will contain all of the type libraries and registry files created when the simulator Beans are packaged. Before I start I'm going to put a copy of *beans.ocx* into this directory so that everything remains together. This is the copy of *beans.ocx* that will be referenced by the ActiveX versions of the simulator Beans. You'll find the *beans.ocx* file in the *bridge\classes* directory of the BDK installation.

Start the ActiveX Packager by entering the following command at a command window prompt:

```
java sun.beans.ole.Packager
```

This starts the packager program, which then guides you through the steps needed to package a Bean:

1. You must specify the JAR file that contains the Bean you want to package. You can type in the full path to the file, or you can use the *Browse* button to search for the file. After selecting *Simulator.jar* from the appropriate directory, press the *Next* button. At this point the packager examines the contents of the JAR file, looking for entries that are Beans.

2. The dialog box changes to show the Beans contained in the JAR file. Select the class `BeansBook.Simulator.Thermostat`, and press the *Next* button.

3. The packager dialog now asks for the ActiveX name that should be used to identify the component. The default is to use the name of the Bean (*Thermostat*). Instead, let's name the component *JavaThermostat*. We'll use this naming convention for the other simulator Beans, so that they all appear together in dialog boxes. After you change the name to *JavaThermostat*, press the *Next* button.

4. Now that we've given the Bean its ActiveX name, we specify the directory where the type library and registry files are to be placed. It is important to put these files in the same directory as the *beans.ocx* file, because this is the location that the registry information for the new component will use to reference *beans.ocx*. Press the *Next* button to get to Step 5.

5. The packager wants to know if events should be cracked or treated as objects.* The alternative is to leave the event object as a single parameter. You have a choice here because of a fundamental difference between the way Java Beans and ActiveX fire events. In JavaBeans, event objects are usually the only parameter to an event listener method. ActiveX passes event information to listener methods by breaking the event into different parameters. The term "cracking" means opening the Java event object to reveal the specific data items that are inside. This means that the event is fired to the ActiveX container using the ActiveX event firing protocol. This is the preferred mechanism, but you do have a choice. We'll look more closely at this later; for now let's crack (or "uncrack" as it is called by the packager) the event into parameters.

6. Start the packaging process by pressing the *Start Generation* button. The packager is now going to create some stub files—new Java classes that create the bridge between the Bean and ActiveX. These classes will be put back into the *Simulator.jar* file when the process completes. But remember that files cannot be added to a JAR file; it has to be created all at once. The packager extracts the entire contents of the *Simulator.jar* file into a temporary directory. It then generates and compiles the Java code for the stubs. After compiling the new classes, everything is put back into a new *Simulator.jar* file, replacing the original. Then the type library and registry files are generated and placed into the directory that was specified in Step 4. The packager then enters the new information into the system registry. A dialog box comes up to confirm that the information from the file was successfully entered into the registry. Finally, the temporary directory that was used for code generation is cleaned up, and the packager informs you that packaging succeeded. You now have an ActiveX control named *JavaThermostat* available on your system.

I won't go through the steps for packaging the other simulator Beans because they are identical. I'm going to package the simulator Beans into ActiveX components with names as shown in Table 11-1.

*Table 11-1. Renaming Java Classes for ActiveX*

| Class Name | ActiveX Name |
| --- | --- |
| BeansBook.Simulator.Thermostat | JavaThermostat |
| BeansBook.Simulator.Boiler | JavaBoiler |
| BeansBook.Simulator.Cooler | JavaCooler |
| BeansBook.Simulator.VisualTemperature | JavaTemperature |

---

* The packager refers to this step as "uncracking," but I believe the correct term is "cracking." Cracking means that you're breaking the event into pieces; uncracking means you are putting it back together. Keep this in mind so that you don't get confused by the choice you'll be given on the packager dialog box.

Now the *Simulator.jar* file contains all of the classes that bridge the simulator Beans to ActiveX. You should note, however, that the stub classes that were generated import classes from `sun.beans.ole`. There is no problem here, unless you try to run BeanBox with the resulting *Simulator.jar* file. When you run BeanBox, a `CLASSPATH` variable is set up that won't be able to locate the `sun.beans.ole` package, resulting in a `java.lang.NoClassDefFoundError` being thrown. You can solve this problem by adding the path that contains these classes to the file that you use to run BeanBox. This can be either the *run.bat* or *run.sh* command scripts, or *Makefile* or *GNUmakefile* if you use a *make* program to run it. Either way, add to the `CLASSPATH` that is assigned in the file so that it includes the *bridge\classes* directory under your BDK installation directory. For example, I've modified my *run.bat* file so that the assignment looks like this: `set CLASSPATH=classes;` `c:\bdk\bridge\classes`.

# Technology Mapping

All of the properties that are exposed by a Bean class can be exposed by the ActiveX component. The data type of the property will be mapped to its corresponding OLE Automation data type, as shown in Table 11-2. These properties are then made available as Automation properties. The types not listed, such as custom classes that you've written, are exposed as Automation objects, using type VT_DISPATCH. Whenever a component's property is accessed, the Bridge calls the corresponding property accessor method on the underlying Bean.

*Table 11-2. Type Mapping Between Java and ActiveX*

| Java Type | OLE Automation Type |
|-----------|---------------------|
| boolean | VT_BOOL |
| char | VT_UI1 |
| double | VT_R4 |
| float | VT_R2 |
| int | VT_I4 |
| byte | VT_I2 |
| short | VT_I2 |
| long | VT_I4 (may be truncated) |
| java.lang.String | VT_BSTR |
| java.awt.Color | VT_COLOR |
| java.awt.Font | VT_FONT |

The methods that you expose from your JavaBeans classes are made available as Automation methods, with the parameters mapped to the appropriate Automation types. When these methods are invoked, the Bridge invokes the corresponding method on your Java Bean. The concept of overloaded methods does not map to ActiveX. If your Bean class exposes two methods of the same name, only one of these will be exposed. You don't really have control over which one is chosen. The ActiveX Bridge makes this choice for you, selecting the overloaded method with the largest number of parameters.

All of the events that can be fired by a Bean are collected into a single set of events for ActiveX. The notion of classifying the events into listener interfaces is dissolved away in the translation from Java to ActiveX technology. For this reason it is important that you don't have two event notification methods with the same name in two different event-listener interfaces, because this results in a name clash.

ActiveX has a persistence model that is mapped to Java Object Serialization. As long as your Beans are serializable, they can be properly saved and restored by the ActiveX persistence mechanism. The limitation is that the serialization of your Bean must take place on a single thread. This means that if you implement your own serialization through `readObject()` and `writeObject()` methods, you must not ask another thread to do the work. The ActiveX persistence interfaces supported by the Bridge are `IPersistStorage`, `IPersistStreamInit`, and `IPersistPropertyBag`. These interfaces are likely to be sufficient for the vast majority of applications.

## *Using Beans in Visual Basic*

Now that there are ActiveX wrappers for the Beans in the simulator, let's create a sample Visual Basic (VB) application that uses them. This is not going to be a tutorial, though you might want to follow along even if you're not familiar with Visual Basic. This will give you the chance to see one way in which the Beans can be used in an ActiveX environment.

Start up VB and create a project for a standard application. I'm using Version 5 of VB, but the concepts are essentially the same for Version 4. This starts you out with an empty form, as well as a component toolbox with some basic Windows controls to choose from.

In order to make the simulator components available for use on the form, we have to add them into the component toolbox. Go to the *Project* menu and select the *Components* item. This launches a dialog box that allows you to identify the components to include in the toolbox for this project, as shown in Figure 11-2. Select the *JavaBoiler*, *JavaCooler*, *JavaTemperature*, and *JavaThermostat* Bean controls to be added to the toolbox.

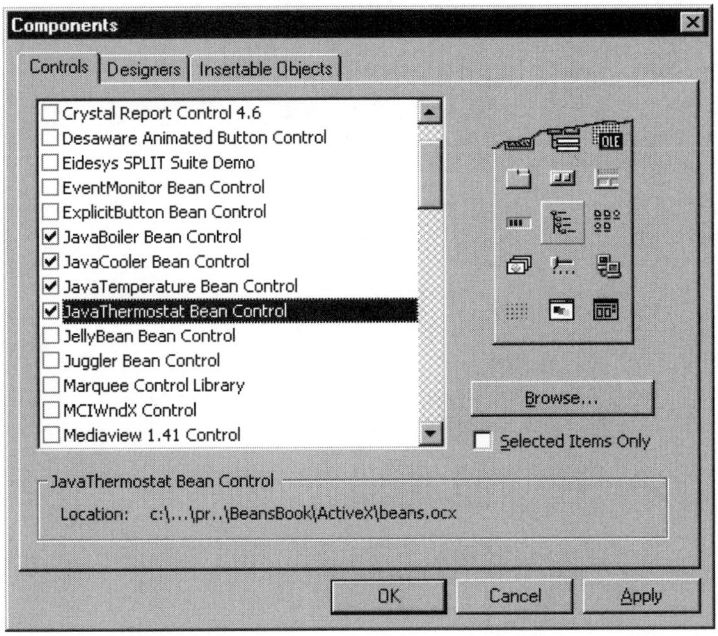

*Figure 11-2. Adding Java Beans to the Visual Basic toolbox*

After you press the *OK* button, the selected simulator components are added to the VB toolbox, as shown in Figure 11-3. Notice that all four of the simulator components appear in the toolbox using the same icon. This is the default specified by the registry information for the component.* As you move the mouse pointer over the icons in the toolbox, the name of the component will be displayed in a tooltip window. This is the little rectangular window that appears next to the mouse cursor. In Figure 11-3, I've placed the mouse over the icon for the *JavaThermostat* component.

Let's talk about the application we're building for a moment. We can create something similar to the previous examples that we created when we wrote Java applet code or used BeanBox to wire components together. These examples had an instance of a thermostat, boiler, cooler, and temperature component. We'll do the same thing here, but let's add something else. In addition to the simulator components, we'll also provide a label component that keeps track of the temperature property of the temperature object. In our previous simulator examples, we could only track the current temperature of the system by setting the thermostat

---

* The image is actually a bitmap resource from *beans.ocx*. There is no reason for all of the Beans to show up in the toolbox with the same image if you expend the effort to change them. If you're familiar with how resources work in ActiveX, and how they are specified in the registry, you could change these icons to something more meaningful, but that's not the topic of this discussion.

*Figure 11-3. Java Beans in the Visual Basic toolbox*

to display the ambient temperature. When we switched the thermostat display to comfort temperature, we could no longer see the ambient temperature of the system. This has nothing to do with Java or ActiveX; it is simply because we didn't provide this feature in our previous examples.

For this example, we need one instance of each of the simulator components, so I'll place one of each on the form. Next I want a label component that will be used to display the current ambient temperature of the system, and I'll use another label to provide a static text description of the ambient temperature label. These labels aren't Beans; they are Windows components that are available from the VB toolbox. Arrange these components on the form however you like. My form is shown in Figure 11-4. The component named *Label1* is the one that will be used to display the ambient temperature. I've placed the other label below it with the text *Degrees Celsius*, and I've used a rather large font for both of these labels so that they stand out.

You've probably noticed that there is a black rectangle in the upper-left area of the form. This is actually the instance of *JavaTemperature*. Remember that this is a very simple Bean that extends `java.awt.Panel`. I've changed the value of two of its properties to suit the example. (These changes are made by selecting the *JavaTemperature* component on the form and then manipulating the property

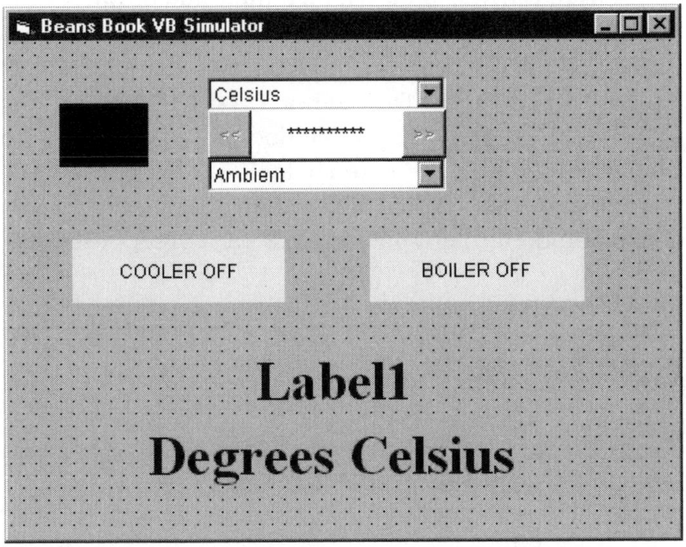

*Figure 11-4. Building the simulator in VB*

values using the VB property sheet.) The first change was to set its *Background* property to black, so that we can actually see where it is on the design-time form. The default color that is used by this component is the same as the color of the form, so it's hard to see if we don't change it. Remember that this component is a subclass of java.awt.Panel, but that we don't do anything with the functionality that we get from that class. We could have written some code into the class to paint itself black, but it's just as easy to make the change here in VB. We also don't want this component to show up at all at run-time, so I've set the value of its *Visible* property to False using the VB property page.

The properties of the simulator Beans are manipulated in the VB property sheet, the same as for any other component on the form. Properties exposed by the Bean are combined with those that are provided as an ActiveX component. Figure 11-5 shows the property page for the instance of the *JavaThermostat* component we placed on the form. Some of these properties are exposed by BeansBook.Simulator.Thermostat, some by its base class java.awt.Panel, and some are standard ActiveX properties. It turns out that all of the properties exposed directly by the BeansBook.Simulator.Thermostat class are read-only properties. They still appear in the property sheet, but you won't be able to change their values. (The properties *TooHot* and *TooCold* were never really discussed. They appear here because of the public methods getTooHot() and getTooCold() in the Thermostat class.) Many of the other properties are read/write, so you can change their values. For instance, you can use the property sheet to change the *Font* property. The result is that the *JavaThermostat* displays text using the new font you selected. If you try to change the value of one of the read-only properties exposed by BeansBook.Simulator.Thermostat, such as *ComfortTemperature*, VB displays a dialog box that informs you that the object doesn't support this property or method. This message occurs because the method that VB wants to call to set the property's value does not exist. This is, in fact, what makes the property read-only. Take another look at the code for the BeansBook.Simulator.Thermostat class. You'll find that there is a public getComfortTemperature() method, but no public setComfortTemperature() method.

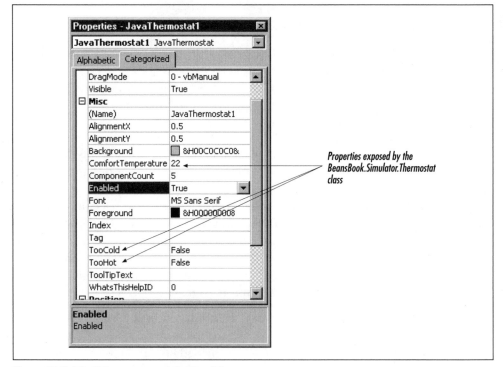

*Figure 11-5. The VB property page for JavaThermostat*

Try selecting one of the other simulator components and looking at the property page again. You can use the property page to change the value of read/write properties exposed by the Bean. These changes result in a call to the appropriate property set method.

Let's look at the property page of the *JavaBoiler* component, shown in Figure 11-6. The *Rate* property is shown in the property sheet, but it seems that the *Running* property is missing. This is because we've changed the value of the *Running* property to be an instance of class BeansBook.Simulator.Running.

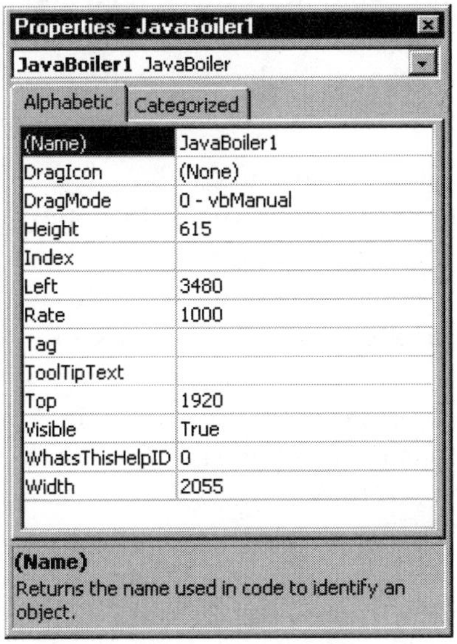

*Figure 11-6. The VB property page for JavaBoiler*

The ActiveX Bridge maps Java data types to their corresponding Automation type. The problem here is that the corresponding type for BeansBook.Simulator.Running is VT_DISPATCH, which simply represents an interface pointer to an object that supports Automation. Without knowing the exact type, the property sheet has no way of knowing how to present the property to the user, so it isn't shown at all.

What we need is another way to manipulate the properties of a component, regardless of whether its properties can be shown in the property page. This can be handled by the customizer class for the Bean. The BeansBook.Simulator.Boiler class has an associated customizer called BeansBook.Simulator.BoilerCustomizer. The user interface on the customizer provides access to the *Running* property. If you click with the right mouse button over the *JavaBoiler* component on the design-time form, you'll get a popup menu that contains an item called *Properties*. If you select the *Properties* menu item, the customizer for the Bean will be launched. Go ahead and change the *Running* property value on the customizer to *YES*. The result is that the instance of the *JavaBoiler* on the form changes its color to red and changes its text to *BOILER ON*. The *Properties* menu item will be available only if the Bean has an associated customizer class.

## Writing Code

So far all we've done is create instances of the components we want on the form. Now we have to write some code to get them talking to each other. Double-click on an empty area of the form to bring up the code window. A quick note about the way subroutines are named in VB: all event-handler subroutines are named *Object_Event*, where *Object* is the instance name of the object that fired the event, and *Event* is the name of the event.

The Form_Load routine is called when the form is first instantiated. This is a good time to set up communications between the components. As I said before, this is not a tutorial on VB, so I'll assume you understand most of the syntax of the code. The first step is to make *JavaCooler1* a listener for cooling request events fired by *JavaThermostat1*. Note that we use JavaCooler1.Object to pass the instance of the object to the thermostat. The addCoolingRequestListener() method takes an instance of Object as its parameter. The Object property of the component is used to get its Object representation. We also make *JavaBoiler1* a listener for heating request events from *JavaThermostat1*, and *JavaThermostat1* is registered for property change events from *JavaTemperature1*. When we wrote similar examples in Java, we registered the temperature object as a temperature pulse event listener on the boiler and cooler objects. We can't do that here, however, because temperature pulses are unicast events, and the ActiveX Bridge has already registered itself as a listener for temperature pulses. We'll work around this shortly. When the application starts I want the system temperature to start at 50 degrees, so I set the *Temperature* property of *JavaTemperature1* to 50. I've created a subroutine called UpdateLabel that is called whenever the ambient temperature label should be updated. All it does is use the *Temperature* property of *JavaTemperature1* to set the *Caption* property on *Label1*. I'm calling this routine now so that it starts out with the right value on display. The code for the Form_Load and UpdateLabel routines are shown below:

```
Private Sub Form_Load()

  ' make the cooler a cooling request listener of the thermostat
  JavaThermostat1.addCoolingRequestListener JavaCooler1.Object

  ' make the boiler a heating request listener of the thermostat
  JavaThermostat1.addHeatingRequestListener JavaBoiler1.Object

  ' make the thermostat a property change listener of the temperature
  JavaTemperature1.addPropertyChangeListener JavaThermostat1.Object

  ' start the system going at 50 degrees
  JavaTemperature1.Temperature = 50

  ' update the temperature label
  UpdateLabel
```

```
End Sub

Private Sub UpdateLabel()

' update the temperature label with the temperature property
Label1.Caption = JavaTemperature1.Temperature

End Sub
```

The last thing we need to do is to route the temperature pulse events to the temperature object. Instead of making the temperature object a direct listener for temperature pulse events, we'll handle those events in our VB code and route the result directly to *JavaTemperature1*. When you're in the code window in VB, you can get started on an event handler by selecting the source object from the drop-down menu as shown in Figure 11-7. The source of the temperature pulse is the boiler, so we choose the object named *JavaBoiler1*. Now we can select an event method from the method dropdown list as shown in Figure 11-8. Select the `temperaturePulse` method and VB will generate a skeleton event handler for you. This is how you generate handlers for the events that are fired by ActiveX components. Note that the name of the event method is the same as the one specified in the `BeansBook.Simulator.TemperaturePulseListener` interface. The only real difference is that the temperature pulse event object has been broken down into its constituent parts as parameters. The parameter we're interested in is the `pulseTemperature` parameter; we'll be passing this value directly to *JavaTemperature1*.

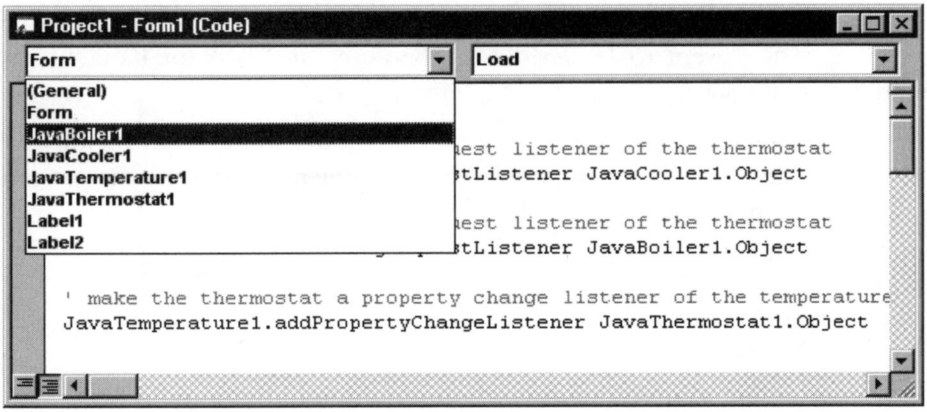

*Figure 11-7. Selecting an event source*

The event handler subroutine name, `JavaBoiler1_temperaturePulse`, is based on the instance name of the object that fires the event and the name of the event

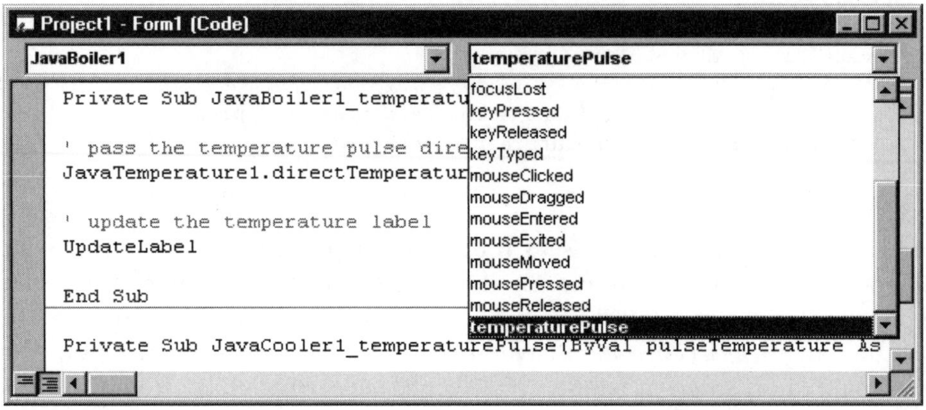

*Figure 11-8. Selecting an event handler*

method. Let's fill in the rest of the code. When the temperature pulse is received
we want to pass its value to the temperature object. Earlier in the chapter we
created the directTemperaturePulse() method for class BeansBook.Simu-
lator.VisualTemperature. So now all we need to do is call this method on
*JavaTemperature1*, passing it the pulseTemperature parameter that was passed into
the event handler. Since we know the temperature object is going to modify the
value of the *Temperature* property, we call the UpdateLabel routine to keep the
ambient temperature label on the form up to date. By the way, the source parameter that is passed into the event handler routine represents the object that is the
source of the event. This is done because the event object was cracked open and
the source is one of the pieces of information that it contained. We already know
the source of the event to be *JavaBoiler1*, because the VB event handlers are
written for specific source/event combinations.

Take exactly the same approach to create a temperature pulse event handler for
pulses that come from *JavaCooler1*. The code that implements this handler is virtually the same as that for the boiler pulse.

```
Private Sub JavaBoiler1_temperaturePulse(ByVal pulseTemperature As _
Double, ByVal source As Object)

' pass the temperature pulse directly to the temperature object
JavaTemperature1.directTemperaturePulse pulseTemperature

' update the temperature label
UpdateLabel

End Sub
```

```
Private Sub JavaCooler1_temperaturePulse(ByVal pulseTemperature As _
Double, ByVal source As Object)

' pass the temperature pulse directly to the temperature object
JavaTemperature1.directTemperaturePulse pulseTemperature

' update the temperature label
UpdateLabel

End Sub
```

When we were packaging the simulator Beans, we chose to break the contents of the event objects into individual parameters. Let's take a look at what the event handler would have looked like if we had chosen to keep the event object intact. The following code implements the `JavaBoiler1_temperaturePulse` event handler method that would have been used if we had decided not to break up the event object:

```
Private Sub Boiler1_temperaturePulse(ByVal TemperaturePulseEvent1 As _
Object)

' pass the temperature pulse directly to the temperature object
JavaTemperature1.directTemperaturePulse _
TemperaturePulseEvent1.getPulseTemperature

' update the temperature label
UpdateLabel

End Sub
```

Since the entire event object is passed as a single object named *TemperaturePulseEvent1*, we need to extract the value of the pulse temperature from it so that it can be passed to *JavaTemperature1*. The `BeansBook.Simulator.TemperaturePulseEvent` class has a method named `getPulseTemperature()` which is used to get the value of the temperature pulse. This is the same method that we call on the *TemperaturePulseEvent1* object that was passed to the event handler; the result of which is being passed to *JavaTemperature1* via a call to the `directTemperaturePulse` method.

That's all there is to it. Most of the properties, methods, and events from the simulator Beans have direct counterparts in ActiveX. We had to clear a few obstacles along the way, but for the most part the process is straightforward. Figure 11-9 shows what the application looks like when it is running.

The screen shot in Figure 11-9 shows the application while the cooler is attempting to bring the ambient temperature down to a comfort temperature of

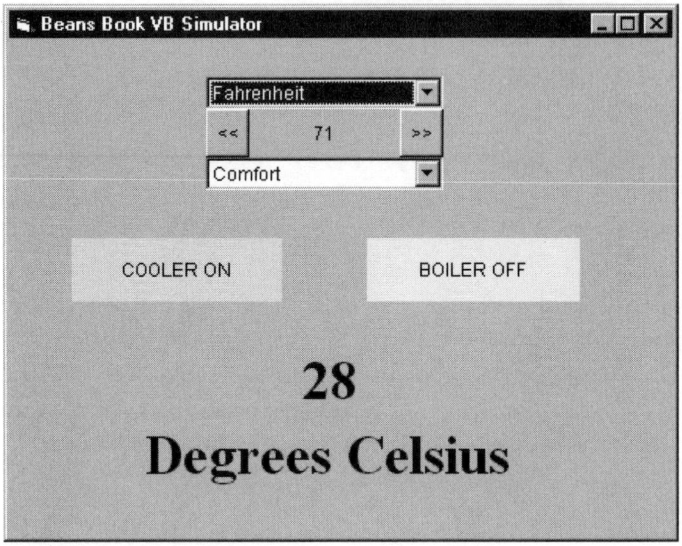

*Figure 11-9. The finished simulator*

71 degrees Fahrenheit. The large ambient temperature label keeps track of changes to the ambient temperature of the system as they happen.

# A

# Design Patterns

## Event Objects

Whenever you define an event object for passing information related to a particular event, you should create a subclass of `java.util.EventObject`. By convention, these classes should end in the word *Event*. This helps to quickly identify their purpose to programmers. All of the event subclasses provided by the core Java class libraries follow this convention.

## Event Listeners

The convention for all event-listener interfaces is for names to end in the word *Listener*. Like the convention for event objects, this helps to identify the purpose of the interface. All of the event-listener interfaces provided by the core Java class libraries follow this convention.

The methods that are defined in the event-listener interfaces should conform to the standard design pattern for event-notification methods. This allows the programmer to understand the purpose of the methods without having to dig through piles of documentation. The method signature for an event-listener method is as follows:

```
void <eventOccurenceMethodName>(<EventObjectType> evt);
```

The event occurrence method name should describe the event. The event object is passed when the event is fired. This object should be derived from the class `java.util.EventObject`. You can also include a `throws` clause that lists any checked exceptions that might be thrown when this method is invoked.

# Registering for Event Notification

The methods used for registration of event notifications should conform to the standard design pattern for event-listener registration. The method signatures are:

```
public void add<ListenerType>(<ListenerType> listener);
public void remove<ListenerType>(<ListenerType> listener);
```

This pattern identifies the object that implements these methods as an event source for the event-listener interface of type <ListenerType>. The client object invokes the add<ListenerType>() method to register an interest in the events supported by the associated interface. When the client object is no longer interested in receiving these event notifications, it invokes the corresponding remove<ListenerType>() method.

# Registering for Unicast Event Notification

The design pattern for registering interest in a unicast event is almost identical to that of a multicast event. It looks like:

```
public void add<ListenerType>(<ListenerType> listener)
                     throws java.util.TooManyListenersException;
public void remove<ListenerType>(<ListenerType> listener);
```

The only difference between the unicast pattern and the multicast pattern is the use of the throws clause with the exception java.util.TooManyListenersException. This pattern indicates that the source object supports only one listener for the specified listener type. Invoking the add<ListenerType>() method on a unicast source registers the specified listener only if no other listener is currently registered; if a listener is already registered, java.util.TooManyListenersException is thrown.

# Multiple Parameter Event Methods

Although it is not recommended, you can define event-notification method signatures that contain any number of parameters. The design pattern for the signature is:

```
void <eventOccurenceMethodName>(<parameter list>);
```

The parameters of this method do not have to be instances of EventObject. They can be any valid class or Java primitive.

# Property Access Methods

The methods used for getting and setting property values should conform to the standard design pattern for properties. These methods may throw checked exceptions. The method signatures are as follows:

```
public void set<PropertyName>(<PropertyType> value);
public <PropertyType> get<PropertyName>();
```

The existence of a matching pair of methods that conform to this pattern represents a read/write property with the name <PropertyName> of the type <PropertyType>. If only the get() method exists, the property is considered to be read-only, and if only the set() method exists the property is considered to be write-only. If the <PropertyType> is boolean, the get() method can be replaced or augmented with a method that uses the following signature:

```
public boolean is<PropertyName>();
```

# Indexed Property Access Methods

There is an additional design pattern for indexed properties. The <PropertyType> in the standard property method design pattern may be an array:

```
public <PropertyType>[] get<PropertyName>();
public void set<PropertyName>(<PropertyType>[] value);
```

These methods are used to access the entire array of property values at one time. An additional pair of methods can provide access to individual values in the property array. The method signatures for this pattern are:

```
public <PropertyType> get<PropertyName>(int index);
public void set<PropertyName>(int index, <PropertyType> value);
```

As with the single value pattern, these methods are allowed to include a throws clause for throwing checked exceptions. Specifically, the indexed methods may throw a java.lang.ArrayIndexOutOfBoundsException if an index is used that is outside the bounds of the property array. Although this is an important aspect of indexed properties, it isn't required for the indexed properties pattern. Since the indexed properties are considered ordered collections, the indexed get() and set() methods should always declare the ArrayIndexOutOfBoundsException. It might have been better to make it a requirement for this pattern.

# Constrained Property Access Methods

The design pattern for setting and getting constrained properties is similar to those of properties that are not constrained. The difference is that the set()

method declares that it throws the exception `java.beans.PropertyVetoExcep-`
tion. The method signatures are:

```
public <PropertyType> get<PropertyName>();
public void set<PropertyName>(<PropertyType> value)
                throws java.beans.PropertyVetoException;
```

# Registering for Bound and Constrained Property Event Notifications

There is a design pattern for registering and unregistering event listeners for
changes to specific bound properties. The method signatures are:

```
public void add<PropertyName>Listener(PropertyChangeListener p);
public void remove<PropertyName>Listener(PropertyChangeListener p);
```

There is also a design pattern for registering and unregistering event listeners for
vetoable-change events for specific constrained properties. The method signatures are:

```
public void add<PropertyName>Listener(VetoableChangeListener p);
public void remove<PropertyName>Listener(VetoableChangeListener p);
```

# Naming a BeanInfo Class

The naming of a BeanInfo class uses a design pattern of its own. The name of the
class is a concatenation of the class name for the Bean with the string *BeanInfo*. So
if you have a Bean class named `Xyz`, its BeanInfo class must be named `XyzBean-`
`Info`. Normally, the BeanInfo class belongs to the same package as the Bean class
it describes, but this is not a firm requirement. When a BeanInfo class is being
located, the package path for the associated Bean class is searched first; so for
Bean `Package.Xyz`, the class `Package.XyzBeanInfo` is looked for first. If this class
is not found, the `XyzBeanInfo` class is searched for in the packages specified by
the BeanInfo package search path. This search path can be accessed using the
`getBeanInfoSearchPath()` and `setBeanInfoSearchPath()` methods of the
`java.beans.Instrospector` class.

# B

# The java.beans
# Package

This appendix summarizes the classes and interfaces in the *java.beans* package. It isn't intended as a reference, but as a brief quick-reference guide.

## Class java.beans.BeanDescriptor

### Description

A BeanDescriptor describes the attributes of a Bean. These include its display name and description, as well as the classes that implement the Bean's customizer and the Bean itself.

### Class Definition

```
public class BeanDescriptor extends FeatureDescriptor
{
    // constructors
    public BeanDescriptor(Class beanClass);
    public BeanDescriptor(Class beanClass, Class customizerClass);

    // methods
    public Class getBeanClass();
    public Class getCustomizerClass();
}
```

### See Also

FeatureDescriptor

# Interface java.beans.BeanInfo

## Description

BeanInfo is an interface implemented by a class that provides explicit information about a Bean. It is used to describe one or more feature sets of a Bean, including its properties, methods, and events.

## Class Definition

```
public interface BeanInfo
{
    // methods
    BeanInfo[] getAdditionalBeanInfo();
    BeanDescriptor getBeanDescriptor();
    int getDefaultEventIndex();
    int getDefaultPropertyIndex();
    EventSetDescriptor[] getEventSetDescriptors();
    java.awt.Image getIcon(int iconKind);
    MethodDescriptor[] getMethodDescriptors();
    PropertyDescriptor[] getPropertyDescriptors();

    // fields
    final static int ICON_COLOR_16x16 = 1;
    final static int ICON_COLOR_32x32 = 2;
    final static int ICON_MONO_16x16 = 3;
    final static int ICON_MONO_32x32 = 4;
}
```

## See Also

BeanDescriptor,    EventSetDescriptor,    MethodDescriptor,    PropertyDescriptor

# Class java.beans.Beans

## Description

This class provides some general methods for instantiating a Bean, and for setting and getting the availability of the graphical user interface. It also provides methods for establishing the design-time state of the environment.

## Class Definition

```
public class Beans
{
    // methods
```

```
    public static Object getInstanceOf(Object bean, Class targetType);
    public static Object instantiate(ClassLoader cls, String beanName)
        throws java.io.IOException, ClassNotFoundException;
    public static boolean isDesignTime();
    public static boolean isGuiAvailable();
    public static boolean isInstanceOf(Object bean, Class targetType);
    public static void setDesignTime(boolean isDesignTime)
        throws SecurityException;
    public static void setGuiAvailable(boolean isGuiAvailable)
        throws SecurityException;
}
```

# Interface java.beans.Customizer

## Description

The Customizer interface is implemented by classes that provide a custom user interface for customizing a Bean. The customizer class should inherit from java.awt.Component so it can be added to a dialog box or panel.

## Class Definition

```
    public interface Customizer
    {
        // methods
        void addPropertyChangeListener(PropertyChangeListener listener);
        void removePropertyChangeListener(PropertyChangeListener listener);
        void setObject(Object bean);
    }
```

## See Also

PropertyChangeListener

# Class java.beans.EventSetDescriptor

## Description

An EventSetDescriptor describes a group of events that a Bean can fire. This group of events is sent to the target object via method calls on an event-listener interface. Another object can register itself as an event listener for the described listener interface by calling the associated registration method on the event-source object.

## Class Definition

```
public class EventSetDescriptor extends FeatureDescriptor
{
    // constructors
    public EventSetDescriptor(Class sourceClass,
                            String eventSetName,
                            Class listenerType,
                            String listenerMethodName)
            throws IntrospectionException;
    public EventSetDescriptor(Class sourceClass,
                            String eventSetName, Class listenerType,
                            String listenerMethodNames[],
                            String addListenerMethodName,
                            String removeListenerMethodName)
            throws IntrospectionException;
    public EventSetDescriptor(String eventSetName,
                            Class listenerType,
                            Method listenerMethods[],
                            Method addListenerMethod,
                            Method removeListenerMethod)
            throws IntrospectionException;
    public EventSetDescriptor(String eventSetName,
                            Class listenerType,
                            MethodDescriptor
                                listenerMethodDescriptors[],
                            Method addListenerMethod,
                            Method removeListenerMethod)
            throws IntrospectionException;

    // methods
    public Method getAddListenerMethod();
    public MethodDescriptor[] getListenerMethodDescriptors();
    public Method[] getListenerMethods();
    public Class getListenerType();
    public Method getRemoveListenerMethod();
    public boolean isInDefaultEventSet();
    public boolean isUnicast();
    public void setInDefaultEventSet(boolean inDefaultEventSet);
    public void setUnicast(boolean unicast);
}
```

## See Also

FeatureDescriptor, IntrospectionException, MethodDescriptor

# Class java.beans.FeatureDescriptor

## Description

FeatureDescriptor is the base class for BeanDescriptor, EventSetDescriptor, MethodDescriptor, ParameterDescriptor, and PropertyDescriptor. It provides methods for accessing the information that is common among the various introspection descriptors. It also provides a mechanism that allows arbitrary attribute/value pairs to be associated with a design feature.

## Class Definition

```
public class FeatureDescriptor
{
    // constructors
    public FeatureDescriptor();

    // methods
    public java.util.Enumeration attributeNames();
    public String getDisplayName();
    public String getName();
    public String getShortDescription();
    public Object getValue(String attributeName);
    public boolean isExpert();
    public boolean isHidden();
    public void setDisplayName(String displayName);
    public void setExpert(boolean expert);
    public void setHidden(boolean hidden);
    public void setName(String name);
    public void setShortDescription(String text);
    public void setValue(String attributeName, Object value);
}
```

## See Also

BeanDescriptor, EventSetDescriptor, MethodDescriptor, ParameterDescriptor, PropertyDescriptor

# Class java.beans.IndexedPropertyDescriptor

## Description

The IndexedPropertyDescriptor class is used to describe a property that appears to be an ordered collection. This property has an indexed read or indexed write method to access specific elements of the collection. An indexed property may also provide non-indexed read and write methods which are used to read and write the values of the property as a single array.

### Class Definition

```
public class IndexedPropertyDescriptor extends PropertyDescriptor
{
    // constructors
    public IndexedPropertyDescriptor(String propertyName,
                        Class beanClass)
            throws IntrospectionException;
    public IndexedPropertyDescriptor(String propertyName,
                        Class beanClass,
                        String getterName, String setterName,
                        String indexedGetterName,
                        String indexedSetterName)
            throws IntrospectionException;
    public IndexedPropertyDescriptor(String propertyName,
                        Method getter, Method setter,
                        Method indexedGetter, Method indexedSetter)
            throws IntrospectionException;

    // methods
    public Class getIndexedPropertyType();
    public Method getIndexedReadMethod();
    public Method getIndexedWriteMethod();
}
```

### See Also

IntrospectionException, PropertyDescriptor

# Class java.beans.IntrospectionException

### Description

This exception is thrown when an exception occurs during the introspection of a Bean. Some causes are not being able to map a class name to a Class object, or specifying a method with a type signature that does not map to its intended use.

### Class Definition

```
public class IntrospectionException extends Exception
{
    // constructors
    public IntrospectionException(String mess);
}
```

## See Also

EventSetDescriptor, IndexedPropertyDescriptor, Introspector, Property-Descriptor

# Class java.beans.Introspector

## Description

The Introspector analyzes a Bean's class and superclasses looking for either explicit or implicit information. This information is then used to build a BeanInfo object that completely describes the Bean.

## Class Definition

```
public class Introspector
{
   // methods
   public static String decapitalize(String name);
   public static BeanInfo getBeanInfo(Class beanClass)
           throws IntrospectionException;
   public static BeanInfo getBeanInfo(Class beanClass, Class stopClass)
           throws IntrospectionException;
   public static String[] getBeanInfoSearchPath();
   public static void setBeanInfoSearchPath(String path[]);
}
```

## See Also

BeanInfo, IntrospectionException

# Class java.beans.MethodDescriptor

## Description

A MethodDescriptor describes a single method that a Bean exposes for public access by other objects.

## Class Definition

```
public class MethodDescriptor extends FeatureDescriptor
{
   // constructors
   public MethodDescriptor(Method method);
```

```
        public MethodDescriptor(Method method,
                                ParameterDescriptor parameterDescriptors[]);

        // methods
        public Method getMethod();
        public ParameterDescriptor[] getParameterDescriptors();
    }
```

## See Also

FeatureDescriptor, ParameterDescriptor

# Class java.beans.ParameterDescriptor

## Description

The ParameterDescriptor class provides additional descriptive information for each of the parameters of a method described by a MethodDescriptor. This class relies entirely on its base class, FeatureDescriptor.

## Class Definition

```
    public class ParameterDescriptor extends FeatureDescriptor
    {
    }
```

## See Also

FeatureDescriptor, MethodDescriptor

# Class java.beans.PropertyChangeEvent

## Description

Whenever the value of a Bean's bound or constrained property is changed, a property change event is fired to all of the registered event listeners. The PropertyChangeEvent contains information about the change, and is passed as an argument to the event notification methods of the PropertyChangeListener and VetoableChangeListener interfaces.

## Class Definition

```
public class PropertyChangeEvent extends java.util.EventObject
{
    // constructors
    public PropertyChangeEvent(Object source, String propertyName,
                               Object oldValue, Object newValue);

    // methods
    public Object getNewValue();
    public Object getOldValue();
    public Object getPropagationId();
    public String getPropertyName();
    public void setPropagationId(Object propagationId);
}
```

## See Also

PropertyChangeListener, VetoableChangeListener

# Interface java.beans.PropertyChangeListener

## Description

A property change event is fired to any registered event listeners after the value of a Bean's bound property has been changed. The PropertyChangeListener interface is implemented by objects that register themselves for notifications of these property value changes.

## Class Definition

```
public interface PropertyChangeListener extends java.util.EventListener
{
    // methods
    void propertyChange(PropertyChangeEvent evt);
}
```

## See Also

PropertyChangeEvent

# Class java.beans.PropertyChangeSupport

## Description

PropertyChangeSupport handles the registration and unregistration of property change listeners, and implements the firing of arbitrary property change events. The class is designed so that you can either inherit from it, or you can delegate work to an instance of it.

## Class Definition

```
public class PropertyChangeSupport implements java.io.Serializable
{
    // constructors
    public PropertyChangeSupport(Object sourceBean);

    // methods
    public synchronized void addPropertyChangeListener(
                              PropertyChangeListener listener);
    public void firePropertyChange(String propertyName,
                              Object oldValue, Object newValue);
    public synchronized void removePropertyChangeListener(
                              PropertyChangeListener listener);
}
```

## See Also

PropertyChangeListener

# Class java.beans.PropertyDescriptor

## Description

A PropertyDescriptor describes a single exposed property of a Bean. This property is associated with a pair of accessor methods.

## Class Definition

```
public class PropertyDescriptor extends FeatureDescriptor
{
    // constructors
    public PropertyDescriptor(String propertyName, Class beanClass)
            throws IntrospectionException;
    public PropertyDescriptor(String propertyName, Class beanClass,
                              String getterName, String setterName)
            throws IntrospectionException;
```

```
        public PropertyDescriptor(String propertyName, Method getter,
                               Method setter)
                throws IntrospectionException;

    // methods
    public Class getPropertyEditorClass();
    public Class getPropertyType();
    public Method getReadMethod();
    public Method getWriteMethod();
    public boolean isBound();
    public boolean isConstrained();
    public void setBound(boolean bound);
    public void setConstrained(boolean constrained);
    public void setPropertyEditorClass(Class propertyEditorClass);
}
```

## See Also

FeatureDescriptor, IntrospectionException

# Interface java.beans.PropertyEditor

## Description

The PropertyEditor interface is implemented by classes that are used by user
interfaces that allow users to edit a property value of a specific type. The PropertyEditor can support different ways of displaying and updating property values.

## Class Definition

```
    public interface PropertyEditor
    {
      // methods
      void addPropertyChangeListener(PropertyChangeListener listener);
      String getAsText();
      java.awt.Component getCustomEditor();
      String getJavaInitializationString();
      String[] getTags();
      Object getValue();
      boolean isPaintable();
      void paintValue(java.awt.Graphics gfx, java.awt.Rectangle box);
      void removePropertyChangeListener(PropertyChangeListener listener);
      void setAsText(String text)
              throws java.lang.IllegalArgumentException;
      void setValue(Object value);
      boolean supportsCustomEditor();
    }
```

## See Also

PropertyChangeListener

# Class java.beans.PropertyEditorManager

## Description

The `PropertyEditorManager` is used to locate a property editor for a specific property type. This property editor must implement the `PropertyEditor` interface. This class also supports the registration and unregistration of property editors at run-time.

## Class Definition

```
    public class PropertyEditorManager
    {
        // methods
        public static PropertyEditor findEditor(Class targetType);
        public static String[] getEditorSearchPath();
        public static void registerEditor(Class targetType,
                                          Class editorClass);
        public static void setEditorSearchPath(String path[]);
    }
```

## See Also

PropertyEditor

# Class java.beans.PropertyEditorSupport

## Description

`PropertyEditorSupport` is used as a base class for other property editors. Its default method implementations are designed to be overridden for the features that are supported for a particular property editor. Work can also be delegated to an instance of this class.

## Class Definition

```
    public class PropertyEditorSupport implements PropertyEditor
    {
        // constructors
        protected PropertyEditorSupport();
```

```
    protected PropertyEditorSupport(Object source);

    // methods
    public synchronized void addPropertyChangeListener(
                        PropertyChangeListener listener);
    public void firePropertyChange();
    public String getAsText();
    public java.awt.Component getCustomEditor();
    public String getJavaInitializationString();
    public String[] getTags();
    public Object getValue();
    public boolean isPaintable();
    public void paintValue(java.awt.Graphics gfx,
                        java.awt.Rectangle box);
    public synchronized void removePropertyChangeListener(
                        PropertyChangeListener listener);
    public void setAsText(String text)
            throws java.lang.IllegalArgumentException;
    public void setValue(Object value);
    public boolean supportsCustomEditor();
}
```

## See Also

PropertyChangeListener, PropertyEditor


# Class java.beans.PropertyVetoException

## Description

A PropertyVetoException is thrown whenever a proposed change to a constrained property is vetoed by a registered VetoableChangeListener.

## Class Definition

```
    public class PropertyVetoException extends Exception
    {
        // constructors
        public PropertyVetoException(String mess, PropertyChangeEvent evt);

        // methods
        public PropertyChangeEvent getPropertyChangeEvent();
    }
```

## See Also

PropertyChangeEvent, VetoableChangeListener

# Class java.beans.SimpleBeanInfo

## Description

SimpleBeanInfo is a support class designed to make it easier to implement Bean-Info classes. Its default implementation provides no information. The various feature set methods can be overridden to provide explicit information on their associated feature sets. When the Instrospector encounters the default null values provided by the methods of this class, it will apply low-level introspection and design patterns to analyze the target Bean.

## Class Definition

```
public class SimpleBeanInfo implements BeanInfo
{
    // constructors
    public SimpleBeanInfo();

    // methods
    public BeanInfo[] getAdditionalBeanInfo();
    public BeanDescriptor getBeanDescriptor();
    public int getDefaultPropertyIndex();
    public int getDefaultEventIndex();
    public EventSetDescriptor[] getEventSetDescriptors();
    public java.awt.Image getIcon(int iconKind);
    public MethodDescriptor[] getMethodDescriptors();
    public PropertyDescriptor[] getPropertyDescriptors();
    public java.awt.Image loadImage(String resourceName);
}
```

## See Also

BeanDescriptor, BeanInfo, EventSetDescriptor, MethodDescriptor, PropertyDescriptor

# Interface java.beans.VetoableChangeListener

## Description

A vetoable-change event is fired to any registered event listeners when the value of a Bean's constrained property is going to be changed. The VetoableChangeListener interface is implemented by objects that register themselves for notifications of these proposed property value changes. These listeners throw a PropertyVetoException if they want to veto the change.

## Class Definition

```
public interface VetoableChangeListener extends java.util.EventListener
{
    // methods
    void vetoableChange(PropertyChangeEvent evt)
            throws PropertyVetoException;
}
```

# See Also

PropertyChangeEvent, PropertyVetoException

# Class java.beans.VetoableChangeSupport

## Description

VetoableChangeSupport handles the registration and unregistration of vetoable-change listeners, and implements the firing of arbitrary vetoable-change events. The class is designed so that you can either inherit from it, or you can delegate work to an instance of it.

## Class Definition

```
public class VetoableChangeSupport implements java.io.Serializable
{
    // constructors
    public VetoableChangeSupport(Object sourceBean);

    // methods
    public synchronized void addVetoableChangeListener(
                        VetoableChangeListener listener);
    public void fireVetoableChange(String propertyName,
                        Object oldValue, Object newValue)
            throws PropertyVetoException;
    public synchronized void removeVetoableChangeListener(
                        VetoableChangeListener listener);
}
```

# See Also

PropertyVetoException, VetoableChangeListener

# Interface java.beans.Visibility

## Description

This interface can be implemented by Beans that may run on systems where a graphical user interface isn't available. The methods of this interface can be invoked to determine if a Bean requires the GUI to accomplish its task, as well as to inform the Bean as to whether the GUI is available.

## Class Definition

```
public interface Visibility
{
    // methods
    boolean avoidingGui();
    void dontUseGui();
    boolean needsGui();
    void okToUseGui();
}
```

# Index

## About the Author

Rob Englander is the President and Principal Engineer at MindStream Software, Inc., a firm specializing in custom software development in Java and C++ for a wide range of application areas.

This is Rob's first book, and so for the first time in his career he can actually hold his work in his hands.

## Colophon

Edie Freedman designed the cover of this book, using an image she created and shot, then manipulated in Adobe Photoshop. The cover layout was produced with Quark XPress 3.3 using the Bodoni Black font from URW Software and BT Bodoni Bold Italic from Bitstream. The inside layout was designed by Nancy Priest and implemented by Mike Sierra in FrameMaker 5.0. The heading font is Bodoni BT; the text font is New Baskerville. The illustrations that appear in the book were created in Macromedia Freehand 5.0 by Chris Reilley and Robert Romano. Whenever possible, our books use RepKover™, a durable and flexible lay-flat binding. If the page count exceeds RepKover's limit, perfect binding is used.

# Java

## Creating Effective JavaHelp

*By Kevin Lewis*
*1st Edition June 2000*
*188 pages, ISBN 1-56592-719-2*

JavaHelp is an online help system developed in the Java&#153; programming language. *Creating Effective JavaHelp* covers the main features and options of JavaHelp and shows how to create a basic JavaHelp system, prepare help topics, and deploy the help system in an application. Written for all levels of Java developers and technical writers, the book takes a chapter-by-chapter approach to building concepts, to impart a complete understanding of how to create usable JavaHelp systems and integrate them into Java applications and applets.

## Java Native Methods

*By Alligator Descartes*
*1st Edition November 2000 (est.)*
*300 pages (est.), ISBN 1-56592-345-6*

Although Java offers the promise of platform-independent programming, there are situations where you may still need to use native C or C++ code compiled for a particular platform. Maybe you have to tie some legacy code into a Java application. Or maybe you want to implement some computationally intensive methods for a performance-critical application in native code. *Java Native Methods* tells you everything you need to know to get your native code working with Java, using either Sun's Java Native Interface (JNI) or Microsoft's Raw Native Interface (RNI).

## Java Internationalization

*By Andy Deitsch & David Czarnecki*
*1st Edition November 2000 (est.)*
*350 pages (est.), ISBN 0-596-00019-7*

*Java Internationalization* shows how to write software that is truly multi-lingual, using Java's very sophisticated Unicode internationalization facilities. *Java Internationalization* brings Java developers up to speed for the new generation of software development: writing software that is no longer limited by language boundaries.

## Java Performance Tuning

*By Jack Shirazi*
*1st Edition November 2000 (est.)*
*446 pages (est.), ISBN 0-596-00015-4*

*Java Performance Tuning* contains step-by-step instructions on all aspects of the performance tuning process, right from such early considerations as setting goals, measuring performance, and choosing a compiler. Extensive examples for tuning many parts of an application are described in detail, and any pitfalls are identified. The book also provides performance tuning checklists that enable developers to make their tuning as comprehensive as possible.

## Learning Java

*By Pat Niemeyer & Jonathan Knudsen*
*1st Edition, May 2000*
*726 pages, Includes CD-ROM*
*ISBN 1-56592-718-4*

For programmers either just migrating to Java or already working steadily in the forefront of Java development, *Learning Java* gives a clear, systematic overview of the Java 2 Standard Edition. It covers the essentials of hot topics like Swing and JFC; describes new tools for signing applets; and shows how to write networked clients and servers, servlets, JavaBeans, and state-of-the-art user interfaces. Includes a CD-ROM containing the Java 2 SDK, version 1.3.

# More Titles from O'Reilly

## Java

### Java Cryptography

By Jonathan B. Knudsen
1st Edition May 1998
362 pages, ISBN 1-56592-402-9

*Java Cryptography* teaches you how to write secure programs using Java's cryptographic tools. It includes thorough discussions of the java.security package and the Java Cryptography Extensions (JCE), showing you how to use security providers and even implement your own provider. It discusses authentication, key management, public and private key encryption, and includes a secure talk application that encrypts all data sent over the network. If you work with sensitive data, you'll find this book indispensable.

### Java Distributed Computing

By Jim Farley
1st Edition January 1998
384 pages, ISBN 1-56592-206-9

*Java Distributed Computing* offers a general introduction to distributed computing, meaning programs that run on two or more systems. It focuses primarily on how to structure and write distributed applications and discusses issues like designing protocols, security, working with databases, and dealing with low bandwidth situations.

### Java Network Programming, 2nd Edition

By Elliotte Rusty Harold
2nd Edition August 2000
760 pages, ISBN 1-56592-870-9

*Java Network Programming, 2nd Edition,* is a complete introduction to developing network programs (both applets and applications) using Java, covering everything from networking fundamentals to remote method invocation (RMI). It includes chapters on TCP and UDP sockets, multicasting protocol and content handlers, and servlets. This second edition also includes coverage of Java 1.1, 1.2 and 1.3. New chapters cover multithreaded network programming, I/O, HTML parsing and display, the Java Mail API, the Java Secure Sockets Extension, and more.

### Java Security

By Scott Oaks
1st Edition May 1998
474 pages, ISBN 1-56592-403-7

This essential Java 2 book covers Java's security mechanisms and teaches you how to work with them. It discusses class loaders, security managers, access lists, digital signatures, and authentication and shows how to use these to create and enforce your own security policy.

### Java Threads, 2nd Edition

By Scott Oaks & Henry Wong
2nd Edition January 1999
336 pages, ISBN 1-56592-418-5

Revised and expanded to cover Java 2, *Java Threads, 2nd Edition* shows you how to take full advantage of Java's thread facilities: where to use threads to increase efficiency, how to use them effectively, and how to avoid common mistakes. It thoroughly covers the Thread and ThreadGroup classes, the Runnable interface, and the language's synchronized operator. The book pays special attention to threading issues with Swing, as well as problems like deadlock, race condition, and starvation to help you write code without hidden bugs.

### Database Programming with JDBC and Java, 2nd Edition

By George Reese
2nd Edition August 2000
352 pages, ISBN 1-56592-616-1

This book describes the standard Java interfaces that make portable object-oriented access to relational databases possible, and offers a robust model for writing applications that are easy to maintain. The second edition has been completely updated for JDBC 2.0, and includes reference listings for JDBC and the most important RMI classes. The book begins with a quick overview of SQL for developers who may be asked to handle a database for the first time, and goes on to explain how to issue database queries and updates through SQL and JDBC.

## O'REILLY®

TO ORDER: **800-998-9938** • *order@oreilly.com* • *http://www.oreilly.com/*

*OUR PRODUCTS ARE AVAILABLE AT A BOOKSTORE OR SOFTWARE STORE NEAR YOU.*

FOR INFORMATION: **800-998-9938** • **707-829-0515** • *info@oreilly.com*

# How to stay in touch with O'Reilly

## 1. Visit Our Award-Winning Web Site

*http://www.oreilly.com/*

★"Top 100 Sites on the Web" —*PC Magazine*
★"Top 5% Web sites" —*Point Communications*
★"3-Star site" —*The McKinley Group*

Our web site contains a library of comprehensive product information (including book excerpts and tables of contents), downloadable software, background articles, interviews with technology leaders, links to relevant sites, book cover art, and more. File us in your Bookmarks or Hotlist!

## 2. Join Our Email Mailing Lists

### New Product Releases

To receive automatic email with brief descriptions of all new O'Reilly products as they are released, send email to:
**listproc@online.oreilly.com**
Put the following information in the first line of your message (*not* in the Subject field):
**subscribe oreilly-news**

### O'Reilly Events

If you'd also like us to send information about trade show events, special promotions, and other O'Reilly events, send email to:
**listproc@online.oreilly.com**
Put the following information in the first line of your message (*not* in the Subject field):
**subscribe oreilly-events**

## 3. Get Examples from Our Books via FTP

There are two ways to access an archive of example files from our books:

### Regular FTP

- ftp to:
  **ftp.oreilly.com**
  (login: anonymous
  password: your email address)
- Point your web browser to:
  **ftp://ftp.oreilly.com/**

### FTPMAIL

- Send an email message to:
  **ftpmail@online.oreilly.com**
  (Write "help" in the message body)

## 4. Contact Us via Email

**order@oreilly.com**
To place a book or software order online. Good for North American and international customers.

**subscriptions@oreilly.com**
To place an order for any of our newsletters or periodicals.

**books@oreilly.com**
General questions about any of our books.

**software@oreilly.com**
For general questions and product information about our software. Check out O'Reilly Software Online at **http://software.oreilly.com/** for software and technical support information. Registered O'Reilly software users send your questions to: **website-support@oreilly.com**

**cs@oreilly.com**
For answers to problems regarding your order or our products.

**booktech@oreilly.com**
For book content technical questions or corrections.

**proposals@oreilly.com**
To submit new book or software proposals to our editors and product managers.

**international@oreilly.com**
For information about our international distributors or translation queries. For a list of our distributors outside of North America check out:
**http://www.oreilly.com/www/order/country.html**

## 5. Work with Us

Check out our website for current employment opportunites:
**www.jobs@oreilly.com**
Click on "Work with Us"

O'Reilly & Associates, Inc.
101 Morris Street, Sebastopol, CA  95472  USA
TEL    707-829-0515 or 800-998-9938
          (6am to 5pm PST)
FAX    707-829-0104

# O'REILLY®

# International Distributors

http://international.oreilly.com/distributors.html

## UK, EUROPE, MIDDLE EAST AND AFRICA (EXCEPT FRANCE, GERMANY, AUSTRIA, SWITZERLAND, LUXEMBOURG, AND LIECHTENSTEIN)

**INQUIRIES**
O'Reilly UK Limited
4 Castle Street
Farnham
Surrey, GU9 7HS
United Kingdom
Telephone: 44-1252-711776
Fax: 44-1252-734211
Email: information@oreilly.co.uk

**ORDERS**
Wiley Distribution Services Ltd.
1 Oldlands Way
Bognor Regis
West Sussex PO22 9SA
United Kingdom
Telephone: 44-1243-843294
UK Freephone: 0800-243207
Fax: 44-1243-843302 (Europe/EU orders)
or 44-1243-843274 (Middle East/Africa)
Email: cs-books@wiley.co.uk

## FRANCE

**INQUIRIES & ORDERS**
Éditions O'Reilly
18 rue Séguier
75006 Paris, France
Tel: 33-1-40-51-52-30
Fax: 33-1-40-51-52-31
Email: france@oreilly.fr

## GERMANY, SWITZERLAND, AUSTRIA, LUXEMBOURG, AND LIECHTENSTEIN

**INQUIRIES & ORDERS**
O'Reilly Verlag
Balthasarstr. 81
D-50670 Köln, Germany
Telephone: 49-221-973160-91
Fax: 49-221-973160-8
Email: anfragen@oreilly.de (inquiries)
Email: order@oreilly.de (orders)

## CANADA (FRENCH LANGUAGE BOOKS)

Les Éditions Flammarion ltée
375, Avenue Laurier Ouest
Montréal (Québec) H2V 2K3
Tel: 00-1-514-277-8807
Fax: 00-1-514-278-2085
Email: info@flammarion.qc.ca

## HONG KONG

City Discount Subscription Service, Ltd.
Unit A, 6th Floor, Yan's Tower
27 Wong Chuk Hang Road
Aberdeen, Hong Kong
Tel: 852-2580-3539
Fax: 852-2580-6463
Email: citydis@ppn.com.hk

## KOREA

Hanbit Media, Inc.
Chungmu Bldg. 210
Yonnam-dong 568-33
Mapo-gu
Seoul, Korea
Tel: 822-325-0397
Fax: 822-325-9697
Email: hant93@chollian.dacom.co.kr

## PHILIPPINES

Global Publishing
G/F Benavides Garden
1186 Benavides Street
Manila, Philippines
Tel: 632-254-8949/632-252-2582
Fax: 632-734-5060/632-252-2733
Email: globalp@pacific.net.ph

## TAIWAN

O'Reilly Taiwan
1st Floor, No. 21, Lane 295
Section 1, Fu-Shing South Road
Taipei, 106 Taiwan
Tel: 886-2-27099669
Fax: 886-2-27038802
Email: mori@oreilly.com

## INDIA

Computer Bookshop (India) Pvt. Ltd.
190 Dr. D.N. Road, Fort
Bombay 400 001 India
Tel: 91-22-207-0989
Fax: 91-22-262-3551
Email: cbsbom@giasbm01.vsnl.net.in

## CHINA

O'Reilly Beijing
SIGMA Building, Suite B809
No. 49 Zhichun Road
Haidian District
Beijing, China PR 100080
Tel: 86-10-8809-7475
Fax: 86-10-8809-7463
Email: beijing@oreilly.com

## JAPAN

O'Reilly Japan, Inc.
Yotsuya Y's Building
7 Banch 6, Honshio-cho
Shinjuku-ku
Tokyo 160-0003 Japan
Tel: 81-3-3356-5227
Fax: 81-3-3356-5261
Email: japan@oreilly.com

## THAILAND

TransQuest Publishers (Thailand)
34 Pracharat-Bampen Road
Soi 9 Huay Kwang
Bangkok 10320, Thailand
Tel: 662-2767582
Fax: 662-6902235
Email: puripat@.inet.co.th

## ALL OTHER ASIAN COUNTRIES

O'Reilly & Associates, Inc.
101 Morris Street
Sebastopol, CA 95472 USA
Tel: 707-829-0515
Fax: 707-829-0104
Email: order@oreilly.com

## AUSTRALIA

Woodslane Pty., Ltd.
7/5 Vuko Place
Warriewood NSW 2102
Australia
Tel: 61-2-9970-5111
Fax: 61-2-9970-5002
Email: info@woodslane.com.au

## NEW ZEALAND

Woodslane New Zealand, Ltd.
21 Cooks Street (P.O. Box 575)
Waganui, New Zealand
Tel: 64-6-347-6543
Fax: 64-6-345-4840
Email: info@woodslane.com.au

## ARGENTINA

Distribuidora Cuspide
Suipacha 764
1008 Buenos Aires
Argentina
Phone: 5411-4322-8868
Fax: 5411-4322-3456
Email: libros@cuspide.com

# O'REILLY®

TO ORDER: **800-998-9938** • **order@oreilly.com** • **http://www.oreilly.com/**
OUR PRODUCTS ARE AVAILABLE AT A BOOKSTORE OR SOFTWARE STORE NEAR YOU.
FOR INFORMATION: **800-998-9938** • **707-829-0515** • **info@oreilly.com**

## O'REILLY WOULD LIKE TO HEAR FROM YOU

Which book did this card come from?

_____

Where did you buy this book?
- ❏ Bookstore
- ❏ Direct from O'Reilly
- ❏ Bundled with hardware/software
- ❏ Computer Store
- ❏ Class/seminar
- ❏ Other _____

What operating system do you use?
- ❏ UNIX
- ❏ Windows NT
- ❏ Macintosh
- ❏ PC(Windows/DOS)
- ❏ Other _____

What is your job description?
- ❏ System Administrator
- ❏ Network Administrator
- ❏ Web Developer
- ❏ Programmer
- ❏ Educator/Teacher
- ❏ Other _____

❏ Please send me O'Reilly's catalog, containing a complete listing of O'Reilly books and software.

Name _____  Company/Organization _____

Address _____

City _____ State _____ Zip/Postal Code _____ Country _____

Telephone _____  Internet or other email address (specify network) _____

Nineteenth century wood engraving of a bear from the O'Reilly & Associates Nutshell Handbook® *Using & Managing UUCP.*

POST CARD

# BUSINESS REPLY MAIL
FIRST CLASS MAIL   PERMIT NO. 80   SEBASTOPOL, CA

*Postage will be paid by addressee*

**O'Reilly & Associates, Inc.**
101 Morris Street
Sebastopol, CA 95472-9902